PSYCHO-SOCIAL FACTORS
LEARNING ENGLISH AT SCHOOL

PSYCHO-SOCIAL FACTORS LEARNING ENGLISH AT SCHOOL

Kusum Sharma

GYAN

GYAN PUBLISHING HOUSE

NEW DELHI - 110002

PSYCHO-SOCIAL FACTORS LEARNING ENGLISH AT SCHOOL
(Education)

ISBN : 81-212-0707-X

Published in 2000 in India by
Gyan Publishing House
5, Ansari Road
New Delhi 110 002
Phone : 3282060, 3261060 Fax : 3285914
E-mail : gyanbook@del2.vsnl.net.in

Laser Typesetting: Grow Computers, Delhi
Printed at: Mehra Offset Press, New Delhi

Contents

List of Figures

List of Tables

Preface

The present book "Psycho-social Factors Learning English at School" is an attempt to peep into the minds of young learners of English Language. English, being a second language in India has always remained a language of important status. Hence, a special attention has always been given to its learning, both on the part of teacher as well as the learner. Reading is one of the major important skills of language learning due to its innumerable significant aspects.

The book introduces us to the two major correlates of reading; the psychological and the social factors. There are many other factors affecting reading such as biological factors, but those require more of clinical treatment. Hence, these two factors are taken for study in detail. This book is a valid document developed on the basis of in-depth survey and observation of the Young English Language Learners.

Is language learning a mechanical process based on share rote memorization or is it the acquisition of certain basic skills? Does acquisition of one skill affect learning the other skills? Can every one be a good reader? These mind-boggling questions are dealt with in the present book.

Besides this, the book also provides a number of recommendations for parents to take care of their young children. At the same time, it also offers a few guidelines to English teachers for improving their classroom teaching. Certain sensitive issues like parents' attitude towards reading and its impact on their childrens' reading proficiency have also been discussed elaborately.

The findings of the survey have revealed and highlighted certain alarming facts too. The readers would very well appreciate the effect of their level of aspiration on their children's performance or effect of their reading habits on their next generation.

To summarize, it can be said that good reading lends a soothing hand of comfort to the lonely, dejected and isolated souls. This book is a humble venture to provide not only the solace, but also provide an information regarding how to be a good reader and how to utilize the various Psycho-social Factors Learning English at School.

Kusum Sharma

General Introduction

Language is, perhaps, man's most basic tool. It would be difficult for men to live together, think or act without the sounds and symbols of language. It is almost impossible to imagine life without language—a life without conversation, writing, books, mass communication media and thoughts based on developed language concepts. There is little doubt too, that as the complexity of our civilization increases, the importance of language as a tool increases as well. As scientific achievement shrinks the world, people are giving greater and greater attention to the development of universal communication in order to maintain civilisation. In the same way the family group must communicate in order to live a human life, so must all people communicate to preserve an increasingly complex world with a common world of sounds and symbols.

Though using language is not an innate human ability—it must be learnt; yet this ability of language development separates human beings from all other species. Although animals have the physical capability and capacity to produce sounds and in some instances, they may even have learnt that particular reactions occur when they make these sounds, only humans have the physical and mental endowment necessary to develop true language.

Language is more than instinctive sounds given in response to environmental conditions. It is a system for interpreting and organising experience, as well as for communicating ideas and feelings. Language and the thoughts and feelings derived from experience are highly interrelated.

Man's use of language is the result of long trial, imitation and practice. He found the need for making responses to situations especially those involving feelings and emotions. At first, this was done by gestures, facial expressions and cries. Once the situation began stimulating the response, the primitive communicating act itself and the subsequent response from all other human beings which this act stimulated, became common to all members of a group, definite meaning began to be attached to these gestures, facial expression and cries and they became natural signs with meaning.

As the use of natural signs became common, the next logical step was taken when man recognised that sounds and later, written symbols—could be attached not only to the communicative act itself (or to a portion of it), but also to the reaction it caused in other men. With the development of these symbols, man began to use them in his thinking process. Thinking itself is actually the manipulation of various symbols which have meaning attached to them. Thus, before systematising language symbols as we know them, man made use of other symbols in his thinking; but the process of living with others—particularly as society became more and more complex—brought a greater need for the development of language symbols and for their use in man's thinking.

While language is used primarily for communication and for thinking, a third function derives from the other two. As man communicated, thought and developed new ideas, he found the need for passing on to succeeding generations more than the very simplest thing. Thus, language became his means for transmitting culture from generation to generation. Without language, men would be isolated from one another, would not be able to share thoughts and ideas and would know little of other people, places and times. Though language is used in performing the functions of communication, thinking and recording, yet it is not the same for each individual. Even within an identical cultural setting, each individual's language is uniquely his. Since a word is a symbol, it has no meaning or even sound of its own. It is true, that agreement between sound and meaning has to be made, but these are general in nature. For each individual there is a personal meaning to each language symbol that he knows; no one else knows exactly what this meaning is. Each person using a language symbol has had a personal experience with that symbol. This fact in the nature of language cannot be ignored, since communication is the chief function of language and is dependent on common understanding of the symbols used. The implications of common experience in helping language function are clear.

The Purpose of Language Instruction

Teachers, in the past, considered language to be a static, unchanging subject—as something taught and used only in the English class. There was a "correct" language, one that was always the same, and one that when learnt was suitable for all times and places. Teachers gave no thought to change, but concentrated on maintaining the purity which they felt was the tradition, that must be upheld. Perhaps, if this were true, the task of instruction in the use of language would be relatively simple. But this is not true, and most of the educators today are aware of the vital nature of language and of how it changes. It is recognised more and more that an acceptable usage in one situation is not necessarily suitable in another; that words and meanings have been added and that others have been lost or have changed; and that language is functional and fluid, with its principal purpose being to promote communication. Language is now recognised as something alive, changing and breathing, and alongwith the culture, evolving. Thus, language must be functional for communication actually to occur.

The major purpose of the school is to help prepare children to meet adequately the problems of life, and to find their place in the expanding culture. This may be best done through the language instructions provided at school. The knowledge, habits, attitudes and skills determine the personality of a child and it largely exhibits itself in use of language—the words most frequently employed in writing or speech, the punctuation most needed, the usages of proper stress and intonation which make effective communication possible and handwriting that is legible.

Language Learning Mechanism in Children

Children these days come to school with a considerable knowledge in using language. They have initially heard a language spoken for five or six years, and have spoken it themselves for nearly that long.This is mostly true as far as their first language acquisition is concerned and partly true in case of second language learning. Their achievement has largely been accomplished by initiating those with whom they have been in contact. They have heard the sounds made by others and have themselves gradually formed words; they have observed the effect of these words when spoken and have thus become aware of the meaning. Their adjustment to a language world has been gradual and has varied from child to child. The factors that influence language growth of a child are the rate of his maturation and the world that constitutes his knowledge. Limitation in maturity and in experience certainly delimit language growth.

Second language learning is a little more complex phenomenon. Besides other factors, certain kinds of direct and indirect inputs influence second language learning. These may be either creating favourable attitude or providing exposure to language.

Second language learning is either a process of creative construction or a skill learning process. When we say that learning a second language is a process of creative construction, we imply emphasis on certain "cognitive processing strategies" that the learner brings to task in order to develop internal representation of the second language system. The more convincing view advocates use of second language as a performance skill which has a cognitive as well as behavioural aspect. The learner has to build up the internal cognition first and also fluently practice it. The cognitive aspect involves the internalisation of plans for creating appropriate behaviour. For language use these plans derive mainly from language system. They include grammatical rules, procedures for selecting vocabulary and social conventions governing speech. The behavioural aspect involves the automation of these plans so that they can be converted into fluent performance in real time. This occurs mainly through practice in converting plans into performance, i.e., through productive language activity, with receptive activity playing a less clearly defined role.

Amongst the four skills of English language learning, listening and reading are considered as receptive skills and speaking and writing are termed as productive skills.

According to Pinnell and Galloway (1987:354): "Becoming literate is accomplished within language process." Children seek to become literate for both survival and pleasure. Hence the opportunities to use language in both spoken and written forms must be given to children. Salinger asserts that "Wherever possible, children should see a written copy of what they are hearing... even if they are not able to read; seeing the graphic image helps children make connections between what is heard and said and the written symbols of language." (1988:38). Schickedanz (1986) asserts that we can always find ways to include print—and the print must make sense! Children need to view others around them as being literate; and then, as maturation, readiness and experience allow, they need to be given many opportunities to talk, read and write.

Literacy development includes listening, speaking, reading and writing. The interrelationship among these component skills should be obvious since they all involve words. In listening, ideas are received through words while in speaking and writing, ideas are expressed through words and in reading, which is mainly focussed in the present book, ideas are communicated through printed words. Language learning must focus on the development of all four skills—listening, speaking, reading and writing in integrated form. This may also be termed as whole language approach.

Listening and Speaking

It is rightly said that children need to listen better and not to listen more. Listening skills include auditory perception (the ability to perceive by listening) and auditory association, (the ability to associate sounds/words with experience, objects, ideas or feelings and rhyming skills). Oral communication skill influences and is influenced by every other aspect of development. Oral language can be encouraged by conversing, discussing, clarifying, reporting, explaining, reacting, dramatizing, story telling, poems and rhymes recitation.

Reading and Writing

These are the other two ingredients of language skills. Reading cannot be taught; reading readiness can be nurtured, facilitated and developed. Learning to read may take time. This varies from child to child. It may require time, patience, desire or readiness. Other skills which are prerequisites to fluent reading include large and small muscle development, social and emotional maturity and intellectual and language experience. The other factors will be thoroughly discussed in the later chapters of the book. Consequently, Johnson, (1983:118) suggested that to begin to read fluently, the child must master certain sub-skills such as association of sounds and letters, recognition of words, connection between speech and print, relationship between letters and words and sentences and sequential reading procedure.

Another ingredient in language learning is writing. Writing cannot be developed in isolation. There has to be a connection between listening, speaking, reading and writing. They have to be overlapping in the experience with using alphabets and sight word manipulative toys. Learning to write is a difficult, slow and challenging task; hence a lot of patience is required as not to be too fussy or tense about committing mistakes. According to Alkins (1984:5): "Children's early writing is totally an egocentric self-expression; fun and play are the real objectives." Writing should be taken for meaningful communication rather than accurate and correct expression.

Our main focus in the present work is on reading and the development of reading skills. Besides the very basic nature of reading, the study will focus on the various factors that affect the reading skills of the beginner for the second language learning that is English.

It is imperative to get acquainted with reading initially. The very basic queries of reading are 'what is reading?' or 'what is the mechanism of reading?' or 'whether reading is a natural, automatic process which takes place gradually along with other developments?' or still 'Is reading an acquired ability which has to be learnt consciously?'

A sincere effort has been made not only to familiarize the reader with the process of reading and its various affecting indicators, but also to clear certain doubts and misconceptions about reading. This book will also unveil certain myths and age-old beliefs about reading.

1

Significance, Objectives and Design of the Study

Introduction

Reading is one of the most important approaches to knowledge and understanding for an individual, whether at school or elsewhere. Melkin and Merrit (1974) called 'reading' as the 'keystone to the arch of education.' Reading involves the whole personality and it promotes countless personal and social values. It also provides entrance into almost all vocations. Reading may thus be considered as one of the life's inexhaustible pleasures and blessings. It is one of the major means of communication, hence is essential to the survival of our complex system of social arrangements.Thus, teaching reading is indeed a very humanizing process and can be termed a cultural endeavour. Reading moulds the personality of the child, who then becomes a right-thinking and cultured citizen of tomorrow.

"Reading, typically is the 'bringing of meaning to' rather than 'gaining of meaning' from the printed page;" (Smith, Dechant and Emrald, 1961). Reading is an aspect of communication which involves transmission of meaning and this occurs in the reading process. Reading is a receptive skill which subsumes receiving, understanding and interpreting meaning. "The real problem in reading is not that of getting the material to the brain but of assimilating after it arrives there" (Sommerfield, 1954). Thus, it is evident that reading is inextricably interwoven with life experiences.

It provides a variety of experiences which directly or indirectly affects one's thinking a lot.

Importance of Reading in Schools

Reading is a much-prized life-long gift of formal schooling to the individual. The importance of the printed word continues unabated in spite of the ever-increasing popularity of new information technologies. Learning is now considered a life-long process of which formal education including schooling constitutes a significant part. It is in the school that the cornerstone of this edifice is laid. In school, reading is taught as a part of a comprehensive process of communication. Children are guided to speak clearly, write effectively, listen attentively, read critically and respond to various types of writing as well as to develop information retrieval strategies.

Reading is, in fact, the heart of literacy. Reading, at its basic level, is the recognition of printed or written symbols which serve as stimuli to recall meaning, built up through various past experiences of the reader. New meanings are derived through manipulation of concepts already learnt. The organization of these meanings is governed by the purposes clearly defined by the reader. Reading is an important means of introducing the initiated to the surrounding world. Through reading, the initiated or the child can view ever widening horizons and explore new areas in the world of things, peoples and events. Reading feeds as well as thrives on different aspects of learning. It focuses on the development of various cognitive skills in the student.

At school level, reading is simple or relatively complex according to the material or the text type which the student reads and processes for comprehension. The main text types are:

- Novels, short stories, fables, literary texts and passages
- Plays
- Poems, limericks, nursery rhymes
- Letters, post-cards, telegrams, notes

- Newspapers and magazines (headlines, articles, editorials, letters to the editor, classified advertisements, weather forecasts, radio/television/theatre programmes)
- Specialized articles, report, reviews, essays, business-letters, summaries, precis-accounts, pamphlets
- Handbooks, textbooks, guidebooks
- Recipes for snacks, meals and concoctions
- Advertisements, travel brochures, catalogues
- Puzzles, problems, rules for games
- Instructions, directions, notices, rules and regulations, posters, menus, price-lists, tickets
- Statistics, diagrams, flow charts
- Telephone directories,dictionaries, phrase-books

For proper comprehension of all these text types and many more, we need efficient reading comprehension skills. The process of reading comprehension is a form of thinking, problem-solving or reasoning which involves analyzing and discriminating, judging, evaluating and synthesizing. Therefore any definition of reading comprehension must include interpretation and evaluation of meaning as well as construction of meaning. In order to encourage full comprehension of the text by students, the teacher should ensure that the student is able to understand the concepts presented and also assess the ideas in the light of his own memorial knowledge and experience.

Levels of Reading

Reading can be thought of at two levels at school. First the reader should grasp the objective facts. This requires some interpretation or judgement. This being the lower level, it is the initial stage of acquiring skills of reading. On a higher level, the reader should get the subjective information. This subjective information might include such things as the tone and the mood of the passage read. It is for the reader to bring his own background knowledge and thinking ability to bear on the text in order to get the main idea. "The child reads with his biology and his geography, with his nature and his nurture" (Dechant, 1969).

Readers who can only read facts and nothing more can never be called good readers. On the other hand, readers who cannot grasp the facts, seldom reach the subjective points. Therefore, reading has to take place in levels, lower or subtle level, and deeper or higher level to understand the text. According to Chase (1962), "Reading is more than a process of abstracting quickly what the author has to say. The reader should raise questions, establish relationships among items of information and be led to search for added and deeper understanding... It is one step to absorb and repeat ideas found on the printed page and another step to relate these to life around." Sommerfield (1954) held a similar view that "Real problem of reading is not that of getting the material to the brain but of assimilating after it arrives there." Thus, it is evident that reading is inextricably interwoven with life experiences.

Kinds of Reading Comprehension

Different kinds of reading comprehension have been described by various reading experts. Gray (1960) suggested that various levels of meaning could be obtained from the same text. He identified these levels as follows:

(i) Literal level which involves translation of words

(ii) Interpretative level which relates material to its context

(iii) Significance level which involves implications

(iv) Evaluative level which requires the reader to react to the material on his own terms.

(v) Gray's entire discussion on reading amounts to an elaboration to Thorndike's main thesis regarding the process of reading comprehension (Thorndike, 1917). Interpretation in reading, according to Gray (1955) comprises three broad aspects:

(a) Word knowledge

(b) Apprehending meaning

(c) Thoughtful reaction to and use and application of ideas to read.

Thus, Gray defined reading as "a process of gathering information or meaning contained in a piece of writing and how one comprehends it."

While Gray describes these levels of comprehension, Robinson (1966) developed a model in which different aspects of reading at school level are discussed. The four quadrants in her model comprise:

(i) Word perception
(ii) Comprehension
(iii) Reaction
(iv) Assimilation

One of the most elaborate descriptions of the reading process is *Barrett's Taxonomy* (Barrett, 1972) which described the levels of comprehension as:

(i) Literal comprehension
(ii) Reorganization
(iii) Inferential comprehension
(iv) Evaluation
(v) Appreciation.

Within each of these categories Barrett provides examples of specific types of tasks in the form of purposes of reading which the teacher might utilize. The five major categories move from easy to difficult in terms of the requirement each category appears to demand. These skills are concerned with the location, identification, reorganization, interpretation and evaluation of the points of information retrievable from a printed text. Together these skills comprise the skills of reading comprehension.

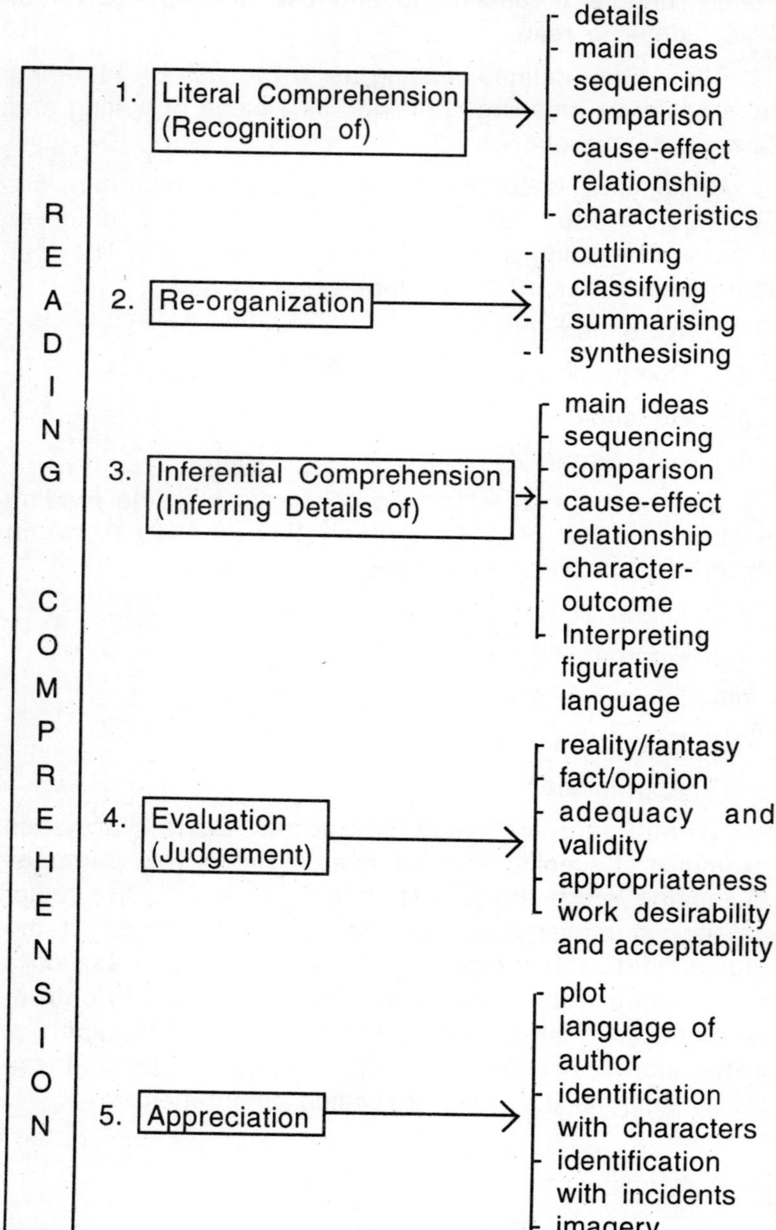

Fig. 1.1. Barrett's Taxonomy of Reading Skills.

(Barrett, Thomas, C. 1972)

Another broad classification of reading skills has been given by John Munby (1978) in his 'Communicative Syllabus Design'. This classification involves a set of reading-related behaviours given below:

- Recognizing the script of a language
- Deducing the meaning and use of unfamiliar lexical terms
- Understanding explicitly stated information
- Understanding information when not explicitly stated
- Understanding conceptual meaning
- Understanding the communicative value of sentences and utterances
- Understanding relations within sentences
- Understanding relation between the parts of a text through grammatical cohesion device
- Interpreting text by going outside it
- Recognising indicators in discourse
- Identifying the main point or important information in a piece of discourse
- Distinguishing the main idea(s) from supporting details
- Extracting salient points to summarize the text or an idea
- Selecting/Extracting relevant point(s) from a text
- Using basic reference skills
- Using skimming for main ideas
- Using scanning to locate specifically required information
- Transcoding information to diagrammatic display

Significance of Reading in Life After Schooling

Inspite of competing mass media, reading in our space age is becoming increasingly important as our society continues to change to a more technological one. As long as competition among nations is largely based on technological advancements and achievements, there will be a premium on the knowledge that can best be attained through reading. The printed page reaches millions, still untouched by electronics and for those who can take advantage of the newer devices, reading still serves unique purposes. Reading is indeed many things to many people. It can be a telescope to take you to the distant stars and speculate about life on them. It can also be a microscope to reveal to you the microorganism. It is a never-ending wide-screen film on which life's pageant passes in review. It is still the only known time machine that can recreate the events of the past and open up the vistas of the future. Primitive humans called reading a 'magic' and perhaps they were right.

Reading is essential to the existence of our complex system of social arrangements. But it is more than that; it is the means by which every age is linked to every other. It makes possible humans' capacity for 'time-binding', the ability to perceive themselves and the fluid universe around them in the historic process. If all the inventions of a hundred years were destroyed and only books were left, humans could still be humans, in the sense intended by the idealists, the poets, and the great creators. Hence it is worthwhile to call reading a humanizing process.

Reading involves application of innate and acquired skills and thinking; in its broader sense, it affects the entire personality of the person. The world of people and events encountered on the printed page may shape a reader's attitude towards fellow-beings, school, parents and towards life in general. Francis Keppel 1964, thus highlighted the value of reading, "every examination of the problem of our schools, every learning disorder seems to show some association with reading difficulty." The introduction to the report of the Carnegie Conference of Reading Experts (1965) included the statement: "Reading is the most important subject to be learned by children; a child will learn little else in today's world if he does not first learn to read properly...."

Reading is an entrance to almost all vocations. Every routine mechanical work demands reading of some kind of material such as basic rules and regulations and safety signs. The skilled traders require considerably more reading for the best quality of work and integration of new practices.

In all professions, of course, one must read a great deal after graduation to keep pace with the new developments. For a lawyer, the ability to read well, to skim through an article, to pick out the important ideas in a paragraph and make deductions from the passage, is the single most important factor for a successful legal practice. The best administrators and teachers demonstrate in their own lives the value of efficient reading. Reading provides the most rewarding use of expanded leisure that comes as a result of automation. At its best, recreational reading affords more than mere entertainment. Reading often relieves emotional tension and gives insight into personal problems. Frequently the right book will fill the psychological need at a critical moment when nothing else works. Reading provides experience through which the individual may expand horizons; it shall identify, extend and intensify interests and help gain deeper understanding of the individual, of other human beings and of the world. Reading organizes experience as it relates ideas from many sources. It is a path to new experiences. Using first hand experiences as a point of departure, the reader reaches out to those of the author consequently transcending the limitations of time and space. As Stevenson 1959 observed, "Reading is a creative art. As the writer creates a structure of thought, so the reader recreates the pattern of words, in the process discovering the essence of the author's idea."

Social Value of Reading

The value of reading among the educated elites of a democracy quickly overreaches the purely personal and merges into social values, in fact, the general values. The general attitude toward reading is largely pragmatic, regarding it as an avenue to financial and social status. For its best welfare, a society requires its members to have a minimum level of education. Surveys show, how the poor readers later become delinquents, unemployed or misfits in a society which progresses to the extent that its mental resources allow it to.

In general, reading disabilities severely restrict the adolescent's development. According to Krugman (1956), "mental hygiene and reading underly all teaching in school and adjustment in living. Reading disability has the same profound influence on educational growth as a severe emotional involvement. Both restrict successful functioning, cause feelings of inadequacy and frustration, bring about disturbed relationships, influence a negative outlook on life and result in a variety of undesirable behavioural manifestations."

Repeated academic failures caused by reading disabilities give rise to a feeling of insecurity and frustration. Penty (1956) obtained clear evidence from data in the Battle Creek, Michigan school system, that preponderance of early school learners stood in the lowest quarter with respect to reading ability. Failure in reading may cause emotional disturbances. Reading retardation often produces a chain of consequences, e.g. inability to do the assignments and non-participation in discussions leading to the feelings of inferiority, hopelessness and even hostility.

Democracy cannot succeed when people are ignorant and can not and will not think for themselves. If citizens fail to become cognizant of the implications of historical trends, to discriminate fact from opinion, or to detect and resist propaganda, both they and their nation are open to exploitation and manipulation. Thus, reading has international significance. In all nations, an awareness has developed of the importance of world-wide literacy as a means of promoting the individual's welfare, social progress and international understanding. Reading is a complex process integrating all aspects of human behaviour and demanding varied and continued instructional guidance to read accurately, efficiently, to appraise what is read and to relate what is read in a significant way to other areas of life. All would agree that reading is the key to the wealth of experience that links people in a way not limited by distance or time. "Reading provides experience through which the individual may expand his horizons; identify, extend and intensify his interests and gain deeper understanding" (Strong, R., 1961).

Finally, we can say reading as a process and as a social phenomenon, is of major concern to the parents, philosophers, psychologists, sociologists, and linguists as well as educationists.

Major Areas in Contemporary Reading Research

Research on reading instruction comprises more material than does research in any other part of the curriculum. In one of the summaries, W.S. Gray (1960) estimated that some 4000 careful, scientific studies of sociology, psychology and teaching of reading were available. Availability of materials in such quantity is a mixed blessing; it provides not only a wealth of facts and opinions to guide teachers' and pupils' procedure but it also creates the problems of organizing and focusing these findings so that current knowledge can be comprehended and the need for further research laid bare. Reading research includes all those studies which may affect the method of teaching reading. These influences include the opinion of parents or the teachers based on their personal experiences, accounts of action research in particular situations, careful description of applied research in classroom and individual situations and scholarly account of basic investigations in laboratory and other settings. But instead of reporting evidence on these topics, one should centre on the methods and materials of teaching reading. All methods of instruction give considerable place to the ability to recognize symbols. In essence, the reading act is divisible into two processes:

(i) Identifying the symbols

(ii) Obtaining meaning from recognized symbols

At the initial level of reading, the child begins to identify and recognize letters, syllables, words phrases and perhaps short sentences with the help of the teacher. This two-fold process of identification—recognition may involve meaning. 'Meaning can assist relationship between them' (Betts, 1953).

Holmes, J.A. (1953) suggested that word discrimination, word-sense and span of recognition account for 56 per cent of the variance in speed and power of reading, while factors like vocabulary in context, intelligence and perception of verbal relationship may provide for 77 per cent of the variance in the reading ability. Holmes' theory concerning the role of the brain in discrimination and appraisal of symbolic meanings seems to agree in principle with the work of other modern writers. D.E.P. Smith (1958), who developed the Synoptic Transmission Theory of Perception, and Gilbert (1959), whose work on the after-image and memory-after-image, appear to support Smith's theory. These two aspects of visual perception in reading and development of visual perception in the child are worth consideration.

Among those who attempted to classify perceivers were M.C. Pettey (1939), Goins (1958) and D.E.P. Smith 1958. Petty concluded that children who had high drawing but low reading ability exercised high synthetic method of perception. These children succeeded at drawing because of attention to details but did not succeed at reading because of inconsistency in selecting details. Petty classified readers as subjective readers (who recognized words from total character) and objective readers (who recognized words from details).

Smith (1958) classified children as placid, hyperactive and alexic groups. The placid child sees letters clearly but cannot shift attention rapidly enough to blend the unfolding sequence of letters into a word. The hyperactive child can easily blend the stimulus letter for such a short time that it makes no impression. The alexic group has both difficulties.

Goins (1958) attempted to classify perception rather than perceivers. On the hypothesis that perception is a primary mental ability, she sought to determine the relationship between competence in visual perception and reading achievement in first grade children. She identified two components, viz. (a) ability to keep in mind a perceptual gestalt during rapid perception, and (b) ability to keep in mind a configuration against distraction. She supported Gray's emphasis on the value to the reader of perceiving several words or a 'thought-unit' as a unit. "If a thought unit is considered as the goal, this heading would include phrase, sentences and larger units such as paragraphs and stories" (Gray, 1956).

According to Cole (1946) concepts are symbolised but the symbols are often non-verbal. Verbals are usually considered to be those standardized oral and written symbols which form the vocabulary of a language. Research on verbals has also been concerned with the following problems:

(i) Total meaning vocabulary where a word is considered to have but one meaning which includes
   (a) measures of vocabulary;
   (b) size of vocabulary; and
   (c) methods of building vocabulary
(ii) Breadth and depth of vocabulary which includes
   (a) multiple meanings;
   (b) implied meanings, e.g. denotation, connotation and figures of speech
(iii) Word order which comprises
   (a) grammar and syntax, punctuation;
   (b) contraction, initials, formulas
(iv) Verbalism
(v) Total vocabulary

Attempts to measure segments and estimate children's total vocabulary have indeed been numerous during the past 75 years. Notable among the summaries of these researches are those by McCarthy (1946), D.H. Russell (1954) and Dale and Reinhart (1957). Such sources indicate that teachers can distinguish among a child's understanding, speaking, reading and writing vocabulary:

D.H. Russell (1954) concluded that measures of children's vocabulary were confined to simple recognition of a synonym in a multiple-choice situation. McCullough (1959) listed factors which affect children's vocabulary, viz. socio-economic status, television-viewing, experience, background intelligence and sex. Larrick (1953) suggested the following methods for estimating children's vocabulary

1. Counting different words used in a natural oral language situation.
2. Counting different words used in a natural written language situation.
3. Counting different words in a free-association situation.
4. Counting different words in a stimulus-response situation.
5. Estimating vocabulary from words recognized on a selected list.

The two most commonly used lists for estimating total vocabulary are a random sample from an unabridged dictionary and a sample from a teacher's work-book (Thorndike and Lorge, 1944). N.B. Smith (1952) reviewed 11 students and concluded that different reading purposes are used in different subject matter fields and that specialized reading skills can be improved with direct instruction. Fifteen purposes have been identified. The major four among these are as follows:

(a) Reading for the Main Idea

This skill is often acquired in parts in the first grade. It is sometimes used by children and adults in casual reading, such as casually reading the newspaper when one is not deeply concerned with the newsitems. McCollough (1957) showed that children can grasp the main idea of a story or reading material even at the readiness stage. Although there is a positive relationship among skills in different types of reading at the second or fourth grades, there is some evidence that children tested are better at reading for specific facts than at reading for main idea or drawing conclusions.

(b) Reading for Sequence

This skill often begins in the first grade with the ability to follow the main events of the story; an ability also related to reading readiness. Children may be encouraged to check word clues such as then, next or after some time to develop reading for sequence.

(c) Reading to Follow Directions

This skill may involve detailed reading, but it seems to require an additional factor of translating the presented symbols into some sort of action. This type of reading is probably close to the reading of verbal problems in arithmetic. Carroll (1926) has shown that reading directions improve with specific practice.

(d) Reading to Draw Conclusion

Such reading may be defined as picking up ideas explicitly stated by the author, rearranging them as needed and formulating some fresh or original generalizations. Such reading is described as problem-solving. It may be included under the broader label of 'creative reading' or 'critical reading'.

Critical Reading

In a world full of conflicting opinions, propaganda, high pressure advertising and specialized points of view, a reasonable aim of language education is teaching to evaluate critically what is read and heard. Quite a few studies have shown that critical reading should be distinguished from literal comprehension in reading.

McCollough (1957) found correlation between various tests of literal comprehension and creative reading (drawing conclusions and making judgement) that ranged from 0.26 to 0.63 with a median of 0.47. Maney (1958) found a correlation of only 0.11 between general reading ability and critical reading scores in science. Similarly Sochor (1958) found a correlation of only 0.23 between literal comprehension and critical reading scores on social studies. Such results suggest that there are certain critical reading abilities which may be distinguished from factual reading.

Reading Research : Sociological, Psychological and Physiological Aspects

Many studies have been conducted on sociological aspect of reading. Gray and Rogers (1952-53) made an analysis of the responses of 400 young people and adults to questions about purposes of reading through structured interviews. Sixty-two specific purposes were identified. Each of the purposes varied in its connotation according to the time and place of reading, the personal urges and the social pressures present in each reading situation.

Research in the field of physiology and psychology of reading began in the middle of the nineteenth century. As generally defined, the physiology of reading relates to the visual, auditory, speech or articulatory or other bodily processes that function in the act of reading. In 1915, Schmidt photographed eye movements in both oral and silent reading of children of grades II to XII. His findings led to the conclusion that the eyes of good readers proceed along the lines in a series of quick movements alternating with longer pauses. During these pauses or fixations, familiar words are recognized as wholes, often in units of two or more. When the eyes reach the end of a line, they make a return sweep to a point near the beginning of the next line.

Gray (1953-54) in his book *Maturity in Reading* secured photographic records of the eye movements of mature readers and concluded that the grosser movement of the eyes in reading are essentially the same the world over, independent of the form or structure of the language or culture involved. Since eye movements are greatly influenced by mental activities that occur during reading, these findings indicate that the basic processes in reading are similar throughout the world.

The relationship between visual defects and reading efficiency has for long been a subject of research. Robinson (1946) gave two very important conclusions in her study on visual anomalies dislineated below:

(i) Visual difficulties which are most frequently linked with reading are due to hyperopia, hyperopic astigmatism, binocular incoordination.

(ii) Cooperative research on the part of refractionists and specialists in reading is greatly needed.

'The role of speech and articulatory processes in oral reading is no doubt clear but even for silent reading, articulation accompanies the process to some extent,' was concluded long ago by Pinter (1913). The findings of studies reported by Bord (1935) reveal that good readers in general ranked higher than poor readers in auditory activity and were somewhat superior in auditory discrimination. Good and poor readers exhibit wide differences in auditory activity, blending, memory of rhythm and auditory discrimination.

The mental processes involved in reading are quite subtle, complex and difficult to study. Yet notable progress has been made through research in identifying their nature, the way in which they function and the factors influencing these processes. The studies reported relate either to progress in reading in relation to total growth pattern or factors relating to progress in specific areas of reading.

Anderson and Huges (1955) emphasised the fact that boys who began to read late were physically less mature than boys who began to read early. This finding is particularly significant since the boys were originally matched for intelligence. It was later concluded that mental age alone may not be an adequate measure of maturing. It was also found that sex differences in the age of learning to read were absent in the higher intelligence quotient (IQ) group. In the past, social and emotional factors affecting reading have been studied largely in relation to retarded readers. The results of numerous studies supply clear evidence of a positive correlation between progress in reading ability and mental capacity. The correlation reported varied from 0.20 to 0.60. The fact that these were not high, indicates that there are factors other than intelligence that influence progress in reading.

Crossen (1948), Groff (1955) and McKillop (1952) have all shown that the attitude of the reader affects his/her comprehension as well as the ability to make inference in reading. Other factors which may affect reading are the nature of material and the setting in which they are read.

Reading Interests

Most of the research studies in this area show that mentally superior children usually continue to do much personal reading and their reading interests vary significantly in both kind and amount with age, sex, intelligence, social background, reading competence and experience.

Gaps and Priorities in Reading Research

During the last three decades, a lot of research work has been done on reading in general, as well as in specific areas. Physiological, sociological and psychological aspects of reading have also been investigated under reading research. Mental processes involved in reading have also been an area of major concern during the first half of the twentieth century. Studies have been conducted on the social role of reading, motives of reading, influence of other mass-media on reading and also on social effects on reading.

Under physiological aspects of reading, studies have been conducted on visual processes, visual anomalies, speech and articulatory process, etc. Effect of environment, e.g. race, socio-economic status, social mobility, parental influence, bilingualism and mass-media other than the printed word have been explored in relation to reading.

A number of research studies have been conducted on reading readiness and on developmental reading practices, oral as well as silent. Research into ways of improving meaning and vocabulary has been scanty since the early work of Gray and Holmes in 1938 in summarizing the apparent effectiveness of many specific techniques such as the use of context, word list and dictionaries. Studies by Eickholz and Barbe (1961) reported self-instructional techniques to be a more effective technique than the conventional ones in improving vocabulary. A valuable source for studies relating to vocabulary, including many studies of the frequency and difficulty of words and their meaning, is found in Dale and Razik's *Bibliography of Vocabulary Studies* (1963).

There is, in contrast, a dearth of research on techniques to improve the basic aspects of comprehension and on ways to improve the more complex aspects of interpretation involving inferential processes often associated with thinking. Little is likewise known in a research sense about techniques for the improvement of reading tastes, of attitudes and appreciation towards reading and of reading interests. The improvement of reading in content areas has long been an objective of development reading consistent with its broad conception of the scope and continuity of reading programme. The available research literature on reading disabilities is extensive, as summaries and studies by Robinson (1946), Vernon (1957), Gray (1960) and Maney (1962) show. Research regarding the study of variables of reading included many studies such as the study on reading attitude, achievement and teacher-pupil relationship by Hilary L. Schofield (1979). He concluded that a significant and positive correlation exists between reading and reading attitude. Jimmy Chan (1986) concluded that favourable parent-child interaction and less autocratic behaviour of parents were positively related to reading ability of the child. Engle, Carulld and Collins (1990) were of the opinion that reading comprehension of the child is affected by his working memory capacity and there are individual differences in this regard. Rowe (1991) stated that parental support and involvement play an important role in the development of reading abilities. Hickman and Greenward (1992) also confirmed in their study that there exists a positive correlation between high verbal achievement and parental involvement.

Indian teachers and researchers have also been constantly facing as well as tackling up to a certain level, in the school situation, many immediate problems regarding specific activities and aids that could improve learning or controlling certain variables that affect the child's achievement, viz. intelligence, study habits, different aspects of child's personality, socio-economic status, etc., which directly or indirectly influence academic achievement.

During the 1960s, in India, many researches were conducted to study the correlates in general, personality correlates, backwardness and failure, over and under-achievement in different school subjects. Patel (1967) investigated some of the factors which influence memory, reasoning and mastery over the English language at high school level. Singh (1965) studied some non-intellectual correlates of academic achievement. Srinivasan (1969) conducted a comparative study of language ability and scholastic achievement of secondary school children. Pal (1984) concluded that socio-economic status, leadership traits and anxiety level of the child influence his reading abilities. This was also supported by Joshi (1984) in his study revealing a significant relationship between reading ability and intelligence, SES, caste and locality of the child. Mohan, (1991) investigated the role of aptitude, attitude and motivation in English language acquisition. She concluded that certain motivational aspects, linguistic aptitude and parental encouragement are significantly related to English language acquisition. Alavander (1992) in his study revealed that reading competency in English is influenced by parental education and occupation, locality, facilities available and the passive vocabulary of the child.

Much of the research conducted in the field of English language in India is related to material development, correlates of achievement, reading disabilities, development of strategies for improvement of reading skills, investigation into the various components of text books in English at various levels, etc. Still there are many areas in which more research needs to be done such as reading attitudes and interest and the psychological and parapsychological correlates of reading comprehension. Since 1970, many researches have been conducted in the field of language teaching. Most of the researches were related to the factors related to reading, material development for developing reading skills and developing strategies for reading comprehension. Only a few studies were based on the affective domain of the reading comprehension.

Statement and Definition of the Problem

Keeping in view the importance of reading skills for a beginner and its correlates, the present problem has been formulated as follows:

"A Study of Psycho-Social Factors Affecting Reading Skills in English"

Definition of Key Terms

As the proposed study has many key words such as 'Reading', 'Reading skills' and 'Psycho-social factors', it would be worthwhile to define and explain the key words in the above-stated problem.

Reading has been defined in several different ways. Some of the authoritative definitions are as follows:

1. "Reading is the process of giving significance intended by the writer to the graphic symbols by relating them to one's own fund of experience" (Dechant, 1970).
2. "Reading is an act of communication in which information is transferred from a transmitter to a receiver" (Smith, Frank, 1971).
3. "Reading is responding. The response may be at the surface level of 'calling' the word. It may be at some-what deeper levels of understanding the explicit meaning of sentence, paragraph or passage... It may involve going beyond the facts to the discovery of new and personal meanings" (Russell, D. 1961).
4. "Reading is a social interaction between the author of the book and the reader" (Ziller, 1964).

5. "Reading is a meaningful interpretation of printed or verbal symbols" (Harris and Sioay, 1971).

From these definitions, one can conclude that reading is more than knowing what each letter of the alphabet stands for. Comprehension is an essential part of reading; without comprehension no reading takes place. Thus, one can say that reading is a highly skilled process of meaningful interpretation of printed or verbal symbols. We can define reading to be anything we choose but certain evident aspects of the process which should be focused on are as follows:

1. Reading begins with the recognition of graphic symbols, print, script, etc.
2. The purpose of reading is the reconstruction of meaning.
3. There is a direct relationship between oral and written language.
4. Visual perception must be involved in reading.
5. Meaning is in the mind of the reader and the writer.
6. Reading is successful when the reader reconstructs a message which agrees with the writer's intended message.

Reading skills can be broadly categorized into following seven areas (Dechant, 1961):

1. Perception skills
2. Literal comprehension skills
3. Word recognition skills
4. Interpretive and appreciative skills
5. Reading study skills
6. Rate of comprehension skills
7. Oral reading skills.

Reading comprehension as treated in *Barrett's Taxonomy* is divided into five major skill categories or levels

1. Literal comprehension
2. Re-organization
3. Inferential comprehension
4. Evaluation
5. Appreciation.

Within each of these categories Barrett provides examples of specific types of tasks which the teacher might utilize. The five major categories range from easy to difficult in terms of the requirement(s) each category appears to demand. These skills are concerned with location, identification, reorganization, evaluation and interpretation of the points of information recoverable from a printed text. Together these skills comprise skills of comprehension. A diagrammatic presentation showing the details thereof has been given in Fig. 1.1.

Another broad classification of reading skills given in *Communicative Syllabus Design* (John Munby, 1978) is as under:

- Recognizing the script of a language.
- Deducing the meaning and use of unfamiliar lexical items.
- Understanding explicitly stated information.
- Understanding information when not explicitly stated, e.g. metaphor, simile, rhetorical questions, etc.
- Understanding that material will differ greatly in validity and reliability because of time, pressure of circumstances, biased opinion of the writer and many other facts.

As the investigator has planned to take class VI students as sample of the study who have just mastered the basic word-skills, it would be worthwhile to delimit the reading skills. The skills that have been selected for the study are as follows:

1. Literal comprehension skills, i.e., recognition of:

(a) details

(b) main idea

(c) sequencing

(d) comparison

(e) cause-effect relationship

(f) characteristics.

2. Re-organization skills by:

(a) outlining

(b) classifying

3. Inferential comprehension, i.e., inferring details of:

(a) main idea

(b) sequencing

(c) comparison

4. Evaluation, i.e., judgement of:

(a) reality versus fantasy

(b) appropriateness

5. Appreciation of:

(a) plot

(b) identification with characters

The other skills of reading have not been included in the study as these would have been too complex and beyond the level of grade VI students.

Psycho-social factors is the other key phrase which needs to be explained. We can broadly categorize the factors that influence reading skills as under:

1. Physical or biological factors
2. Psychological factors
3. Social factors
4. Cognitive and linguistic factors

A diagrammatic representation of these factors is given in Fig. 1.2.

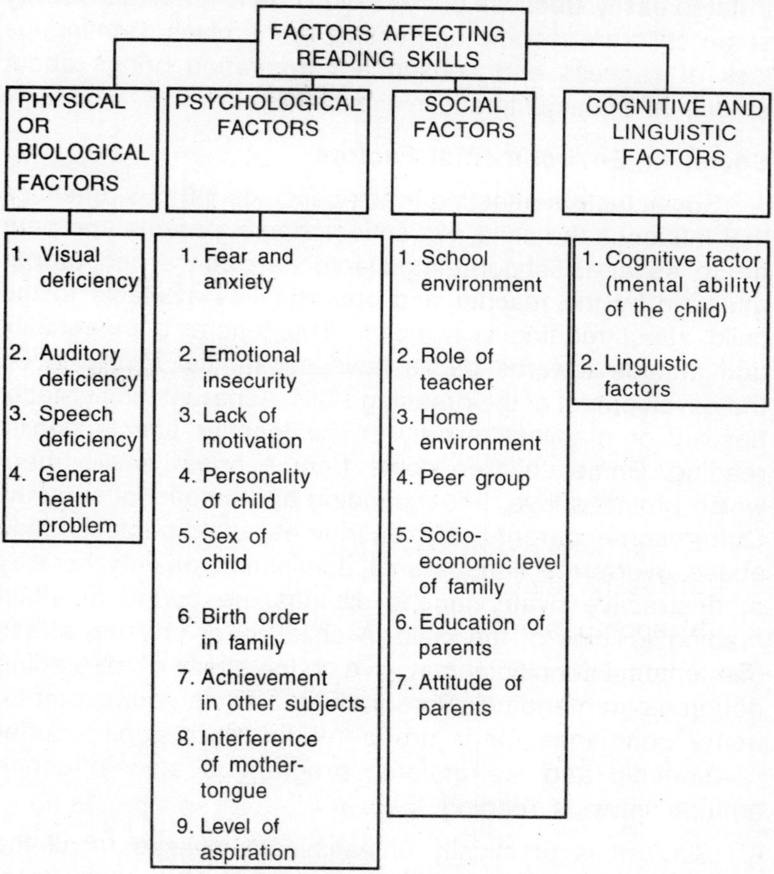

Fig. 1.2: Factors Affecting reading Skills of the Child.

Psychological Factors

Factors like fear and anxiety, emotional insecurity, lack of motivation, introvert personality of the child, sex, birth order of the child in the family, achievement in other subjects and interference of mother tongue have considerable influence on reading. Children with reading problems also manifest symptoms of stress in various ways. Some reading disabled children appear shy or restless, some seem to be unable to concentrate, others show nervous mannerism such as nail biting. Often children with reading problems lack self-confidence and consequently get discouraged and irritated easily. Because of frustration due to reading disability some children become aggressive in the class. Continuous lack of success and consequent frustration brings about emotional maladjustment in the child.

Social or Environmental Factors

Social factors affecting reading include various agencies that influence the child, viz. school, home, parents and peer group. As far as school-related factors are concerned, proper attention by the teacher and opportunities available to the child affect reading very much. The teacher's personality and attitude towards pupils have substantial influence on the development of their reading skills. Apparent indifference, hostility or manifest anxiety in the teacher affects pupils' reading. Some children come from a home environment which provides love, understanding and emotional security. Quarrelsome parents, broken homes, child-neglect, child abuse, over-protection, parental domination, anxiety, hostility or destructive rivalry among siblings are bound to affect reading abilities of the child. A child under unusual stress due to home conditions may give up too easily when reading becomes demanding. Personal and social adjustments, home conditions, peer group relationship, pupil-teacher relationship and instructional programme also influence attitude towards reading.

Since it is practically unfeasible to investigate all the factors related to reading skills in a study, the investigator has chosen relatively more significant psychological, parapsychological and social factors for the study. These are given as follows:

(i) Visual perception (through sight-vocabulary)

(ii) Level of aspiration

(iii) Sex of the child

(iv) Socio-economic status of family

(v) Parental support to reading

Besides these, intelligence of the child has also been taken into account as an important correlate of the study.

These factors would be discussed further under the topic construction of tools (Chapter III).

Delimitation of the Study

The proposed study has been planned to be delimited in two ways:

(a) Delimiting the factors

(b) Delimiting the skills of reading.

As shown in Fig. 1.2 there are many variables, viz. physical, biological, cognitive, psychological and social factors, and it would not be practically feasible for any investigator to include all of them.

Besides, physical or biological factors are beyond one's control; hence are recommended for clinical study separately. Therefore the author has taken into consideration the psychological and social factors. A number of research studies have been conducted on these correlates, e.g. the mother-tongue interference, achievement in other subjects, personality of the child, birth order in the family, role of school, teacher and home environment and so on.

In view of studies, the author has listed out certain variables for the study, which are as follows:

1. Psychological factors
   (a) Visual perception of the child (through sight vocabulary)
   (b) Level of aspiration of the child
   (c) Sex of the child
2. Social factors
   (a) Socio-economic level of the child/family
   (b) Parental support to reading
3. Cognitive factors—mental ability of the child.

As there are various skills involved in reading at various levels, the author felt the need to delimit reading skills for the present study according to the level of the sample. The study was conducted on class VI students of Kendriya

Vidyalayas of Delhi region where English is taught as a subject right from class I. As all Kendriya Vidyalayas follow the NCERT curricula, broad uniformity in terms of learning experiences can be assumed. The chief reasons for selecting this particular group was that the students of class VI have already learnt English as a subject for five years; consequently they possess certain level of reading skills including reading comprehension skills and word-identification skills.

On the basis of the above-mentioned the author listed out the following reading skills for the study:

1. Literal comprehension skills or recognition of
   (a) details
   (b) main idea
   (c) sequencing
   (d) comparison
   (e) cause effect relationship
   (f) characteristics
2. Re-organization
   (a) outlining
   (b) classifying
3. Inferential comprehension, i.e., inference of
   (a) main idea
   (b) sequencing
   (c) comparison
4. Evaluation i.e. judgement of
   (a) reality vs fantasy
   (b) appropriateness
5. Appreciation of
   (a) plot
   (b) identification with characters

Significance of the Study

Reading is one of the major important skills of language learning. It relates and introduces an individual to the world of information. It lends a soothing hand of comfort and solace to the lonely, dejected, isolated souls who are devoid of friends. Reading provides them a partner, a soulmate with whom they can very well pass their leisure time. "A good book is far better than boring friends" goes the adage. Reading not only recreates a person, but provides a number of significant psychological reliefs also such as:

(a) Reading a book takes away depression.

(b) Reading a book or a magazine before sleep, gives a comfortable nights sleep.

(c) Reading develops many other language proficiencies such as eye-span, concentration of mind and of course enrichment of vocabulary.

(d) Good reading propagates good thinking leading to a positive bent of mind. It helps to develop a positive attitude towards life and society.

(e) Reading broadens the mental horizons of people. It not only makes people more open and broad-minded, but also makes them more receptive and flexible.

It has been observed that a well-read man has more patience and openness to others' thoughts than those who don't read much. Reading provides a variety of experiences. It is said correctly that "It is good to learn through experience; but it is always better to learn from others' experiences." Reading provides a lot of scope to learn from others' experiences. It is not always feasible to have a first-hand experience of all happenings. Neither is it possible and nor is it desirable. Reading provides us the opportunity to learn about various happenings and incidents. Of course visuals do give us information, but the effect of visuals such as television or a movie is temporary; just short-lived, whereas reading has an everlasting effect. It is a famous saying that:

"Some books are to be tasted,

Some are to be chewed;

and, some are to be chewed,

assimilated and digested."

Hence, the effect of a good book leaves a permanent impression on one's mind.

When the significance of this particular language skill is universally accepted why should our young Indian readers be deprived of using this skill? Our Government school children are not good readers. This is a bitter fact, but one has to accept it. The scenario is very pathetic when talking of reading as far as the second language English is concerned, English is taught as one of the subjects. At primary level, none of the aforementioned four language skills is given proper attention.

The research studies reveal that more than 50 per cent of the students at class VI level are familiar only with the very basic elementary level language skills. A class V student can read only a few familiar words and sentences. The reading ability of children even at upper primary level is not better. Reading skills even at upper primary level are developed till the lower comprehension level. The higher level of skills such as analysis, evaluation and interpretation are not expected at this level.

Keeping these things in mind, the author selected this topic to study the various factors affecting reading skills of the young readers. These young readers would be students of class VI, those who have just stepped out of primary education. These children have the elementary, word-level knowledge of the English language. By word-level knowledge is meant that these children are familiar to certain words and structures and their vocabulary is very limited. Class VI students of Kendriya Vidyalaya were selected for the study. These students have studied English as a subject from Class I. Kendriya Vidyalayas have a judicious mixed grouping of students coming from all socio-economic levels. The children of senior defence officers study in the same class with the children of soldiers. Some of the parents are highly educated and highly placed while the other parents are illiterates. In a way, a true picture of Indian society with all its different colours, castes and creed can be found in Kendriya Vidyalayas. Hence, the classroom reflects a mini-India in these schools.

Reading skills of the students in these schools are not so developed. There could be a number of factors responsible for these not so well developed reading skills. Some of the factors may be biological while others may be related to the environment. The author selected the area of study and delimited it to the psychological and social factors. The study will take care of the factors that are very personal to the child. The first and foremost reason for taking psychological and social factors is that these factors are either related to the child itself or his/her family, parents and siblings. The study concentrates only on the child as an individual or its home. Therefore, the author is hopeful that the study would reveal certain important factors which would help to take some reformative steps in improving reading skills of the young children. The author is also optimistic that the study will provide valuable suggestions for the parents for improvement of the reading skills of their children.

Objective of the study

Keeping in view the rationale and the significance of the problem, the proposed study has the following objectives.

To Investigate the Various Psycho-social Factors Affecting Reading Comprehension.

Reading comprehension of the students reflect a poor understanding of the content and the process of reading comprehension is undesirably slow and yielding insignificant results. The author probes into the various factors especially the psycho-social factors that attribute to this state of reading comprehension.

To examine the influence of Socio-economic level of the Learner's Family on his Reading Comprehension at both Literal and Inferential Level

Reading comprehension takes place at various levels such as literal level where the child comprehends the meaning of the text as it is projected to him/her. He/she does not deploy any other means or thought process or his/her creative imagination to analyse the text. He/she does not try to interpret the text. On the contrary, at inferential level the child uses the various sub-skills such as analysing the situation or extrapolating the text in his/her own way. One can say, the child flies high in the world of imagination, on the wings of the content provided by the author. The investigator desires to find out whether the socio-economic level of the family influences the learner's reading comprehension skills both at literal and inferential level or not. The socio-economic level of the family may be ascertained by taking many aspects together such as the educational level of both the parents, professional status of both the parents, facilities and comfort at home, home environment, social status of the family and so on. The author took up some of the important factors and saw their effect on the reading comprehension of the learners.

To Study the Role of Parental Support to Reading on the Learner's Reading Comprehension Skills at Various Levels

It is true that the attitude of parents does have a major influence on the child's learning. The author would wish to find out the effect of parental support to reading on the child's reading comprehension. By parental support, the investigator does not mean providing instructions, but inspire them towards reading. It also includes their own interest in reading, their reading habits and amount of time they devote to reading. By attitude, the author also means the opportunity for good reading the parents provide to their children or the parent-child interaction about good literature.

To Examine Whether the Learner's Sex Affects his/her Reading Comprehension

Does it really matter whether a learner is a boy or a girl for acquisition of skills for reading comprehension? The author desired to find out the effect of the individual's sex on his/her reading comprehension. There are several misconceptions such as:

(a) Boys perform better than girls in acquisition of literal level of comprehension.

(b) Girls perform better in extrapolation and explaining the text.

(c) Boys have more analytical mind, hence they perform well in making tables or analysing the factual data.

(d) Girls, since childhood, are more interested in reading fantasy novels whereas the boys are keen on reading mysteries or adventure novels.

How far do these myths hold any substantive basis? Are these only the hearsay/misconceptions or there lies any hidden truth beneath? The author desired to find out in the fourth objective of the study.

To Examine the Contribution of Learner's Sight Vocabulary Towards Reading Comprehension

The sight vocabulary of an individual is the ability to recognise, understand and use the commonly-used words. The author desired to ascertain whether the students' treasure of vocabulary, i.e., familiarity with the words which are commonly used in his/her literal surrounding help them for their reading comprehension or not. It is true that the more you have encounters with the written text, more will you develop familiarity with words. This will certainly build the sight vocabulary of an individual. But whether it has any direct influence on the development of reading comprehension of the learner is yet to be investigated according to the fifth objective of the study.

To Assess the Learner's Level of Aspiration and its Correlation with Reading Comprehension

The sixth objective is related to the learner's goal setting, his own desire and achievement level. Most of the learners set their goals first and then make their efforts to achieving those goals. The author set out to find out whether the learners set their goals for high achievement in English too or they kept their goals set only for subjects like Science and Mathematics. Whether any correlation exists between the level of aspiration of the child and his reading comprehension level was also observed.

To Study the Contribution of General Mental Ability towards Reading Comprehension at Various Levels

The general mental ability is the intelligence of a person. It is perceived that the general level of achievement of an individual is directly correlated to intelligence. But how far is the acquisition of reading comprehension skills affected by the general mental ability of the individual learner is the seventh and last objective of the proposed study.

Hypothesis of the Study

On the basis of the review of the related studies conducted in India and abroad in the past few decades, the proposed study had the following hypotheses:

1. Various psychological and social factors affect a learner's reading comprehension individually as well as collectively.
2. Socio-economic status of the family does influence the reading comprehension skills of the learner positively.
3. Parents' support in reading reinforces the learner's reading comprehension skills.
4. The learner's reading comprehension skills are independent of learner's gender.
5. More developed sight vocabulary of the learner promotes reading comprehension.

6. The level of aspiration of the child is positively related to his acquisition of reading comprehension skills.
7. There exists a positive correlation between the general mental ability and reading comprehension skills of a learner.
8. Various levels of reading comprehension have a hierarchical relationship.

Design and Procedure of the Study

The author planned a line of action to carry out the study such as:

(a) selection of sample
(b) selection and preparation of tools
(c) standardization of tools
(d) collection of data
(e) analysis of data

The author selected 250 students comprising 125 girls and 125 boys of 5 Kendriya Vidyalayas of Delhi region, geographically located in north, east, west, south and central Delhi. 25 girls and 25 boys comprising a group of 50 students, studying in class VI from each school were randomly picked up. As Kendriya Vidyalayas reflect a true picture of students coming from different socio-economic level families, no further stratification was thought to be required.

Selection and development of tools had been planned which were as follows:

- Reading passages for testing various comprehension skills
- Sight vocabulary test
- Parental support to reading questionnaire
- Socio-economic status scale questionnaire
- Level of aspiration test
- A non-verbal general mental ability test

Some of the tests such as Raven's Standard Progressive Matrices (RSPM) were used but the other tools were developed and standardized by the author. The data collected through various sources was subjected to both qualitative as well as inferential statistical devices. Suggestions and recommendations were made for enhancing the role of these factors in attaining greater mastery of reading skills.

2

Resume of Related Literature

Introduction

For any worthwhile study in any field of knowledge after formulation of hypothesis, the researcher needs an adequate familiarity with the library and its main resources to acquire up-to-date information about what has been thought and done in a particular area from which he/she has selected the problems for research. The review of educational research gives the researcher an excellent overview of the work that has been done in the field and helps him/her keep up with recent developments.

Keeping this in mind, in the present chapter, the studies related to the research problems have been reviewed selectively. Besides a brief historical perspective, the studies have been classified under two broad categories:

(i) Studies conducted in India

(ii) Studies conducted abroad.

A Historical Perspective

Reading has been always an area of interest since the beginning of the 20th century. Thorndike (1917) hypothesized that adequate comprehension in reading comes about as a result of the reader's use of all his reasoning faculties and skills in problem solving.

Gray (1925) on the basis of his research provided four tentative conclusions on reading comprehension. These were:

readiness in a predictable manner (Scott and Kobbe, 1975).

As far as studies on reading in India are concerned, these gained recognition in the 1970s. Shastri (1972) studied that performance of students on vocabulary test had a significant correlation with their performance in Senior School Certificate (SSC) examination. Deshpande (1973) made a methodological study to teach reading to beginners through improvement in the preparation of reading material and through evaluation in reading. Parikh (1976) inquired into the factors affecting reading speed and comprehension and found that reading speed was influenced positively by printing and size of letter.

Verbal intelligence and language proficiency were identified as important variables in reading comprehension by Pal (1977).

Studies Conducted in India

Kopper, B. (1970) conducted a study on "An inquiry into factors affecting reading comprehension in English." The main objectives of the study were:

(i) to study the level of reading comprehension of class XI students; and

(ii) to study the relationships of reading comprehension with attitude towards reading, anxiety, academic motivation, socio-economic status and dependence.

The study sample included 555 students of class XI of nine Gujarati medium schools of Baroda. The tools used were silent reading comprehension list in English by Patel, reading attitude scale by Patel, junior index of motivation scale by Frymier, test anxiety scale for children constructed by Nijhawan, the socio-economic status scale by Mehta and pre-adolescent dependence scale developed by Pareek and

(i) The ability to interpret simple passage accurately increases rapidly in the lower grades and reaches a very high level by the end of grade III.

(ii) The speed with which the reader interprets simple passages improves rapidly with the class level.

(iii) The depth of interpretation increases steadily throughout the elementary and higher level.

(iv) The ability to pronounce words usually exceeds the ability to comprehend them by the end of grade III.

Bridges (1941) compared the effect of specific training for speed with specific training for reading comprehension. He concluded that training which stressed reading comprehension resulted in better achievement than training which emphasized only speed. Cutts (1953) in his study gave greater emphasis to comprehension and development of study skills than rate of reading. Smith and Carrigan (1959) have reported that indications are there that reading comprehension, cognitive skills and memory are directly affected by the body's chemical reactions.

Till the end of 1960, most of the studies were conducted on reading abilities. The 1970's were the time of large-scale studies on reading comprehension. These were set off by a series of conferences sponsored by the National Institute of Education and the establishment of a centre for the study of reading at the University of Illinois in USA in 1976.

Reading readiness is one of the few technical terms that has a direct counterpart in the non-technical language of ordinary conversation. This concept is associated with maturation issues, development and environmental situation. It is generally assumed that learning occurs best when people are ready to learn (Sawyer, 1975). A major component of reading is maturation based on biological

Rao. Descriptive analysis and product-moment correlation were used for data-analysis. The major findings were that:

(i) Reading comprehension was positively correlated to reading attitude;

(ii) Anxiety was negatively correlated to reading comprehension; and

(iii) Some other factors such as reading readiness, academic motivation, attitude towards the English language, quality of classroom, status of parents and social and economic compulsions were found to be related to reading comprehension.

From the above-stated study, it may be concluded that reading attitude certainly affects the reading comprehension and anxiety plays a negative role for reading comprehension. Though the author mentioned some other variables affecting reading comprehension, these are yet to be studied in detail.

Shah, J.H. (1979) conducted a comparative study of some personal and psychological variables and reading comprehension on 412 pupils of VIIIth and IXth grades selected randomly from four different secondary schools of Bhavnagar city. The main objectives of the investigation were to compare intra-group differences in subject scores on Trivedi and Patel's reading comprehension test with respect to six personal variables, i.e., gender grade, age, parental education and occupation and also three psychological variables namely reading rate, intelligence and meaning vocabulary.

The study revealed that:

(i) No significant differences existed between the reading comprehension of boys and girls;

(ii) A significant difference appeared in the frequencies of high and low group pupils on variables like parental income, education and occupation; and

(iii) All the three psychological variables, viz. reading rate, intelligence and meaning vocabulary showed positive correlation with reading comprehension.

Thus, it is indicated in this study that gender of an individual does not have any relationship with reading comprehension. But at the same time variables like parental education, occupation and income as well as reading rate, intelligence and meaning vocabulary are positively correlated with reading comprehension.

Bhishikar, L. (1980) conducted an experimental analytical study of the acquisition of reading skills. The main objectives of this study were:

(i) To prepare a training programme in reading skills;

(ii) To design and construct reading test for evaluating training;

(iii) To study the effect of intelligence and sex on reading skills acquisition;

(iv) To study reading interest and reading habits of students; and

(v) To study the interrelationship among sub-skills of reading and the relationship of reading performance with language scores, general scholastic achievement and socio-economic status (SES) of students.

The tools used in the study were a verbal test of intelligence, Raven's progressive matrices, reading skill test, critical reading test and reading inventory. The randomised sample comprised 400 boys and girls of various schools of Pune. The data were analysed through various statistical techniques. These were product-moment correlation, chi-square test, Hartley's test and analysis of variance.

The study revealed that intelligence plays a significant role in acquisition of reading skills. The training programme brought about significant improvement in the performance of students. It was seen that the low intelligence group enjoyed perception exercise while the high intelligence group preferred vocabulary contexts. The study also confirmed the fact that gender of the child does not affect the acquisition of reading skills. But at the same time SES, reading habits, reading interest, health, and scholastic achievement were found to be positively related to reading achievement.

Thus, it may be concluded that the personal correlates like intelligence, reading habits and interests, SES, health and scholastic achievement are significantly correlated to the acquisition of reading skills whereas the gender of the child does not influence the reading skills.

Agrawal, V.R.A. (1981) studied reading ability in relation to certain cognitive and non-cognitive factors. In his study, the main focus was on examining the role of some personal, cognitive and non-cognitive factors in reading ability. The sample comprised 400 grade IX boys and girls. Personal data blank, Krishna's reading ability test battery, Jamdar's study habits inventory, Mohsin's test of general intelligence, Nafde's non-verbal intelligence test, Eysenck's personality inventory and Worchel's self-activity inventory were used. Two-way analysis of variance was used for data analysis.

The major findings were that:

(i) Caste or personal occupation did not affect the reading ability of males as well as females;

(ii) High and low reading ability group in boys differed significantly in ordinal position. Economic status and parents' educational level created significant difference in high and low reading ability groups;

(iii) Gender of the child was related significantly to study habits, academic achievement, verbal and non-verbal intelligence, anxiety and parental attitude; and

(iv) A significant relationship was indicated between reading ability and study habits, verbal and non-verbal intelligence.

Thus, the study confirms that gender has no correlation with the acquisition of reading skills but at the same time variables like SES, parents' education, study habits and intelligence show significant correlation with reading.

Pal, R. (1984) conducted a factorial study of socio-psychological variables related to scholastic achievement of higher secondary school-going pupils in Uttar Pradesh.

The study aimed at the following objectives:

1. To find out how far family relations; intelligence, self-concept, aspiration and anxiety were responsible for scholastic achievement in higher secondary pupils;
2. To study the interaction of bivariate as well as trivariate independent variables (scholastic achievement, sex and SES);
3. To factor analyse the performance in terms of achievement of high and low scholastic achievers.

The sample included 240 boys and girls belonging to different SES and scholastic achievement levels. The various tools used were Sherry and Verma's family relationship inventory (FRI), Singh and Saxena's socio-economic status scale, Singh and Tiwari's level of aspiration test, Rastogi's self-concept scale and Srivastava and Tiwari's anxiety scale. Data were analysed with the help of factorial design analysis of variance of equal size cells, t-test, Duncan's range test and Hotteling's principal axis solution method.

The findings revealed that

(i) The parents' acceptance promoted scholastic achievement;

(ii) There was no impact of gender on mother's acceptance or father's avoidance and concentration;

(iii) SES has no relation with father's acceptance and avoidance, as well as with intelligence;

(iv) High scholastic achievers promoted predominantly verbal, non-verbal and total intelligence in comparison to low achievers;

(v) No significane impact of interaction between scholastic achievement, gender and SES on the intelligence of the students was found;

(vi) Gender had a significant impact on aspiration and anxiety; males promoted aspiration whereas females surpassed them in anxiety; and

(vii) SES had a significant impact on aspiration and anxiety.

Das, P.A. (1984) conducted another study on reading comprehension of class X students of English medium schools in the context of some psycho-social factors in central Gujarat.

The main objectives of the study were

(i) To construct a test to measure reading comprehension of class X students;

(ii) To establish norms for reading comprehension for students;

(iii) To study whether there were any sex differences with regard to reading comprehension; and

(iv) To study reading comprehension in the context of SES, test anxiety, emotional stability, leadership and radicalism.

The randomized sample used for the study comprised 384 girls and 489 boys selected from English medium schools of central Gujarat. A test was constructed and standardized for measuring the various components of reading comprehension. Percentile rank norms and standard score norms were formulated separately for boys and girls. For studying reading comprehension in the context of SES and other psycho-social factors, a 2x2x3 factorial design was used.

Major findings revealed by the study were:

(i) The mean score of girls was slightly higher than that of boys with regard to reading comprehension in English;

(ii) Students with high SES showed better scores in reading comprehension;

(iii) Emotional stability was not found to influence reading comprehension;

(iv) The mean difference in reading comprehension scores was in favour of students having leadership traits; and

(v) Students with low anxiety level showed better scores in reading comprehension than those with high anxiety level.

The conclusion drawn from the study is that the girls perform better at reading comprehension though the difference is very low. The study further establishes that SES, leadership traits and anxiety level of the individual affects his/her reading comprehension.

Srivastava, R.P. (1984) studied the relationship of reading ability with general mental ability, SES and school achievement. The main objectives of the study were:

(i) To study the relationship between various measures of reading ability and general mental ability; and

(ii) To find out the relationship between reading ability, SES and school achievement.

A stratified random sample of 480 boys and girls was taken. The tools used were Raven's advance progressive matrices and Dabas' socio-cultural status scale and reading ability test. The t-test was employed for analysis. The major findings of the study were:

(i) A positive and significant correlation was found between school achievement and reading comprehension;

(ii) No significant correlation was found between SES, intelligence and reading ability with school achievement; and

(iii) Intelligence and SES were found to be significantly related to acquisition of language skills.

Joshi, A.N. (1984) investigated into the factors influencing English language abilities. The objectives of the study were:

(i) To ascertain the growth level of comprehension, vocabulary, language usage and spelling ability;

(ii) To find out the common errors committed in English by the students belonging to different gender, locality, intelligence and SES; and

(iii) To find out the factors which influence the growth of English language abilities.

The study was conducted on a stratified random sample of 720 students (boys and girls) of Scheduled Castes as well as non-Scheduled Castes of both urban as well as rural areas of Moradabad. The tools used were Raven's Progressive Matrices, SES urban scale (Kapoor), SES rural scale (Udai Parikh), sixteen personality factors inventory (Cattell) and English language ability test by Sharma. Mean, percentage, t-test and correlation were used for analysis of data. The major findings of the study were:

(i) The SC students were found to attain average growth level in language abilities whereas non-SC students were found to be higher than average in these abilities;

(ii) There existed a significant relationship between intelligence and growth of various English language abilities;

(iii) The growth of English language abilities was found to be maximum among eighth graders of missionary-run schools followed by state government schools and thereafter by schools run by private agnecies; and

(iv) A significant relationship was found between language abilities and intelligence, caste, SES and locality of the individual.

Joshi concluded that language abilities in English showed a significant relationship with intelligence, caste, SES and locality of the student.

Skantha Kumari, S.K. (1987) conducted a study on development of strategies for improvement of reading skills in English at middle school level. The main objectives of the study were:

(i) To identify the task involved in reading and comprehension;

(ii) To develop strategies that would help students perform the tasks involved in reading and comprehension;

(iii) To develop the skills of reading comprehension through these strategies; and

(iv) To find out the effectiveness of these strategies through an experiment.

A survey-cum-experimental design was used for the study. The sample comprised 937 students, both boys and girls selected by stratified random sampling from 11 schools of both rural and urban areas of Chennai. The sample for experimental study consisted of 58 top ranking and 56 low ranking students in reading and comprehension. The tools used were mental ability test, part I (NCERT), Kuppuswamy's SES scale, self-constructed achievement test and reading comprehension test.

Major findings revealed by the study were as under:

(i) There was a significantly higher reading ability score for male students from English medium urban schools.

(ii) The intervention strategy helped improve the reading ability of both high as well as low scorers; the increase in lower group being higher than that in the higher group.

(iii) The increase in the achievement of reading ability was significantly high in literal comprehension and in inferential comprehension for both high and low groups.

(iv) The percentage of increase in achievement of reading ability of the student and the mental ability scores were significantly related.

From the above-stated study, a conclusion may be drawn that social environment plays a significant role in language learning. The study also shows a significant correlation between reading ability and the mental ability of the child.

Aranha, Mabel (1988) conducted a study on reading attitudes of Indian students. The main objective of the study was to determine the effect of sustained silent reading (SSR) on students' attitude towards reading.

The sample of the study comprised 144 students of grade IV of an English medium school at Goregaon, Mumbai. The randomized sample was of three classes having 48 students each. Out of the three classes one class was the experimental group and the other two were controlled groups. The tools used for the study were, a structured questionnaire, Estes' attitude scale and self-constructed pre-test and post-test.

SSR was introduced in grade IV twice a week beginning from five minutes and later extended up to 25 minutes. Besides this, eighty books on children's literature in English were given to the class to read on rotation basis. Attitude towards reading was scrutinized for variation with reference to language ability and sex. The study revealed that Indian children had good attitude towards reading. It also concluded that boys had a better attitude towards reading than girls.

Singh, Manju (1989) conducted a study of achievement in English in relation to intelligence, interest, socio-economic status and facilities available for learning the language for the students at high school level.

The main objectives of the study were:

(i) To find out the reason for offering English at high school level;

(ii) To know the reasons responsible for unsatisfactory achievement of students in English;

(iii) To find out the average level of performance in English of high school students in relation with their intelligence, interest, SES level and facilities available for learning the language;

(iv) To make a comparative study of the scores of boys and girls on various tests and questionnaires;

(v) To find out the degree of relationship between scores on English achievement test and the correlates; and

(vi) To find out which of the related variables play an effective role in achievement of students in English.

The investigator constructed seven tests and questionnaires as tools of the study which included check-lists, interest-inventory, an SES scale and a questionnaire regarding the facilities available for learning the language. A mental ability test by M.C. Joshi was also used.

There were 908 students of class X from eastern and central Uttar Pradesh who were selected through stratified random sampling for data collection. Statistical techniques employed for the study included mean, SD (standard deviation), correlation-coefficient, regression and standard error of estimate for multiple prediction.

Major findings revealed by the study were as under:

(i) The difference in the mean scores of the boys and girls in English achievement and facilities for learning language was not found significant;

(ii) A significant difference was found between the mean scores of the rural and urban students in all five tests and questionnaires except for interest scores.

(iii) In all the tests, the urban students of both sexes were found to be superior to the rural students.

(iv) The most significant factor of achievement for both boys' and girls' achievement was found to be socio-economic status.

(v) All the five variables–intelligence, English achievement, interest, SES, and facilities for learning had a positive relationship with each other.

Thus, it may be concluded that boys and girls do not differ significantly in their achievement in English. Socio-economic status of the learner and his locality affect achievement in English, intelligence, interest, and educational facilities available for learning the language.

Sabharwal, Veena (1989) concluded a study on reading skills of precocious and average readers in first and second language learning. The main objectives of the study were:

- (i) To analyze the nature of the reading process used by precocious and the average children in terms of various reading skills;
- (ii) To study level of reading comprehension of the precocious and the average on L1 and L2 prose texts;
- (iii) To examine and compare level of factual and interpretive comprehension of prose texts by the precocious and average readers;
- (iv) To examine systematic and semantic acceptability of various types of miscues made by the precocious and the average;
- (v) To study incidence and typology of miscues made by precocious and average readers;
- (vi) To compare and analyse reading performance of the precocious and the average in terms of various aspects of reading process;
- (vii) To propose a model of reading that explains and accounts for various differences between reading performance of precocious and average readers;
- (viii) To study reading behaviour of the precocious and the average readers and their perception of various environmental factors as contributory to their reading proficiency; and
- (ix) To develop a generalised profile of the precocious reader as distinguished from the average.

The initial sample comprised 497 grade IV students who were rated on reading performance rating scale (RPRS) and finally 28 precocious and 28 average readers were selected randomly as student sample. The tools used for the study were self-developed reading performance rating scale

(RPRS), two test batteries, a fifty-item isolated word list and a set of six prose passages along with comprehension questions and teacher record sheet. Besides these tests, interviews were also taken for eliciting additional information on reading behaviour.

Data were analyzed by using mean, SD, range and chi-square test. The t-ratio test and correlation analysis were also carried out. The major findings revealed were that

(i) The precocious children performed at a higher level of reading comprehension than average readers;

(ii) The precocious children did not perform as well or better than the average on factual comprehension of L1 text though they performed better on factual comprehension of L2 text than the average;

(iii) The precocious children performed better than the average in terms of interpretive comprehension of text;

(iv) The average readers made more miscues than the precocious;

(v) Reading skills were transferable across language; reading skills were transferred from the more familiar and the more practiced language irrespective of whether it was L1 or L2;

(vi) The precocious readers excelled the average at transfer of reading skill across L1 and L2;

(vii) The precocious readers relied more on their use of higher reading skills while the average relied more on lower reading skills; and

(viii) The precocious readers perceived their home environment as a major contributing factor to their reading precocity, their home environment contributed through better guidance, greater parental interest and more facilities for personal reading whereas the contribution of school is relatively negligible.

Thus, it may be concluded that precocious children have better reading abilities; they employ higher reading skills for comprehension and they perceive home as a contributing factor to their reading proficiency.

Grover, S. (1991) made an investigation into the standards of reading ability in English in government and central schools. The researcher formulated the following hypotheses regarding her study:

(i) Reading ability is a unitary trait;

(ii) Both boys and girls acquire more or less equivalent reading ability by the time they reach a particular grade level (IX grade);

(iii) Pupils studying in Central Schools and government schools are more or less equivalent in their reading ability at a particular stage (IX grade).

In order to test hypotheses (ii) and (iii), the investigator formulated the following null hypotheses:

(i) There is no significant difference in the reading ability of homogenous groups of boys and girls studying in Central Schools;

(ii) There is no significant difference in the reading ability of Central School boys and government school boys

(iii) There is no significant difference in the reading ability of Central School girls and government school girls.

The sample comprised 400 randomly selected students including boys and girls of both government and Central Schools of Delhi. The tools used for the study were various reading tests constructed by the investigator. The data were analysed using inter-correlation matrices and factor-analysis. The major findings of the study were

(i) Reading ability emerged as a unitary trait partially in case of Central School girls and government school boys and girls;

(ii) Central School girls excelled better than government school boys with substantial margin in their scores on reading ability;

(iii) There was a marked difference between the mean scores of Central School girls and government school girls in reading ability.

(iv) No significant difference was found in the achievement of government school boys and girls;

(v) Almost no significant difference in reading was found between Central School boys and girls;

(vi) Reading emerged as a differentiated trait in case of Central School boys; and

(vii) Central School pupils both boys and girls showed better performance in almost all the six variables of reading ability test as compared to government school pupils.

The researcher, therefore, concluded that reading ability of the individual was influenced by one's socio-cultural background. Reading ability had no correlation with the gender of the individual, but it was certainly affected by the social environment both at school as well as at home.

Mohan, S. (1991) investigated the role of aptitude, attitude and motivation in English language acquisition. The main objectives of the study were:

(i) To investigate the relationship of socio-psychological factors and linguistic aptitude to English language learning of the students;

(ii) To compare the achievement of public school and government school students in reading with regard to the above factors;

(iii) To study the interrelationship among various attitudinal factors as also among various sub-components of English achievement;

(iv) To study if the learner's attitude towards English learning bears significant relationship with achievement in English.

(v) To study the relationship between linguistic aptitude and achievement in English;

(vi) To compare the public school students and government school students in their linguistic aptitude and attitude towards learning English;

(vii) To study the effect of parental encouragement on learner's attitude for English learning;

(viii) To study if a strong reading vocabulary is accompanied by fewer spelling errors in English; and

(ix) To examine whether grammar and vocabulary are related to reading comprehension and language expression in English.

The investigator formulated the following hypotheses:

1 (a) A positive attitude towards English learning has a significant positive relation to achievement in English;

(b) High aptitude for language learning has a significant positive relationship to achievement in English;

2 (a) The public school students have a significant higher attitude towards the English language learning than the government school students;

(b) Public school students have a significantly higher aptitude for English learning and also have higher achievement in English than the government school students.

In all 14 variables were controlled in this study. Of these, seven represented attitudinal and motivational characteristics, two linguistic aptitude and five different facets of English achievement. The tools used were English language attitude and motivation questionnaire (BLAMQ), language aptitude test (LAT) and English achievement test (EAT). The sample comprised 546 senior secondary school students (233 from three public and 313 from six government schools).

The following statistical procedures were used for data analysis:

(i) Step-wise multiple regression was used to analyse the influence of attitudinal and aptitudinal variables on the attainment in English.

(ii) Z-test of significance was used to test whether the mean scores of the attitudinal, aptitudinal and achievement variables differed significantly among the three groups of students.

(iii) Factor-analysis was used to discover a few basic factors that may explain the interrelationship among the attitudinal variables.

The major findings of the study were:

(i) Some aspects of motivation and attitude showed significant correlation with some aspects of English learning;

(ii) Practice and use (a motivational factor) emerged as the most influential attitudinal factor which had significantly positive correlation with the public school students;

(iii) No relation was found between English learning attitudes and the scores in language expression and spellings in any of the three groups;

(iv) Parental encouragement was significantly and positively correlated to government school students' scores in reading comprehension;

(v) Public school students revealed a significantly higher aptitude for English learning and had better attitude towards English than government school students and also showed higher achievement in English;

(vi) Students having high parental encouragement had higher motivation to learn; and

(vii) Those who derive satisfaction from using English were better able to use English.

Thus, we may conclude that a positive attitude towards English, linguistic aptitude, parental encouragement and motivation are significantly related to English language acquisition.

Alavandar, R. (1992) conducted a study of selected variables relating to English reading competency of high school pupils. The main objective of the study were:

(i) To construct and standardize the following tests in English for IX grade students

(a) spelling test

(b) grammar test

(c) silent reading comprehension test;

(ii) To find out the level of English reading competency of high school pupils;

(iii) To study the reading habits and interests of high school pupils;

(iv) To find out the relationship between gender, reading habits and interest of the pupils as well as their parents' education, occupation and income and also with their reading competency;

(v) To find out the relationship between pupils' reading habits, spelling ability, passive vocabulary and grammatical knowledge on one hand and their English reading competency on the other; and

(vi) To find out and compare the level of achievement in English among different groups such as :

(a) English medium and Tamil medium pupils

(b) public schools and government schools pupils

(c) rural and urban schools pupils.

The tools included self-designed test battery for testing spellings, grammar and silent-reading comprehension, questionnaire on reading habits, a test on reading speed, a cloze test in English, a word recognition test and a personal data sheet. The statistical techniques included descriptive analysis test of significance of difference between the means of different groups, chi-square test, correlation techniques and multiple regression equation for prediction of achievement in English reading competency (ERC) from scores on linguistic variables.

The major findings of the study were:

(i) High school pupils differed widely in ERC, i.e., ability in spelling, grammar, word-recognition skill and reading habits;

(ii) English medium pupils showed superior ERC to Tamil medium pupils whose low competency was related to lack of access to books;

(iii) Urban and public school pupils had better ERC than rural and government school pupils;

(iv) ERC was found to be related to the education of the parents especially the mother. ERC was also related to the occupation of parents but not to interests;

(v) ERC was directly proportional to reading habits, spelling, passive vocabulary and grammar which determine 75 per cent of the variance in ERC; and

(vi) The influence of passive vocabulary was found to be four times greater than that of reading habits and spelling and twice that of grammar making, thus, being the most important contributor.

Therefore, it may be concluded that reading competency in English is influenced by parental education and occupation, locality, facilities available and the passive vocabulary of the child.

Sankarappan, R. (1992) studied the relationship of certain variables with the achievement in English of IX grade pupils. The objectives of this study were:

(i) Examining the attitude and the interest of students towards English in relation with their sex, residence and their parents' literacy level;

(ii) Analysing the pupils' level of achievement in English against the respondents' sex, residence and parental literacy level; and

(iii) Finding out the relationship between the attitude, interest, achievement and perception of effectiveness of their teachers of English.

For the study 490 students of class IX were selected through stratified randomization from ten different schools of Madurai district. The investigator used the following tools for data collection:

(i) Attitude scale by Sundarajan and Balakrishanan (1989)

(ii) Interest inventory

(iii) Students' perception questionnaire.

The data was analyzed by using descriptive statistics, Pearson's product–moment correlation, test of significance and graphic presentation. On the basis of the study the following results were obtained:

(i) The gender of the child had no relation with the attitude towards English;

(ii) There was a significant difference between the rural and urban pupils in respect of their attitude towards the study of English;

(iii) Boys and girls differed significantly with respect to their interest in English;

(iv) Rural and urban pupils differed significantly in respect of their interest in English;

(v) Boys and girls did not differ significantly in their perception of the level of effectiveness of their English teachers;

(vi) Boys and girls did not differ significantly in their achievement in English;

(vii) Parental educational level had a positive influence on the achievement of the child in English; and

(viii) Pupils' attitudes and interests in English had a positive and significant influence on their achievement in English.

Thus, it may be concluded that gender of the child has no influence on his achievement in English but his parental educational level, interest, attitude and locality have significant influence on his achievement.

Studies Abroad

Fotheringam, J.B. and Creal, D. (1971) conducted a study on the family's socio-economic and educational characteristics as predictors of school achievement in Ontario, Canada. The main objective of the study was to determine the association between family characteristics and academic achievement. The sample comprised 62 II graders and 83 III graders selected on stratified randomization procedure, having a wide range of academic achievement types of class placements. These children were Canadian-born having both the parents. The tools used for the study were the family functioning scale and Dave's scale of home educational process. Interviews of parents were conducted to access educational and emotional atmosphere at home. A step-wise multiple regression was used for the analysis of data.

The major findings were:

(i) The major influence on the difference in academic achievement among children was of the family;

(ii) A significant relationship was found between parental education, occupational status and mental abilities of the children;

(iii) Curriculum, amount of expenditure, teacher's qualification or experience didn't seem to have a significant effect on achievement; and

(iv) Family background, family physical resources and difference in home educational learning environment had a significant influence on academic achievement of the students.

Thus, the study revealed that family, home atmosphere (both educational and emotional) have a significant effect on learning.

Dori Roettger, Mike Szymczuk and Joseph Millard (1975) conducted a study on elementary school children in Iowa, USA. The objectives of the study were:

(i) To modify the vocabulary and sentence structure of estate scale without changing the concept;

(ii) To validate the modified reading attitude scale; and

(iii) To investigate the relationship between the attitude and reading achievement among elementary school children.

A total of 697 students from urban and rural areas from grade level three through six, were involved. Student and teacher reading criterion measures, used to validate the estate scale, were employed to assure validation consistency. Two-way ANOVA were used for criterion measure. The conclusions drawn from the study were:

(i) That the reading attitude scale can be used with elementary students for measuring levels of attitude towards books and reading;

(ii) The instrument can detect the students having favourable attitude towards reading;

(iii) A positive attitude is essential to learning to read successfully, however, attitudes cannot be used as predictor of academic achievement; and

(iv) The primary value of attitude scale is to answer the questions like (a) what is the students attitude towards books and reading; and (b) following instructions, has there been a change in student's attitude?

Mezynski (1983) investigated in her study whether vocabulary functions as an aid for reading comprehension. The objectives of the study were:

(i) To find out the effect of instructional vocabulary training programme on reading comprehension.

(ii) To understand the mechanism of reading comprehension.

The students of upper-elementary grades were given special instructional training on the words thought problematic. The training was in different modes. One was direct training which was on the target words from the passage and the other was "General transfer training" which was given on a large set of words with the expectations of overall advantage. Word knowledge and passage comprehension were measured by various combinations of recall and recognition test.

The findings of the study reveal that:

(i) Vocabulary training improved performance on vocabulary test but it had little effect on reading comprehension.

(ii) Comprehension of the text of reader is just a free recall/recognition phenomenon.

Gerard, W.G. Spaai, Henk, H. Ellermann and Pieter Reitsma (1987) conducted a study in The Netherlands. The objective of the study was to investigate the learning effect of two different strategies—word analysis and word-supply procedures—in normal beginning readers.

Sixty first grade children (27 girls and 33 boys) from three different classes of a normal primary school were taken. The average age of those children was 7.1 years and they had received about 9 months of formal reading instruction at school using the same reading material. Prior to the experiment a standard reading test that accompanies the reading method was administered. The reading score was the number of words read correctly within one minute. The result revealed certain facts such as:

(i) The corrective feedback of reading error in the form of whole word sound has a positive effect on reading accuracy. When the whole-word sound feedback was provided after every oral reading error, significantly less errors were committed.

(ii) No such strong learning effects were found for the segmented feedback. A memory load of many segments may not facilitate learning.

(iii) A phoneme-by-phoneme feedback does not support or facilitate the process of learning words.

Schofield, H.L. (1976) conducted a study on reading attitude, achievement and teacher-pupil relationship in Australia. The main objectives of the study were:

(i) To find out the influence of attitude towards reading on achievement in reading; and

(ii) To study whether teachers' attitude affects pupils' attitudes and achievements.

The initial pretest sample of the study comprised 251 exit primary school teachers (189 females and 62 males) from 2 vocational colleges. Out of these, 56 teachers who became teachers of classes IV and VI were contacted. The students' sample comprised 595 girls and 624 boys. The tools used for the teachers were ACER's Reading comprehension test and a semantic differential instrument to measure the attitude towards reading and teaching. For reading achievemnt of puplis, ACER's primary reading survey tests were used.

Factor-analysis was done on two scores. One-way analysis of variance was used to investigate the relationship between teachers' reading achievement and pupils' reading attitude and achievement. The major findings were:

(i) There was significant effect of teachers' reading comprehension on pupils; school attitudes and achievement both in vocabulary and comprehension;

(ii) There appeared a significant effect of teachers' reading speed on pupils' reading attitudes and achievement; and

(iii) Teachers' reading attitude had a positive effect on pupils' reading achievement.

Thus, the study concludes that there is a significant and positive relationship between teachers' attitude towards reading and students' reading attitude and achievement.

Neuman, S.B. and Prowda, P. (1979) conducted a study in Connecticut State, USA, on the relationship between television viewing and children's interest and achievement in reading. The study had the following main objectives:

I. To assess the time spent by the children of different age groups for TV viewing; and

II. To analyse the possible relationship between TV viewing and children's reading performance.

A large sample of 7787 students of grades IV, VIII and XI was selected randomly. In addition to the grade consideration, students were selected on the basis of the size of the community and its locality within the state. The tools used for the study were criterion referenced multiple choice tests. The construction of the tests occurred in three stages. First, the objectives reflecting key areas of reading were determined. Seven skill areas were selected and test items were prepared on these. The tests included a number of demographic, attitudinal and general descriptive questions besides reading skills items. Pearson's product moment correlations were computed between the independent variables and the total reading scores. The major findings of the study were that:

(i) Gender was not a dominant factor for reading performance at any grade;

(ii) The number of educational material available at home was positively related to reading; however, the strength of relationship diminished over time;

(iii) Reading for pleasure was indeed associated with achievement gains at all ages; and

(iv) Negative correlation between reading achievement and TV viewing was reported at all grade levels.

Thus, it may be inferred that television viewing does not have a positive impact on reading achievement; instead reading for pleasure has a significant, positive relation with reading achievement.

Searls, D.T, Mead, N.A., and Ward, B. (1979) conducted a study in the same area, i.e., TV's impact on children's personalities, propensity to violence and academic achievement. The main objectives of the study were:

(i) To assess the reading skills of the children;

(ii) To study the amount of TV watched by different groups of students;

(iii) To study the relationship between the achievement on readings kills and TV watching; and

(iv) To analyse the relationship between leisure time reading, TV watching and reading ability.

A large sample of 77,197 children was taken. These included 21,208 nine-year old, 30,488 thirteen-year old and 25,501 seventeen-year olds. The tool used for the survey was a questionnaire related to their background and with a wide range of items probing their reading comprehension skills. The major findings were:

(i) Age was a major factor in determining how much television students should watch and how their TV watching interacted with reading skills;

(ii) Television viewing even up to 3-4 hours daily improved reading performance at younger ages but showed negative association in case of older students;

(iii) TV also appeared to have a differential effect for students in different SES groups; and

(iv) Moderate amount of spare time reading appeared to have a favourable impact on reading.

Thus, it may be inferred that moderate television viewing may have a positive impact at younger ages, but it has a negative effect on reading abilities in case of older students. Spare time reading has a positive effect on the reading ability of the child.

Stevens, K. C. (1980) studied the impact of background information on reading comprehension. The objective of the study was to find out the impact of background knowledge in the acquisition of new knowledge and skills. The study wad conducted on 140 class X students of high school in the south side of Chicago.

Two passages from the 'McCall Crabbs Standard Test Lessons in Reading' were used. The first passage and its nine multiple choice comprehension questions were used as a covariate for reading ability. A second passage, similar to the target passage, was used with a hope to get a more accurate covariate measure. Subjects were given covariate passage and then to the half group, the related main text was given and to the other half of the sample some other text about which no information was given in covariate passage, was taught.

Data was analysed using an analysis of covariance design. The major findings of the study were:

(i) Providing background information on the topic resulted in improved reading of that topic; and

(ii) Spending more time in providing background knowledge directly prior to the main reading, promoted the reading comprehension of the students.

Thus, it may be concluded that the reading comprehension of the child can be improved by providing information about the text that the child is going to read.

Chan, J. (1986) studied the cultural standards and psychological impact of the child's home conditions, in Hong Kongs in relation to the child's total development of verbal and other intellectual abilities.

The research background for this study was cross-cultural studies of Vernon(1969) who concluded that socio-economic level and linguistic background were considerably associated with 'g' or general intelligence. But at the same time, it was noticed that cultural level at home, parental education level, reading facilities seemed to have even higher correlation than 'g' factor.

The main objective of the study was to find out the relationship between parental behaviour and children's verbal and hence reading abilities. A representative sample of 113 students selected through stratified randomization, between the age group of 12 and 18 years was drawn for the study. The tools used for study were:

(i) A Parental-Image-Differential Test covering six concepts of parent-child interaction

(a) father's treatment of the child

(b) mother's treatment of the child

(c) father's approach to teaching the child

(d) mother's approach to teaching the child

(e) father's attitude to child's discipline

(f) mother's attitude to child's discipline

(ii) Reading ability test consisting of 11 passages and 44 test items based on recognition, recall, free expression and general reading ability.

All the scores were analysed through factor analysis. The major findings were:

(i) Favourable parent-child interaction, i.e. less parental autocracy, restrictiveness and demandingness, was correlated with the development of good reading abilities;

(ii) Recall ability was significantly related to mother's less autocracy;

(iii) Free expression was significantly related to father's less restriction;

(iv) General reading ability was significantly related to father's less restriction and mother's less demand; but

(v) Recognition was not related to parent-child relationship.

Thus, it may be inferred that the parent-child relationship and their interaction have a very significant relation with child's verbal abilities.

Engle, R.W., Carulld, J.J. and Collins, K.W. (1990) studied the effect of individual difference in working memory for comprehension and following directions, in Columbia, South Carolina. The main objectives of the study were:

(i) To determine the extent to which individual difference in working memory capacity predicted performance on higher level cognitive tasks in children;

(ii) To determine whether the capacity reflected by this complex memory span was important for listening and reading comprehension; and

(iii) To analyse whether the increase in ability to follow more complex directions with age were related to increase in memory span.

The sample comprised 120 children randomly selected from two school districts in Columbia, USA. The subjects included 40 first graders, 40 third graders and 40 sixth graders. The tools used for the study were Wepman's auditory discrimination test, a word-span task, a listening and reading comprehension test and a 'following direction' test. The subjects were tested individually in two 45 minute sessions separated by at least one day. All the conclusions of the study were based on ANOVAs and Tukey HSD post-hoc comparison on appropriate scores with significance established at .05 level. The major findings of the study were:

(i) The number of words recalled in a simple word-span task or as a part of a sentence span task was found significant for predicting comprehension ability;

(ii) There was no age difference in this relationship;

(iii) The functional storage capacity of working memory did not increase developmentally;

(iv) Simple word-span significantly predicted performance on a measure of reading comprehension. But the magnitude of the correlation was slightly lower between word-span and comprehension than between complex span and comprehension; and

(v) There were individual differences in the working memory capacity and this factor affects the ability of the child to comprehend.

Thus, it may be concluded that reading comprehension of the child is affected by his working memory capacity and there are individual differences in this regard.

Rowe K. J. (1991) conducted a study on the influence of reading activities at home on students' attitudes towards reading in Australia. The objectives of this study were:

(i) To study the influence of home reading on the learning of children; and

(ii) to study the effect of home reading experience on reading and attentiveness in reading.

The study sample comprised 5000 students of 5 to 14 years selected randomly. The tools used for the study were students' home record, reading attitude scale, self-report of reading attitudes and at home reading practice. The coefficient of correlation was estimated and the conclusions drawn were:

(i) Children with more frequent home reading experiences enjoyed higher achievement in reading, better attitude towards reading and more positive rating of attentiveness; and

(ii) There was no effect of age, gender, sex, or socio-economic status of students on these results.

Thus, it may be concluded that parental support and involvement play important role in the development of reading abilities of the child.

Elliott, J.A. and Hewison, J. (1991) conducted a study on the effect of socio-cultural background on reading comprehension and reading interests. The study was conducted in the University of York, England. The main objectives of the study were:

(i) To investigate the kind of context into which a project might be introduced obtaining general educational activities already existing in home;

(ii) To compare and contrast information on educational activities in homes of different socio-cultural groups;

(iii) To identify the reading related activities and their influence; and

(iv) To review the information on parental help with reading in terms of possible implications for home reading projects.

Three of the main target groups were chosen on the basis of difference in social class and ethnicity, i.e., 30 middle class families, 40 working class families and 50 families of Asian origin. The children involved in the study were of average age-group of seven years. The sample consisted of 60 children, i.e., 20 from middle-class, 26 from working class and 24 from Asians by origin selected randomly. The tools used for the study were interview and recording of home reading sessions. The analysis revealed that:

(i) Success in reading was associated with a parental helping style; and

(ii) A positive correlation was seen in parental help and the child's reading comprehension.

Thus, the study concluded that parental help has a significant positive correlation with the child's reading comprehension.

Hashway, R.M., Duke, L.I. and Farmer, V.F. (1993) studied the reading habits of the adult learners. The objectives of the study were:

(i) To study the effect of socio-economic status or cultural/ ethical background on literacy habits of young adult learners; and

(ii) To study the impact of parental socio-economic status as well as personal socio-economic status on reading habits of young adults.

The tool used for the study was a survey conducted in the USA by Educational Testing Service, the Office for Educational Research and Improvement and the Center for

Statistics from 38,400 households in 800 locations across the country. The data was also collected on 3618 young adults of 21-25 years age group for analyzing their habits. The analysis of the data yielded the following findings:

(i) Family SES, defined by mother's and father's education and occupation had little influence on young adults' reading habits;

(ii) The personal SES influenced the reading of the learner;

(iii) As their educational and occupational attainment rose, so did the level of their literacy behaviour; and

(iv) It seemed that goal-orientation rather than home environment was the major determinant of young adult's literacy behaviour.

Thus, the study revealed certain facts that SES influenced the reading; the reading habits and the literacy behaviour of young adult learners is more influenced by their own socio-economic status and goal orientation.

Reutzel, D. Ray and Hollingsworth, Paul M. (1993) studied the effects of fluency-training on second graders' reading comprehension. The objectives of the study were:

(i) To study the impact of using oral recitation as a means for developing second grade students' oral reading fluency;

(ii) To study the effect of this training on reading comprehension; and

(iii) To study the effects of reading fluency on reading comprehension.

A sample of 78, second grade students was selected randomly from two elementary schools representative of the entire socio-economic status of a community of approximately 85,000 in the Rocky Mountain region of USA. The students represented several ethnic groups—African-American, Oriental and American Indians belonging to middle or lower middle socio-economic classes. The study was conducted as an experimental one. Each of the four classrooms in two schools were randomly assigned to one or two conditions or groups : a control group round-robin reading (RR) and oral recitation group (ORL). Thirty-nine students were in each group, i.e., RR and ORL. The students were given the Iowa Test of Basic Skills (ITBS), reading battery including word analysis, vocabulary and reading comprehension sub-tests, prior to beginning, to check the effectiveness. A Wilks' multivariate test of significance indicated no difference among the two groups on ITBS. The other tests used were a norm-referenced standardized achievement test, ITBS, comprehension sub-tests and self-constructed oral reading test based on the *Aesop's Fable*, 'The Fox and the Grapes' adapted by Denise Guynn (1980). Four teachers were especially trained for the implementation of ORL procedures and the control instructional procedure. The amount of time given to both for ORL and RR group was same, i.e., 30 min each day for 4 months (September to December). Then the post-test was administered.

The data was analysed in a four stage process:

(a) First, the mean and SD for each outcome measures were computed;

(b) Second, documented fluency differences were analysed using one-way analysis of variance (ANOVA) between groups;

(c) Third, if a difference in fluency was determined, a multivariate ANOVA was used to determine the influence of ORL fluency training on students' comprehension;

(d) Finally, if a significant MANOVA was found, four separate one-way ANOVAs were used to determine which of the four comprehension measures showed significant differences between the groups on comprehension attributable of fluency training effects.

The major findings were:

(i) The ORL was an effective means of developing second grade students' oral reading fluency;

(ii) The performances of students of ORL group was superior to that of RR group in three out of four comprehension measures;

(iii) The study showed a strong effect of fluency development on second graders' reading comprehension;

Thus, it may be concluded that there exists a casual link between improving students' reading fluency and simultaneously improving their reading comprehension.

Hickman, C.W., Greenwood, G. and Miller, M.D. (1994) conducted a study on High School Parent Involvement : Relationship with achievement, grade level, SES and gender. The main objectives of the study were:

(i) To study the relationship between SES, school achievement and total amount of parent involvement;

(ii) The type of parent involvement related to the achievement of the student; and

(iii) The type of parent involvement related to student's SES, gender and grade level.

The sample comprised 60 parents selected through stratified randomization of schools and grade level of the total number of 6704 public school students of Alachua County, Florida, USA. Parent involvement data were collected by means of a structured interview (PPI) developed by Hickman and Greenwood (1992). The instrument yielded three types of scores:

I. Total scores based on the sum total hours parents participated in parent involvement activity. These type were:

(a) communicator (talking with school representative)

(b) supporter (providing transport).

(c) learner (contacting professionals for child's problem)

(d) advocator (attending school meetings)

(e) decision-maker (participating in school's committee)

(f) volunteer/professional (working in school)

(g) home based activity (help in home-work).

2. A sub-scale based on number of hours a parent participated in home based activity vs school-based activity.
3. Total number of hours parents participated in each seven individual type of activities.

The data were analysed using multiple regression in order to investigate the relationship between the chosen variables. The regression analysis was conducted to examine the relationship between parental involvement and grade level, gender, SES and academic achievement. The major findings were:

(i) There existed a positive relationship between the higher achievement and high parent involvement score;

(ii) Only the home based type of parent involvement were significantly related to SES, gender and grade level;

(iii) Parent as supporter and parent as learner were found to be related to SES;

(iv) Parental involvement was found to be higher at lower grade level and lower at higher grade level; and

(v) Gender was not a significant variable but a substantial parental involvement was seen for girls than for boys.

Thus, it may be concluded that the parental involvement has a positive and significant relationship with the achievement of the child. More parental involvement was seen at lower grade level and for the female child.

Conclusion

The studies mentioned in this chapter both conducted in India and abroad provide a firm foothold to the investigator to work on the existing problem. Some of the broad generalizations that emerge out of the findings of these studies are mentioned below:

(i) Almost all the studies confirm that gender of the child has no significant influence on reading comprehension.

(ii) Parental socio-economic status, their educational level, occupation and income level do affect the reading ability of the child at a younger stage whereas the personal socio-economic level influences the reading ability of the adult learner.

(iii) Certain psychological factors like reading readiness, intelligence, leadership traits, reading interest and attitude towards language have significant positive correlation with acquisition of reading skills.

(iv) Certain sociological factors like parents' involvement, motivation and encouragement have positive correlation whereas too much restriction or interference by parents has negative correlation with acquisition of reading ability.

(v) Some factors like anxiety level and more time spent on television viewing affect the reading ability negatively.

Therefore, these studies do provide substantial help in formulating hypotheses and making the research problem look like an extension of the work done by earlier researchers.

3

Development of Tools

Introduction

The present chapter relates to the development as well as selection of research tools for data collection on various aspects of the study. Any worthwhile description of the development of research tools can't ignore theoretical consideration on which the tools rest. Therefore, the author has tried to relate the theoretical aspects with various phases of tool construction. A variety of tools was used by the investigator for data collection depending upon the purpose and category of the respondents.

Tools Used for the Study

The various tools developed and used for the study by the author were:

(i) Reading Comprehension Passages

(ii) Sight-Vocabulary Test

(iii) Socio-economic-Status Scale

(iv) Parental Support to Reading Questionnaire.

Use was also made of Raven's Standard Progressive Matrices for Testing General Mental Ability and Shah's Level of Aspiration Test.

Tools for Investigating Reading Skills

The author thought it imperative to explore the various reading skills employed in the process of reading comprehension. So, the first attempt was made in this direction only. The reading skills were analysed and identified and these were the bases of the various passages for reading comprehension and the questions based thereon.

Reading comprehension has been a much debated concept in reading research. According to Ruddell (1970) 'language comprehension is a function of a reader's control over grammatical and lexical components of discourse.' He further believes that a reader's comprehension of language precedes and exceeds his ability at producing language. Gray's (1960) description of comprehension at three levels, viz. understanding literal meaning, grasping implied meaning and understanding implications and significance of the author's ideas beyond those actually stated, is essentially conceptual in nature. Attempts at providing an elaborate description of comprehension by Kingston (1961), Leyland (1965), Deighton (1967), and McCullough (1967) have been concerned with specification of major processes that constitute reading and reading comprehension. However, the best known attempt at describing reading comprehension has been made by Barrett in his unpublished paper "Taxonomy of the Cognitive and Affective Dimension of Reading Comprehension." Barrett presented both a manageable and an understandable description of reading comprehension and distinguished five major skill categories or levels of reading comprehension, viz. (a) literal comprehension, (b) reorganization, (c) inferential comprehension, (d) evaluation and (e) appreciation. Reading comprehension, may be understood as the reader's ability to answer questions on a text as a result of reading it. Thus, reading comprehension also implies increase in a reader's knowledge due to reading a text. It is therefore text-dependent. In view of the young age of the study sample, reading comprehension was based on all the general aspects at elementary level, i.e. main idea, details, word-meaning, inference and low level evaluation and appreciation.

Development of Reading Passages

Selection and Development of Reading Passages

Reading skills can never be developed in isolation and therefore, the skills are text dependent. It was obvious to the investigator that a good reading passage had to be selected or developed. The criteria for selecting passages for reading were based on three variables. These were :

(i) The interest level of the passage,

(ii) The language used in the passage, and

(iii) The length of the passage.

Besides these variables, another guiding consideration was that at least three passages should be selected, one of each text type, i.e., narrative, descriptive and expository.

Keeping in mind these variables, initially three passages were selected. These were:

(i) Merciful Radha–Narrative Text

(ii) The Story of Delhi–Descriptive text

(iii) Mr Word or Mr Action–A Short Play.

These passages were later discarded for the reason that these were very long passages which may be useful for classroom reading purposes but not as reading passages for testing reading comprehension. Later on another five passages were chosen. These were:

(i) Holding up the sky

(ii) Asia: Some Facts

(iii) Value of Games and Sports

(iv) The Lotus Temple–Bahai House of Worship

(v) Kapil Dev–The Hero of Indian Cricket.

The first passage 'Holding up the Sky' was a narrative text, a short story by Freda Saxey—from *Guided English for India,* (A course book of English) of 277 words. The second passage 'Asia: Some Facts' was a descriptive text full of geographical information about the continent and its countries. This passage was of 280 words. The third passage

'Value of Games and Sports' was an expository text that emphasized the advantages of games and sports in life. This passage was of about 260 words. 'The Lotus Temple–Bahai House of Worship' was a small descriptive passage of 265 words, developed by the investigator with the help of the information taken from pamphlets and other reading literature collected from the temple. The fifth passage was developed by the investigator on the basis of the information gathered from newspapers and various sports magazines. The period during which this passage was developed, coincided with Kapil Dev's remarkable achievement in the history of cricket. This made this passage of 280 words extremely topical. These five passages were written, edited and rewritten till the required degree of uniformity was attained in all passages. The final versions of these passages were of comparable size and difficulty level as far as language of the passage was concerned.

Development of Comprehension Questions

No learning can take place if the reading is not comprehended well. It goes without saying that reading without comprehension is a futile exercise. Therefore, the investigator having selected the reading passages for comprehension prepared comprehension questions.In this, she was guided by the following considerations:

(i) The questions should be brief and unambiguous;

(ii) The language of the questions should be clear; and

(iii) The questions should be text-dependent.

The reason for not using open-ended questions was that sometimes the writing skill significantly affects the response of the child. The child may tick correct response if the choice is given to him but due to poor writing skills, he may not answer and hence give a wrong impression that he has not comprehended well. Each question and its acceptable answer was based on the reading skill, which the student would employ to answer it. All the passages had similar types of questions testing the same skills, i.e., Q. 1 in all the passages was based on understanding of meaning of words in their contextual use. Similarly Q. 2 in all the passages aimed at testing the understanding of the main idea of the text and so on. The same uniformity was maintained in all questions for each passage. The questions were arranged in an easy-to-difficult sequence. Therefore the last question on each passage was at a higher level of comprehension skill viz. making inference and interpretation of the text. The investigator used various item formats for testing. Some of the questions were to be answered by ticking the most suitable answer. Some of the questions were of matching type. Some of the questions required reorganization of the given statements while some were based on 'fill-in-the-blanks' format, where an appropriate word was to be picked up from the text and filled. In no case a learner was asked to write more than a small phrase on his own, so that the writing skill did not affect the responses on reading comprehension.

Eliciting Students' Opinion about Reading Text

The learner's needs and interest were the most important aspect of the study. Hence, the researcher considered it worthwhile to seek the students' opinion about the reading passages. The five passages were administered to a small sample of grade VI students of a Kendriya Vidyalaya. The sample comprised 20 students in all (6 below average, 8 average, 6 above average). The students were asked to read the passages and attempt all the comprehension questions based on the passages. The time taken by them to complete the whole exercise (reading the passage as well as answering the questions based on it) was noted for each passage. The students were also asked to give their frank opinion about these passages. The investigator gave them only one passage in a day in order to avoid boredom and fatigue. This exercise provided extremely useful information which proved very decisive in selecting the three final passages for the study. The results of this exercise are shown in Table 3.1.

TABLE 3.1

Pupils' Response to the Reading Passages

S.No.	*Passage*	*Student's Opinion*	*Average Time Taken*
1.	Holding up the Sky	90 per cent favourable (Interesting text)	22-24 minutes
2.	Asia: Some Facts	80 per cent unfavourable (boring, difficult text)	30-32 minutes
3.	Value of Games and Sports	70 per cent unfavourable (boring, dry, difficult (text)	35 minutes
4.	The Lotus Temple —Bahai House of Worship	80 per cent favourable (interesting and informative text)	25 minutes
5.	Kapil Dev—The Hero of Indian Cricket	100 per cent favourable (interesting and informative text)	24 minutes

Table 3.1 clearly indicates that passages 2 and 3, i.e., 'Asia: Some Facts' 'Value of Games & Sports' and did not elicit favourable response and hence these passages were rejected. The average time taken by the students showed that an average student required 20-25 minutes to attempt a passage. The three passages finally used have been given in Appendices A-C.

Eliciting Teachers' Opinion About Reading Text

Assessing teachers' opinion about the passages was equally important. Five Kendriya Vidyalayas of Delhi region were randomly selected for this purpose. A questionnaire was developed in order to ascertain the opinion of teachers who were teaching English to class VI. A set of five reading passages along-with comprehension exercises, a questionnaire for teachers (see Appendix-D) and the reading skills on which these were based was sent to 20 TGTs from these Vidyalayas. All respondent teachers were requested to give their frank opinion while answering the questionnaire regarding the length, suitability and difficulty level of class VI students. They were requested to give their suggestions for further improvement of the passages as well as the questions. They were also requested to mention the estimated time that the average class VI student would take to complete the reading comprehension exercise. The results obtained were very interesting and useful for the investigator. The findings are briefly summarized below:

Passage I. 'Holding up the Sky'

The passage was given to 20 teachers of Kendriya Vidyalayas of Delhi region. Thirty per cent of the teachers found the passage most suitable for class VI students whereas 60 per cent of them found it just suitable and appropriate for class VI level. Only 10 per cent teachers felt the passage unsuitable. When asked, the teachers were of the opinion that the passage should have an Indian context. All teachers found the passage interesting. 90 per cent teachers felt that the language of the passage was easy and the students would be able to comprehend it quite easily whereas 10 per cent teachers felt that certain phrases were above students' level of competency. Surprisingly the same teachers commented on the vocabulary of the passage as easy. Ninety per cent teachers felt that the sentence structure used in the passage was of average difficulty level. About the length of the passage, ninety per cent teachers found it appropriate whereas ten per cent teachers found it slightly lengthy. All the teachers found the instructions to the comprehension exercise clear and the questions well framed and text-based. Twenty per cent of the teachers felt that the average child would take 12-15 minutes to complete the whole exercise. Fifty per cent of the teachers felt that an average child would take 20-22 minutes whereas 30 per cent teachers felt that an average child would take 25-30 minutes to read the passage and respond to the comprehension exercise. No adverse comment was received on the passage except that the passage should have had an Indian context. The teachers desired that open-ended questions should also be included in the comprehension exercise. The psychometric aspects of their suggestion were made use of for ensuring that the passage focussed on reading skills and not writing skills. Most of the teachers desired that such type of reading comprehension exercise should be a part of the English textbook.

Passage II. Asia : Some Facts

The passage was given to 20 teachers of different Kendriya Vidyalayas of Delhi region. Care was taken to ensure that the passage was given to only those teachers who were teaching English to class VI at that time. The passage was adjudged suitable and interesting for class VI level by only 10 per cent teachers. Ninety per cent of the teachers found the passage as boring, difficult and above the level of class VI students. All teachers felt that the passage was lengthy and should be a part of the geography textbook only; hence it shouldn't be used as a reading passage. Surprisingly the questions framed on the passage were liked by 75 per cent teachers. They found the questions clear and direct. All teachers felt that the instructions for each question were also clear. They felt that an average child would take at least 40-50 minutes to attempt the passage. Taking these suggestions into consideration, the researcher decided that this passage shouldn't be used as a reading text. Hence the passage was rejected.

Passage III. Value of Games and Sports

This passage was given to 20 teachers teaching English to grade VI students in different Kendriya Vidyalayas. The questionnaire was responded to by all of them individually. Eighty per cent teachers found the passage interesting and suitable for class VI students but 20 per cent teachers felt such a passage had no relevance to language learning. Though they found the topic informative, yet they felt it uninteresting. Fifty per cent teachers found the language easy while others commented that the language of the passage was of average difficulty level. Thirty per cent teachers felt the passage to be lengthy whereas 60 per cent teachers felt the passage just average in length. Ten per cent teachers felt that the instructions given for comprehension questions were not clear enough. None of the teachers found any question ambiguous or defective. The overall response of the teachers regarding this passage was not very encouraging. The passage was considered just an average passage. So the investigator decided not to use the passage as a text for testing reading comprehension.

Passage IV. The Lotus Temple— Bahai House of Worship

This passage was given to 20 teachers teaching English to class VI students of various Kendriya Vidyalayas of Delhi. The questionnaire was attempted by all of them and their responses were quite favourable. Forty per cent teachers found the passage most suitable whereas 60 per cent found it just suitable for class VI students. None of the teachers found it unsuitable. All teachers felt that the passage was quite interesting. Sixty per cent teachers thought the language of the passage easy whereas 40 per cent teachers considered the language to be of average difficulty level. The teachers felt the same for vocabulary used in the passage. The phrase, 'Idol-worship' was considered difficult by 20 per cent teachers but the item based on it, was answered correctly by most of the students. So, the investigator didn't try to replace the word. Ten per cent teachers felt that the passage was lengthy but surprisingly the students didn't complain of the same. So the length of the passage was left unchanged. None of the teachers found any question irrelevant or ambiguous. An important point raised by 30 per cent teachers and later on by one of the experts concerned the previous knowledge of those students who might have visited the temple. They thought that this might affect their performance favourably. The investigator however didn't find any marked difference in the students' scores that could be attributed to this factor. On the whole the passage was considered good, interesting and a challenging text.

Passage V. Kapil Dev : The Hero of Indian Cricket

This passage was given to 20 teachers teaching English

to class VI students in various Kendriya Vidyalayas. All the teachers rated the passage as very interesting and suitable for class VI students. Sixty per cent teachers felt that the language used in the passage was simple and easy, whereas 10 per cent teachers felt that the language of the passage was difficult. As far as the length of the passage was concerned, 90 per cent teachers felt that the children would be able to do the whole exercise in 25-27 minutes and rated it of an average length. All teachers felt that instructions for comprehension questions were clear. Eighty per cent teachers felt that comprehension questions were completely text-based whereas 20 per cent teachers felt that some questions were partially text-based. These teachers were of the view that the students who might have read about Kapil Dev earlier would attempt the questions better. The investigator thought it best to wait for the results of try-out on students and then to make changes if necessary. Surprisingly this was found to be an apprehension only. None of the question was found ambiguous or defective. On the whole the reading passage was considered to be good, effective and interesting.

Experts' Review of Reading Texts

After seeking teachers' opinion about the reading passages, the investigator made the necessary changes and then the three finally selected passages (approved by teachers and also supported by students' performance) were sent to five experts. These experts were from various reputed educational institutions such as Department of Education, Delhi University, State Council of Educational Research and Training, Department of Education, Maharishi Dayanand Univerity and National Council of Educational Research and Training. The experts were also asked to rate each text and comprehension questions based on it on the same criteria as were used by school teachers earlier. An answer key was also sent along with the set so that the experts might look into the suitability of the keyed answers. The experts' opinions were as follows:

'All the three passages were found interesting and suitable for the age group of class VI students. The language of the passages as well as the vocabulary was considered to be of average difficulty level, neither easy nor difficult for the students'. A few changes which were suggested in sentence structure were incorporated. The comprehension questions were rated as text-based and clear. None of the questions was found ambiguous except one question. Consequently, necessary changes were made in the scoring key as well as in the instructions.

Try-out of Reading Passages

After selecting the three reading comprehension passages and modifying them wherever necessary on the basis of experts' remarks, the investigator conducted a tryout. The try-out was carried out on a small group (n=10). The investigator selected ten students of Kendriya Vidyalaya, Lawrence Road randomly for this purpose. The students were given the reading passage. They were asked to read the passage and attempt the questions based on it. They were instructed to attempt all questions. Time taken by each student in completing the whole exercise was recorded by the investigator. All the three passages were tried out on students on three different days, so that fatigue or boredom resulting from doing same activity thrice a day might not affect their performance. The results are shown in Table 3.2.

TABLE 3.2
Try-out of Reading Passages

S.No.	*Passage*	*Average Time Taken*	*Average Marks Scored*
1.	Passage I : Holding Up the Sky	25 Minutes	45 per cent
2.	Passage II: The Lotus Temple Bahai House of worship	20 Minutes	52 per cent
3.	Passage III: Kapil Dev —The Hero of Indian Cricket	22 Minutes	57 per cent

Besides this, the general response of the students about the passages was quite encouraging. Most students wished that such reading passages and comprehension exercises should be given to them more often.

Scoring Scheme of the Reading Passages

In order to assess the performance of students on reading passages, a scoring scheme too was developed. A separate scoring key for each reading passage was prepared. The number of questions for the narrative text was more than those for the other two. Therefore, a common scoring scheme for all the three passages couldn't be prepared. The scoring schemes for all the three passages are given in Appendices E-G.

Development of Sight Vocabulary Test

"In its initial stage, reading is little more than decoding word symbols" (Chall, 1967). Therefore, the skills of greatest concern at initial level of learning a language are those that lead to accurate decoding of word-symbols. These skills are often, grouped under the heading 'word-recognition skills'. Directly related to word-recognition is vocabulary development. Rich and accurate associations for word-symbols are fundamental to success in reading. There are number of techniques for the evaluation of word power like 'Ddch's-list of 220 Basic sight words' which figures heavily in the running service vocabularies of most content text-books. The word-list is given to the student with instructions that he pronounces aloud from sight recognition or analysis if the word is unfamiliar. The examiner marks the number and type of error. This word list consists of functional words only.

Another example of such word-list which is a screening-level list is the 'San Diego Quick Word Test' whose words have been selected on a try-out basis and arranged to correspond with reading levels. The investigator felt that the word list should be a prepared one rather than a ready-made one because the latter would not necessarily cater to the needs of the sample. The investigator had two main objectives while constructing this test viz.

(i) The vocabulary range of the child; and

(ii) The speed with which the child recognises and pronounces the word correctly.

The sight vocabulary list was prepared keeping in mind the age level of the sample. As the sample consists of class VI, the investigator tried to have a balanced distribution of vocabulary items. For that purpose, the English course books of class V, VI and VII were analyzed. It was assumed that a class VI student would be more familiar with those words which he has studied in class V or those which he had been reading in class VI. It was also decided to include some words from class VII course book. The students learn language not only through formal system of class-room teaching but also by acquiring considerable word power during their informal day-to-day transactions. Hence the researcher decided to select words on this criterion as well. the word list contained 100 words in all at the initial stage. Out of these 100 words, 40 words were picked up from class V reader, 20 from class VI reader, 20 from class VII reader and the remaining 20 words were selected on the basis of common usage. These 20 words were very frequently used as a part of learners' active vocabulary. Another criterion of selection of words was their syllabic configuration. The investigator tried to keep maximum numbers of bi-syllabic or tri-syllabic words and only a few poly-syllabic words. Therefore out of 100 words, 45 words were bi-syllabic and 35 were tri-syllabic. Ten mono-syllabic and 10 poly-syllabic words were also included in the list.

Try-Out of the Sight Vocabulary Test

This word list was tried out on 20 students of class VI of Kendriya Vidyalaya, Shalimar Bagh. The students were instructed to read aloud the words in the serial order. The investigator kept a record of correctly read words and also the total time taken by every child to read aloud 100 words. The investigator also noted down those words separately that the children were unable to read. After collecting this data and analysing it, it was found that there were certain common words that all the 20 children couldn't read. The list also contained certain words which were too elementary. Such as chalk, school, etc. There were certain words which couldn't be properly pronounced though children could analyse these words later on. The average time taken by the children for reading aloud the word list was four to six minutes.

Considering these results of the try-out, the investigator selected a list of 50 words from the initial list of 100 words. The list has 12 per cent mono-syllabic, 46 per cent bi-syllabic, 30 per cent tri-syllabic and again 12 per cent poly-syllabic words. Fifteen words are from class V level, 15 from class VI level, 10 from class VII level and 10 words were very frequently used ones. On the basis of the results of try-out, the investigator decided to keep a time limit of two minutes for a child to read 50 words. The final word list was thus, ready for administration (See Appendix-H).

Socio-Economic Status Scale

In such a large democratic set-up like India, the society has diversified living groups. The disparity among these groups could be because of any factors such as their economic level (Income level group), their common interests, their religion or way of living. But do these various disparities affect language acquisition of the child and especially the reading skills? This is the main crux of the problem. The investigator feels the socio-economic level does affect the development of reading skills of child directly or indirectly.

First of all, one has to define socio-economic status of an individual. The position that an individual acquires in his own social group because of his economic level or professional placement or academic achievements. This position or status may be termed as socio-economic status. As far as the child is concerned, all the facilities that he receives at home or the exposure of his environment is due to the economic level of the family. Hence, we can say that upto some extent, the statement of hypothesis holds some weightage of truth.

In order to ascertain the degree of reliability of this hypothetic truths, the investigator decided to use a socio-economic status scale in her study.

Reading this questionnaire has been incorporated in the study. The main objectives of this questionnaire will be:

(i) To assess whether the parents have a positive attitude to reading.

(ii) To find out the amount of time parents devote for children's reading.

(iii) To see the quality of time spent with the children for developing reading.

(iv) To analyse whether the academic-resource support or reading texts are provided to the child.

(v) To find out the quality of reading material provided to the child;

(vi) To see the parent-child relationship in promotion of reading skills.

(vii) To find out the efforts made by the parents in order to develop a positive attitude towards reading in the child.

It is difficult to define the term socio-economic status. The status is the position of a person in the group or community to which he/she belongs. Sometimes the status also means prestige. A person, socially sound may be economically not well off or the reverse may also be the case. Some sociologists have tried to give a formal definition of the term. Chaplin, F.S. (1928) defined socio-economic status as "the position that an individual or family occupies with reference to the prevailing average standard of cultural possessions, effective income, natural possessions and participation in group activities of the community". According to Lovinger, J. (1940), "socio-economic status contains such factors as size of the family, race, locality of residence, education of parents, income and occupation". Young, K.

(1942) laid emphasis on the prestige dimension of status. His contention was that "Status is a function of interaction and that it results from the acceptance by the self and by others, of the role, the person plays in this interaction". Philip, R. (1954) has described socio-economic status as "the economic position and prestige, a way of life and a pattern of values". Later on, the term socio-economic status was broadly defined by Rangaswamy (1969) as, "socio-economic status includes educational, professional, occupational and economic status of parents. It also includes the environmental facilities available for the individual".

Construction of SES Scale

In the present study, socio-economic status includes education of parents, income, occupational level of parents, living conditions at home which include possession of several items which have become symbols of status, size of the family and parents' participation in social activities.

Before constructing the socio-economic status scale, the investigator made a survey of the already existing standardized scales so that she might use one for the present study. For that purpose a number of SES scales available were studied thoroughly. These scales were:

(i) Kuppuswamy's Socio-economic status scale.

(ii) Kapoor and Kochar's Socio-economic status scale.

(iii) Jalota, Pandey, Kapoor and Singh's Socio-economic status scale: Urban.

All these scales, no doubt were very good but these required some modification due to rapid changes in urban society. For example, the total income of the family has been classified in Kuppuswamy's scale as follows:

(i)	Above Rs. 1000 per month	12
(ii)	Between Rs. 750 and Rs. 999	10
(iii)	Between Rs. 500 and Rs. 749	6
(iv)	Between Rs. 300 and Rs. 499	4
(v)	Between Rs. 100 and Rs. 299	3

(vi) Between Rs. 50 and Rs. 99 2

(vii) Below Rs. 50 1

This income chart does not faithfully reflect the present income levels in urban society like that of Delhi. The minimum pay of a part time trained graduate teacher has now been fixed at Rs. 1000 per month. Hence, the need to revise these income slabs was indeed overdue. Similarly, items related to possessions in the house have become more or less redundant in earlier scales. None of the above mentioned scales include common items like colour TV, VCR, air-conditioner, electric oven, cooking range, etc. Therefore, it was felt that a new socio-economic status scale that takes stock of recent changes in our society, should be prepared. The investigator also took care to include factors like mother's education and occupation and the amount of pocket money children get; these factors were totally absent from the existing scales.

Therefore, a socio-economic status scale was developed in the form of a questionnaire for the present study. A copy of the final version (Hindi as well as English) of the SES questionnaire is enclosed in Appendix-I.

Main Components of the Scale

(i) Parental Education - Education of both mother and father.

(ii) Parental Occupation - Occupation of both mother and father.

(iii) Economic Index

(a) Income of the family from all sources

(b) Standard of living (i) Type of House

(ii) Area of House

(c) Material possessions—various items in the house

(d) Number of children

(iv) Cultural level of the family - Expenditure on newspapers and magazines.

(v) Psychological Indicators - Concepts of social prestige and power.

Scoring of SES Questionnaire

The SES questionnaire contained 14 questions in all and the scoring of responses was done component-wise only.

I. Parental Education - (Q. No. 1 and 3): There are eight categories on this variable. Scores allotted to each category are as under:

a	-	12
b	-	10
c	-	8
d	-	6
e	-	4
f	-	2
g	-	1
h	-	0

(For details of each category, See Appendix - I)

The same scoring procedure applies to Q. No. 1 and Q. No. 3.

II. Parental Occupation (Q. No. 2 and 4): This item related to the occupational placement of both parents, i.e., mother and father who support the family. This variable is divided into seven categories according to the social prestige they carry. The scores allotted are:

a	-	10
b	-	8
c	-	6
d	-	4
e	-	2
f	-	1
g	-	0

III. Economic Index

(a) Parental Income (Q. No. 6): There are six income groups and the scoring is as follows :

a	-	12
b	-	10
c	-	8
d	-	6
e	-	4
f	-	2

(b) Standard of living: (Types of House - Q. No. 9) Seven types of houses have been distinguished in this item on the basis of type and area of the house. The scores allotted are:

a	-	12
b	-	10
c	-	8
d	-	6
e	-	4
f	-	2
g	-	1

(c) Material Possessions: (Q. No. 10). This item elicits information about the household items the family possesses and also the number of items which indicates the economic index. Various articles have been grouped under four categories as shown in the Table 3.3 below.

TABLE 3.3
Scoring of Various Items of Material Possession

Vehicle			*Electrical*			*Recreational*			*Kitchen Aids*		
a	-	5	a	-	4	a	-	6	a	-	4
b	-	4	b	-	3	b	-	5	b	-	3
c	-	3	c	-	2	c	-	4	c	-	2
d	-	2	d	-	1	d	-	3	d	-	1
e	-	1				e	-	2			
						f	-	1			

Final scoring of the item is done by adding up the scores for various categories. Though the students are instructed to write the number also for each item, the number has no relevance with scoring but is considered for interpretation only.

(d) No. of the children in the family (Q. No. 5): This item is related to the number of brothers/sisters the child has and also their status, whether they are students or employed persons. The scoring of this item is done on the basis of the family size.

a	-	5
b	-	4
c	-	3
d	-	2
e	-	1

The 'a' category refers to the family having one child and the marks allotted are 5. The scores diminish (4, 3, 2 and 1) as the number of children increases as 2, 3, 4 and more.

(IV) Cultural level of the family (Q. No. 7 and 8): This category includes two items, i.e., purchase of newspapers and purchase of magazines in the family and their details.

(A) Q. No. 7 is related to the purchase of newspaper and the scoring is :

a	-	5
b	-	2
c	-	0

(B) Q. No. 8 is about the purchase of magazines and the scoring is:

a	-	4
b	-	2
c	-	1
d	-	1
e	-	0

Both for categories C and D, 1 mark is allotted because purchase of one magazine per month or purchasing magazines occasionally could mean the same.

(V) Psychological Indicators (Q. No. 11, 12, 13 and 14). This item is related to the concept of social prestige and power.

Q. No. 11 is about the type of tiffin the child brings to school. The scoring is done as follows:

(i) No. of items in tiffin (3 or more)	3 marks
No. of items in tiffin - 2	2 marks
No. of items in tiffin - 1	1 marks
(ii) No. tiffin	0 mark

Q. No. 12 is related to the amount of pocket money the child gets in a month. The scoring is:

(a) Rs. 75 and above	4 marks
(b) Between Rs. 50 and Rs. 74	3 marks
(c) Between Rs. 26 and Rs. 49	2 marks
(d) Rs. 25 and below	1 mark
(e) No pocket money	0 mark

Q. No. 13 seeks information about the social participation of the parents and the scoring is

(a) = 2 marks

(b) = 0 mark

Q. No. 14 concerns active participation of the head of the family in social activities and the scoring for this is as follows:

(a) Yes

(i) 3 marks

(ii) 2 marks

(iii) 1 mark

(b) No 0 mark

The total scores allotted range from 8 to 112 for all the 14 questions.

Standardization of the SES Scale

Before using any tool on the main sample, it is imperative to standardize it; hence the reliability and validity of the SES Scale was computed.

Reliability of the Test

It is a truism that in order to get a reliable test score, the test based data should be stable and trustworthy. This depends on the degree to which the data collected through test or scale is free from chance error. For this purpose, reliability coefficient has to be determined. The investigator used test-retest method to estimate the reliability of the scale. The SES scale was given to 40 students of class VI of Kendriya Vidyalaya, Sainik Vihar. There was an apprehension at that time that the students might not be able to understand the language of the questionnaire and they would not be able to respond well. The investigator decided to prepare a Hindi version of the questionnaire which was given to the students on demand to clear their doubts. The administration of the scale was repeated on the same group after a gap of 30 days. The coefficient of correlation of the two sets of scores was computed and found to be 0.95.

Validity of the Test

The validity of a set of data based on a test depends upon the fidelity with which it measures what it purports to measure. According to Garrett, (1966) "A test is valid when the performance which it measures corresponds to the same performance as otherwise independently assumed and measured or objectively defined. So far as the SES scale is concerned the investigator took care not only to establish face validity of the test but also its concurrent validity.

The SES scale developed for the present study has sufficient face validity as the questionnaire contains items which according to the experts not only seem to be related but are in fact related to various dimensions of the variable being measured. The content of the items in the SES scale seems to be relevant to its stated purpose. Face validity too, is an operational concept of validity, though based on subjective judgement. For the present study, face validity of the SES scale is reflected by analysing and incorporating all those items which directly relate to the dimensions of SES and have been retained in the scale on the basis of consultation with expert educationalists.

In order to test concurrent validity of the scale, the investigator gave the self-constructed scale as well as the standardized SES scale of B. Kuppuswamy to a group of 20 students of class VI of Kendriya Vidyalaya, Sainik Vihar. As Kuppuswamy's SES scale covers three main dimensions viz. education, occupation and income, only the data in respect of these dimensions of the self-constructed SES scale were used. The correlation between the results of standardized SES scale and the self-constructed scale was 0.91. Thus, the SES scale was well-standardized and could be used for data collection.

Development of PSRQ (Parental Support to Reading Questionnaire)

Language learning is a process which cannot take place in isolation. It is more of a social phenomenon because language acquisition is nothing but the communication between two persons or may be among a group of people. Since the parents fall in the first and immediate periphery of the child, their attitudes towards learning a language have significant effects on a child's learning. Heath (1962) conducted her study on "The environmental effect on literacy performances of a child". She analysed that those children who had frequent encounters with printed material at home could learn the words faster than those who were not provided any reading material at home. A nurturing atmosphere of literacy— exposure to books, print, reading and writing, careful selection of reading material, opportunities for ample reading experiences— is all what the child needs at home for developing reading.

This could only be possible if the parents themselves have a supportive and positive attitude towards students' reading. It is not absolutely essential that a positive attitude to reading can only be found in educated and well placed or socio-economically sound parents. It is only a myth with even increasing awareness of education, even the not-so-much educated parent do wish that their children study. But are all parents aware of the importance of reading? If the answer to this question is yes, then upto which extent and what efforts do they actually make in this direction. In order to ascertain this the parental attitude and support to reading questionnaire was evolved.

The investigator had a strong belief that the motivation provided by the parents plays a significant role in developing reading skills in children. Earlier also Mohan, S. (1991) in her study confirmed that parental encouragement, was significantly correlated to achievement in reading comprehension. Chan, J. (1986) in Hongkong also supported that parental support has a significant role in developing reading skills. Hence, the investigator thought of developing a questionnaire which would determine the parental support that the child gets for reading. The PSRQ questionnaire has five major components, viz:

(i) Amount of time given to the child by parents;

(ii) Availability of the reading material for the child;

(iii) Parental guidance provided to the child;

(iv) Motivation provided by parents to the child;

(v) Parents' effort to inculcate good reading habits in the child.

Twenty-five items using multiple-choice format were framed on these components. Three options were given for answering each item. This uniformity of options was meant for scoring each item on a three point scale. The questionnaire was prepared in English as well as in Hindi, assuming that some parents would feel more comfortable in attempting the questionnaire in Hindi. PSRQ (See Appendix-J : i & ii) had a provision for eliciting qualitative responses as well.

Scoring of PSRQ

The PSRQ had 25 questions. Each question carried a maximum of 2 marks for option 'a', 1 mark for option 'b' and zero mark for option 'c'. For example:

Do you buy a newspaper regularly?

The three keyed options provided in the PSRQ were:

A - Yes daily	- allotted marks	- 2
B - Sometimes	- alloted mark	- 1
C - Never	- allotted mark	- 0

This scoring scheme was followed for all the items in PSRQ.

Try-out of the PSRQ

Initially, the try-out was done on a group of parents of 20 children of class VI, studying in Kendriya Vidyalaya, Shalimar Bagh. These parents were contacted in a parent-teacher's meeting arranged in the school. Twenty parents were randomly selected from among those present in the meeting. The investigator had also procured a record of academic achievement of their children's performance. Another try out was done on those 20 students of K.V. Shalimar Bagh whose parents were previously contacted. After consulting various experts, the form of questions were modified. The questions now were framed to be attempted by the students and not the parents seeking information about their parent's role. Hence, the form and the language of the questionnaire was totally changed but the objective remained the same. The investigator found the results of second trial more reliable. Hence, she planned to administer the questionnaire on the students only.

Raven's Standard Progressive Matrices— An Introductior

For assessing the level of intellectual functioning of the children, the use of a non-verbal mental ability test was considered desirable. The selection of a non-verbal mental ability test was based on the consideration that the verbal competency of the child might influence his general ability. For this purpose, Standard Progressive Matrices Test was considered most appropriate. Another reason for selecting SPM was its perceptual nature and easy administration. SPM is a test which is designed to assess a person's intellectual development. In the words of Raven, J.C. (1960)

> It is a test of a person's capacity at the time of test to apprehend meaningless figures presented for his observation, to see the relation between them, conceive the nature of the figure completing each system of relation presented and by doing so develop a systematic method of reasoning".

SPM consists of 60 problems divided into five sets of 12 (set A, B, C, D and E). In each set, the first problem is almost self-evident. The problems become progressively more difficult. The order of the items provides standard training in the methods of working. The five sets provide five opportunities for understanding the method and five progressive assessments of a person's capacity for intellectual activity. To ensure sustained interest and freedom from fatigue, the figures in each problem are boldly presented, accurately drawn and quite pleasing to look at. SPM was designed to cover the widest possible range of mental ability and to be equally useful for persons of all ages, levels of education, nationality or physical conditions. Raven (1960) maintains that 'it is a scale which tests a person's power of observation and clarity of thinking'. All subjects are given exactly the same series of problems in the same order and asked to work at their own speed without interruption, from the beginning to the end of the scale. The scale can be given either as an individual, self-administered or as a group test. A person's total score provides an index of his/her intellectual capacity. The contribution which each of the five sets make to the total provides a means of assessing the consistency of the estimate and the psychological significance of discrepancies in the test results. As an untimed 'capacity' test and even as a 20 minute "speed or efficiency" test, the results have been found to be more reliable and psychologically valid than one might expect from 60 problems arranged in five sets of overlapping difficulty. It must, however be kept in mind that the scale is intended to span the whole range of intellectual development, rather than to differenciate clearly between individual persons. It is assumed in RPMT that till the age of 11, a child's ability to form comparisons and reason by analogy is often too recent an intellectual achievement for it to be exercised with a consistent degree of efficiency (Chauffard and Benassy, 1949). In all cases, the SPM used an untimed test is the most appropriate form to employ.

Standardization of SPM

The SPM was originally developed during the mid 1930s. It was revised and standardized in Ipswich in 1938. Extensive adult norms were collected during the war and the test was again standardized on school children in 1943.

(Raven and Walshaw, 1944). Additional data on old people and other respondent groups were accumulated during the forties. (Foulds and Raven, 1948). During the fifties and sixties several checks were carried out on the accuracy of norms (Adams, 1952 and Skranes, 1967). In 1972, a nationally representative sample of 3700 Irish school children aged 6 through 12 was tested using the machine scorable answersheet. In 1979, a nationally representative sample of 3500 British school children aged 6 to 16, excluding those attending special schools, was tested. The detailed results of the 1979 standardization revealed that:

(i) There is no sex difference in the scores obtained on the SPM except at age 11+ six months;

(ii) Only 9 per crnt of the within age variance is explained by social backgrounds;

(iii) As in the 1938 and 1972 standardization, the test works on scales in the same way for children from different socio-economic status background. It is not "Foreign to the way of thought process of children from certain background"; and

(iv) Once items become too difficult for children, they get the item right less often than would be expected by chance. Their responses are, therefore, not "random" but guided by hypothesis—albeit wrong hypothesis.

The 1984-86 USA standardization was based on a series of local norming studies conducted within particular school districts throughout America. Over 22,000 students were tested. One of the main findings was that the norms varied with the ethnic and socio-economic composition of the school district and its geographical location. Nevertheless item-analysis showed that the test scaled in the same way within each of the ethnic groups and had similar predictive validity. It, therefore, measured the same thing and worked in the same way within each group.

The implication of all these efforts is that as SPM was developed as a research tool, whose results can be relatively unambiguously interpreted. These studies throw new light on the question of 'test bias'. Besides, it is vital for psychological reasons to select the norms they use with any test to suit the purpose for which the test is being used.

Reliability Studies of SPM

Over forty reliability studies of SPM have been reported in the research literature. They cover a very wide age range; many cultural groups and clinical as well as normal population. Some of these studies suffer from inadequate sample size or from application to very young subjects for whom Coloured Progressive Matrices (CPM) would be more appropriate. When these studies were excluded, the general picture is of good reliability, whether in terms of internal consistency or test-retest reliability.

(a) Internal Consistency. The concept of internal consistency adopted for the Progressive Matrices essentially concern the question, "how closely the item-characteristic curves conform to the ideal shape, have few cross overs, are as far as possible, equally spaced and cover a whole range of abilities?" and secondly, "whether the items scale in the same way for different populations". In the British standardization, the correlation between the item difficulties established separately for eight socio-economic groups ranged from 0.97 to 0.99. Since SPM is a homogenous test, one would expect a high correlation with split half measures of reliability. The majority of studies giving consistency data report a correlation of at least 0.90.

(b) Test-Retest Reliability. Reports of retest reliability of SPMT are contained in over twenty papers. They differ widely in their methodoloy and the time intervals between tests range from one week to three years. The shorter intervals are in general associated with higher reliability correlation. Laroche (1960) has reported 0.85 with six grade negro boys. More substantial studies give a clear picture of short-term reliability around 0.90 reducing to around 0.80 at larger intervals; with the higher values being associated with younger subjects (under 30).

In general, the test-retest reliability and the inter-correlation between the matrices and vocabulary tests tend to be lowest of all with very young children and very old people. (Pinkerstom and Kelly, 1952; Burke, 1958; Gill and Byrt, 1973). Under normal conditions scores on the matrices reach their maximum somewhere about the age of 14, remain relatively constant for about 10 years and then begin to decline slowly but with remarkable uniformity Slater, 1947; Vernon, 1947; Foulds and Raven, 1948).

Validity Studies

(a) Criterion Oriented Validity. The concurrent and predictive validity of SPM vary with the age, sex and homogeneity of the sample, the method of assessment of the criterion to which the test will be related and the criterion measures in the context considered. A review of the relevant research, however, allows some general conclusion to be formulated.

(b) Correlation with Concurrent Intelligence Measure. For English speaking children and adolescents, reliable correlation of SPM with Binet and Wechesler Scales ranges from 0.54 to 0.86. Moderate to high correlations are also reported for SPM and various non-verbal and performance intelligence test for use with the children whereas correlations with verbal intelligence and vocabulary tests tend to be slightly lower generally falling below 0.7.

(c) Correlation with concurrent achievement measures. Correlation between SPM and performance on achievement tests or actual scholastic achievement are generally lower than correlation with intelligence and even more variable, ranging from negligible to very high.

(d) Factorial Construct Validity. The progressive matrices have been described as one of the purest and best measures of 'g' or general intellectual functioning available. Evidence for this claim comes from several factor analytic studies involving large number of children and adults. Cross-cultural studies confirm the high 'g' situation of 0.82 of SPM. It is claimed that the test can provide a valid means of assessing a person's capacity for clear thinking and accurate intellectual work.

The author of Progressive Matrices recommends the use of the test in conjunction with Mill-Hill vocabulary scale. Whereas the matrices test provides a reliable measure of a person's intellectual capacity, the verbal scale can indicate the general information a person has acquired up to the present level and his command on language. Both the tests have been standardized on the representative sample of British people of 6-65 years of age. But the inter-correlation between matrices and vocabulary scales tends to be lowest for very young children and very old people.

So, in this investigation, the Matrices Test was administered as a group test strictly in conformity with the procedure outlined in the instruction manual. As the test can be easily administered and requires little verbal instructions, the use of SPMT can be justified for the age group of 11 years. As the sample comprises class VI students aging 11 years, the investigator decided to use SPM only on the basis of the criteria given below:

(i) CPM (Coloured Progressive Matrices) would be too elementary for the sample group of 11 years, hence the idea of using it was discarded.

(ii) APM (Advanced Progressive Matrices) appeared to be too high for the age group of 11 years. This was later on confirmed on the basis of a try-out on 10 students studying in class VI Kendriya Vidyalaya, Lawrence Road. These students could not understand the complexity of the problems. Therefore, it was discarded. Consequently, the investigator decided to use SPM only.

Instructions for SPM-Materials

A set of test-booklets is required which can be used repeatedly. Each child required a record form and a pencil. Illustration of the record form and problems can be drawn on the blackboard at least twice its original size. Stencil keys facilitate rapid scoring of responses.

The SPMT was administered as a group test and also scored according to the instructions provided in the manual.

Level of Aspiration Test - An Introduction

Like other psychological phenomena, motivation factors are important in directing individual behaviour consciously and making him strive to perform certain types of activity in order to achieve a definite goal. Every one aims at reading a definite goal or excellence in performance and in doing so, he reveals a desire for a performance destination which has an inner structure known as 'Level of Aspiration' (LOA). The LOA is usually measured in terms of Goal Discrepancy Score (GDS). When GDS is very high or low, it may be claimed that one is merely imaginative, fantastic, unrealistic, below or above his self-esteem. On the contrary when actual performance and expectancy of the individual is about the same, it may be said that the person is realistic and practical in life. Thus, setting of level of aspiration may itself motivate the individual to try his level best though sometimes acknowledging how well one has performed previously may equally be effective. The performance on the test trial enables one to estimate how well he will do in the next trial-whether he would exceed or fall short of his estimate. It is generally found that majority of people tend to set their level of aspiration slightly above the previous performance and continue to adjust the level of successive trials. If one has reached the level set by him previously, he raises it on subsequent trials, but if one fails to reach the previously set level, it is lowered on the subsequent trials. Thus, the greater the success, the stronger the tendency to raise the level, whereas the greater the failure, the stronger the tendency to lower it. LOA is indicative of an individual's expectations or ambition. It refers to the estimate of one's future performance on a given task.

The concept of Level of Aspiration was first of all introduced in 1931 by Dembo, one of Daruin's students in the course of an experimental investigation of anger. The first experiment directed towards the analysis of the level of aspiration—a translation from German Word *'Anuspruch and Niveau'* was performed by Hoppe in 1930. Hoppe defined Level of Aspiration (LOA) as "a person's expectations, goals or claims on his own future achievement in a given task". Hoppe found that a given performance is accompanied by a feeling of failure if it falls below the LOA and given performance is accompanied by a feeling of success if it goes above the LOA. Therefore, LOA was essentially qualitative in nature. Hoppe ascertained LOA through the following lines of evidence:

(i) The subjective nature of an individual's goal;

(ii) The occurrence of success and failure experienced after the goal is achieved; and

(iii) The influence of immediate past experience on the subsequent level of goal setting behaviours.

Not only this, Hoppe also investigated various factors which affect goal setting behaviour. He concluded that individual variations are found in the level of aspiration. In his view, a realistic person always sets a goal on the basis of his past experience keeping in view his capabilities for doing a particular task. Thus, Hoppe conceived level of aspiration as a technique for studying dynamic factors which operate in the prediction of feeling of success and failure. Later on Frank (1935) redefined Hoppe's concept of LOA as, "Level of future performance on a familiar task which an individual, knowing his level of past performance in that task, explicitly undertakes to reach".

In the words of Hurlock (1967), "Aspiration means the goal an individual sets for himself on a task which has intense personal significance for him or in which he is ego-involved". Drever defined the term LOA as "a frame of reference involving self-esteem".

In short, many researchers have pointed out that level of aspiration is the expected level of achievement of the individual where difference is obtained between person's performance on a task and his estimate of future performance on that task. This concept of level of aspiration taken in the present study is based on the studies of Humphery and Argyle (1962).

Determinants of LOA

Level of aspiration is usually influenced by two types of factors; environmental and personal. The environmental determinants are:

(i) Parental Ambitions

(ii) Social Expectations

(iii) Peer pressure

(iv) Culture

(v) Social Value

(vi) Competition

(vii) Group Cohesiveness.

Personal Determinants are wishes, personality, past experience, values and interest, sex, socio-economic background and racial background.

Description of Level of Aspiration Test

After referring to a number of level of aspiration tests, such as Occupational Aspiration Scale (Grewal), Educational Aspirational Scale (Shanue and Gupta) and Level of Aspiration Test (Bharagava V.P.), the investigator decided to use Shah and Bhargava's Level of Aspiration test. This test was found suitable considering the difficulty level of the task to be performed for class VI level and also the age group of the students and their interests.

The level of aspiration booklet contains the general information instructions to the respondent and the scoring table. The LOA booklet also contains the performance sheets arranged in order of trial numbers. A performance sheet has 50 circles (each of 1 cm. diameter) which are arranged in five rows, ten in each row. Above and below these rows, there are two boxes on the right side, the upper box is for writing the number of expected score (except in practice trial) whereas the lower is for indicating the number of actual score on completed performance. A copy of the first page of LOA test and a performance sheet is given in Appendix 'M'.

Procedure of Administering LOA

Each student was given eleven performance sheets alongwith the first page of the booklet on which the instructions to the respondents are printed. The investigator read out the instructions and then the students were asked to complete their particulars, etc., on page one of the booklet. Then the students were asked to work only in the allotted time and stop working as soon as the allotted time was over. The practice trial sheet was given first; thereafter the actual trials began.

Scoring and Interpretation

The procedure of scoring LOA responses is simple. It provides three types of scores:

(i) Goal Discrepancy Score (GDS)

(ii) Attainment Discrepancy Score (ADS)

(iii) The Number of Times the Goal Reached Score (NTRS).

Goal Discrepancy Score (GDS)

The extent and direction of the difference between actual score on the previous trial and goal set up for the next trial is known as Goal Discrepancy Score (GDS) which is obtained by subtracting the actual score on a trial from the aspiration score (Goal set up score) for the next trial. Thus, in other words, Goal Discrepancy is the gap between aspiration for the next trial (expected score) and the immediate performance on previous trial. A positive goal discrepancy score suggests that the goal is higher and the negative goal discrepancy suggests that one's goal is lower. The size of discrepancy shows how high or low one sets the goal in relation to his performance. The general tendency by and large is to set the goal a little higher than the previous performance leading to positive goal discrepancy. If the differences of the scores are consistently positive, it indicates that the subject is over-aspirant and may be called idealistic. If the difference is consistently negative, the subject may be called under-aspirant. A positive difference may also be interpreted in terms of ego involvement of the subject.

Attainment Discrepancy Score (ADS)

Related to the concept of Goal Discrepancy is the attainment discrepancy. It is the difference between aspiration (expected scores) and the achievement (actual score) on the same trial. Thus, in order to obtain ADS, expected scores are subtracted from the actual scores. The size of the discrepancy shows the extent to which one surpasses or fails to reach one's goal.

Relation Between Goal Discrepancy Score and Attainment Discrepancy Score

Both GDS and ADS cannot be separated in goal setting patterns. But they are found to be inversely related. Eysenck and Himwelweit (1946) have reported a correlation of –0.95 between GDS and ADS. This negative correlation suggests that whatever makes the one higher in the positive direction should make the other higher in the negative direction.

Number of Times the Goal Reached Score (NTRS)

It may be obtained by the numbers of times when an individual's actual score is equal to or more than the expected score. The probability of success can be measured directly through NTR score which provides an index of subject's actual probability of reaching his stated goal. There may be a minimum and maximum score with reference to the number of trials and it is expected that a subject with relatively high motivation will take less trial risk to avoid failure in approaching these two limits minimum and maximum. The subject with minimum NTRS are relatively more ready to risk failure.

Reliability of LOA Test

The reliability of LOA calculated by the test-retest method and the split half method (correcting the first-half trials with the second-half trials). The results of the reliability of LOA test done through the Retest and Split half method, during the investigation, are shown in Table 3.4.

TABLE 3.4
Reliability of LOA Test

Method	*N*	*GDS*	*ADS*	*NTRS*
Retest Method				
Ist Test	100	0.88	0.82	0.86
IInd Test	100	0.72	0.75	0.74
Split half Method	60	0.77	0.69	0.78

Validity of LOA Text

It may be stated that no device or measure of level of aspiration has made any mention of validity coefficient. Perhaps the question of validity is not relevant to the study of level of aspiration. In this context, Muthayya (1959) writes, 'level of aspiration behaviour remains constant regardless of the means used to measure it'. His argument is understandable because the question of validity arises when a behaviour is inferred from another indirect behaviour. In this situation, the respondent is involved in actual task proposed by him and the situation is by and large realistic for him. Nevertheless the present investigator tried to find out the validity coefficients with a few tasks and other available tests of level of aspiration and the results are shown in Table 3.5.

TABLE 3.5
Validity of LOA Test

SN.	*Method*	*N*	*GDS*	*ADS*
1.	Card Sorting Tray Tasks	80	0.63	0.52
2.	Bhargava's Level of Aspiration Test	50	0.67	0.62
3.	Grewal's Occupational Aspiration Scale	60	0.76	0.65
4.	Shanua and Gupta's Educational Aspiration Scale	45	0.48	0.56

Norms of LOA Test

LOA measure was administered by Shah and Bhargava on 600 higher secondary and college-going students and the results obtained in the form of norms for categorization of students are given in Appendix - N.

Thus, the tools were readv for the administration on the actual sample.

4

Analysis of Data

Introduction

Statistics is an indispensable tool in research work. It is a body of mathematical techniques and processes used for organizing, analyzing and interpreting the available data. The data have no meaning in themselves unless they are analyzed appropriately and interpreted logically. Analysis of data involves data reduction including tabulation and use of various tests and techniques in order to determine its inherent meaning or messages. Data analysis may also include breaking up of various composite factors into simpler parts and putting them in new arrangements for the purpose of interpretation. The data deal with the quantitative as well as qualitative characteristics of the variables under consideration and may thus be numerical as well as verbal statements of relevant facts. Suitable statistical techniques are required to understand the significance and implication of such data.

Scheme of Data Analysis

In the present study, there are certain dependent as well as independent variables that have been described in earlier chapters. In the present study, the investigator processed the data at three levels:

(a) Graphical Presentation using frequency polygons and pie diagrams for highlighting dominant trends;

(b) Descriptive Statistical Analysis of data that yielded various statistics about the sample. These were:

(i) Mean

(ii) Standard Deviation

(iii) Range

(iv) Coefficient of Correlation.

The following formulae have been used for calculating Mean, SD and Coefficient of Correlation:

(i) Mean = $\Sigma fx/N$

where 'Σfx' is the sum of mid-points, weighed by their frequencies and 'N' is the number of measures

(Garret, 1961, 28)

(ii) $SD^{\sigma} = \frac{\Sigma fx^2}{N}$

where x is the deviation from mid-point

f is the frequency and

N is the number of measures

(Garrett, 1961, 50)

(iii) Coefficient of correlation may be thought of essentially as the ratio that expresses the extent to which changes in one variable are accompanied by changes in the other variable.

In the present study, the relationship to be established between the sets of measures, is 'linear', i.e., can be described by a straight line. The correlation was computed between reading, comprehension and other variables.

Product-moment coefficient of correlation 'r' was calculated with the help of the following formula:

$$r = \frac{\Sigma x^1 y^1/N - CxCy}{\sigma x^1 \; \sigma y^1}$$

where $\Sigma x^1 y^1/N$ is the sum of deviations from mean.

(Garrett, 1961, 138)

The interpretation of 'r' value in verbal description is:

r from 0.00 to ± 0.20 denotes indifferent or negligible relationship.

r from ± 0.20 to ± 0.40 denotes low correlation.

r from ± 0.40 to ± 0.70 denotes substantial or marked relationship.

r from ± 0.70 to ± 1.00 denotes high to very high relationship.

(Garrett, 1961, 176)

(c) Inferential Statistical Analysis: This included significance of the differences between Means which was tested through:

(i) t-ratio

(ii) F-ratio

The basic formulae used here are as follows:

$$SD = \sqrt{\frac{\sum (X_1-M_1)^2 + \sum (X_2-M_2)^2}{(N_1-1) + (N_2-1)}}$$

$$SED = SD\sqrt{\frac{N_1+N_2}{N_1N_2}}$$

$$\sigma D = \sqrt{(r^2Mx_1+r^2Mx_2)\ (1-r^2xy)}$$

$$t = \frac{Mx_1-Mx_2}{\sigma D}$$

(Garrett, 1961, 224)

Graphic Presentation of Data

Analysis of numerical data may often be obtained through graphic or pictorial treatment of the data through frequency distribution. Such a visual presentation not only catches the eye but also helps in translating numerical facts into more concrete and intelligible form.

In the present study, the investigator uses frequency polygon to study the scores of boys and girls on various dependent as well as independent variables.

The investigator divides the entire data related to 250 students in 3 major groups viz.

Group I	-	Above average boys
		Above average girls
Group II	-	Average boys
		Average girls
Group III	-	Below average boys
		Below average girls.

Sight Vocabulary

Fig. 4.1 gives graphic presentation of data on sight vocabulary scores for above-average boys and girls. This category of students was formulated on the basis of students' scores on Raven's Standard Progressive Matrices Test. The process of recognition of words at a glance requires basic intelligence. It seems that the above average boys and girls have approximately identical scores on the test.

This can be further supported by the near identical range of scores of both groups. The mean of above average boys being 69.95 is not much different from the mean of above average girls of 74.2.

It may be inferred from the frequency polygons that above average girls have greater and sharper individual difference as compared to boys. The unimodal graph indicating boys' scores reflects greater homogeneity than the frequency polygon for girls' scores which is bimodal and shows sharp kinks.

Thus, it may be concluded on the basis of Fig 4.1 that above average boys and girls do not differ much in terms of their sight vocabulary though girls shows sharper individual differences amongst themselves.

Fig. 4.2 gives the graphic presentation of data on sight vocabulary test for average boys and girls. This category of students was formulated on the basis of students' performance on Raven's Standard Progressive Matrices Test. The graph shown in Fig. 4.2 provides a mixed picture of the

FIG. 4.1 : SIGHT VOCABULARY
(ABOVE AVERAGE BOYS AND GIRLS)

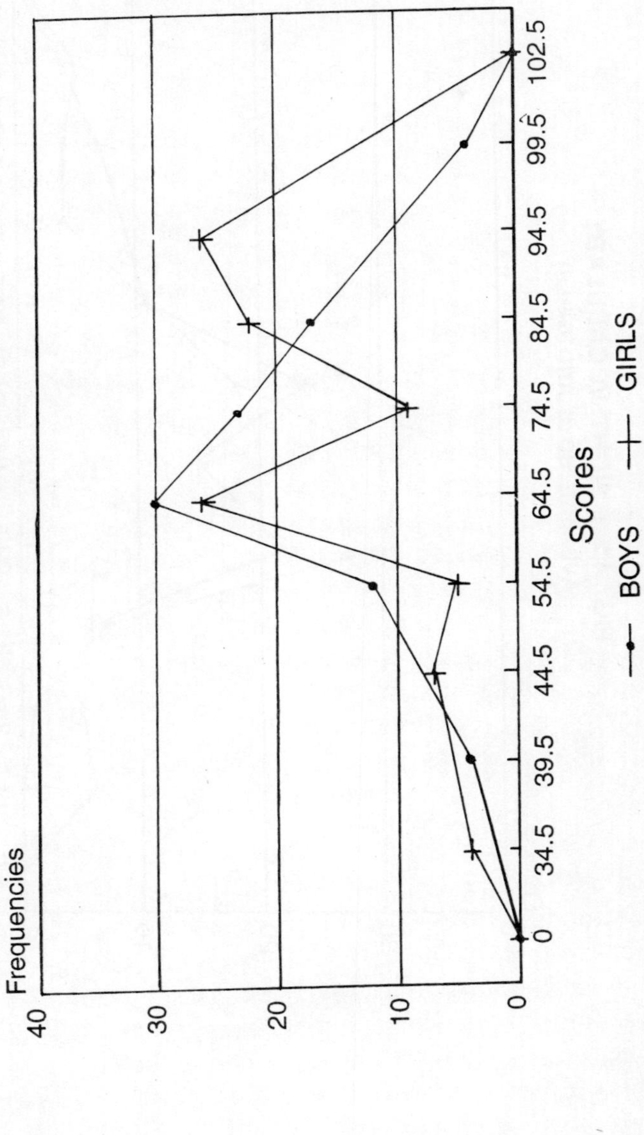

FIG. 4.2 : SIGHT VOCABULARY
(AVERAGE BOYS AND GIRLS)

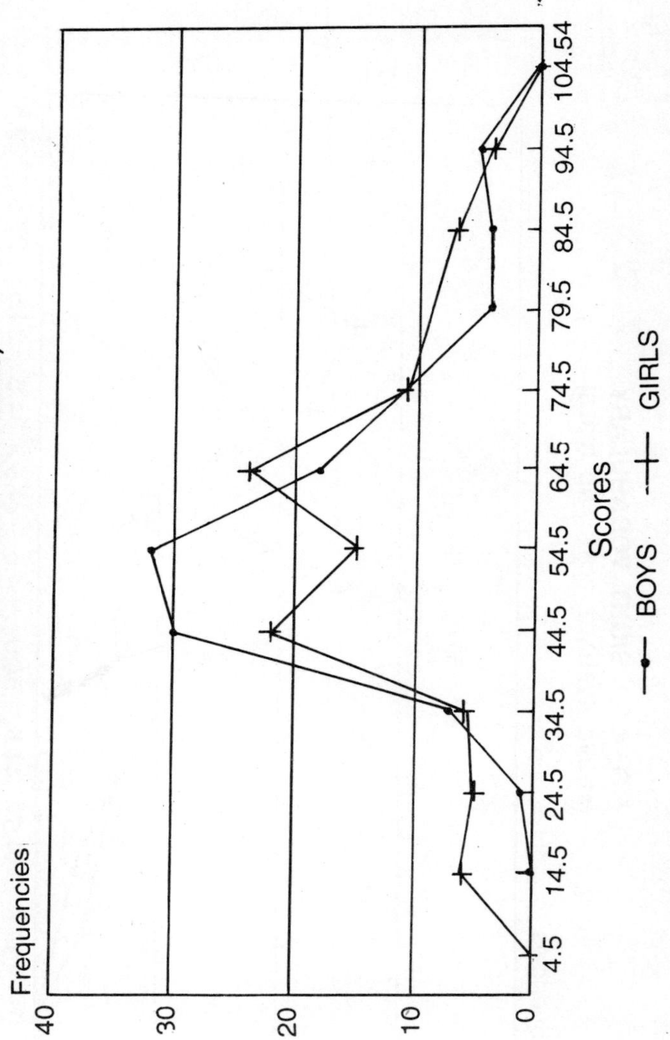

scoring pattern of average boys and girls. Though there is shift in the range of scores of boys on the higher side as compared to girls, yet the girls show sharp modes. There do not appear to be appreciable differences between the score patterns of the two groups. Average boys' mean score is 54.8 whereas that of average girls is 54.34.

It may be concluded that on the whole there is not much significant difference in the sight vocabulary of average boys and girls.

Fig. 4.3 provides graphic presentation of data on sight vocabulary test for below average boys and girls. This category of students was formulated on the basis of students scores on Raven's Standard Progressive Matrices Test. It is well known that the process of recognition of words at first sight requires basic intelligence.

The graph reveals a mixed picture of scores of both the groups. The boys' scores are concentrated within the middle range, whereas' the girls' scores are on the higher side of the scale. Apparently, the girls show better performance on sight vocabulary but at the same time their scores show sharp individual differences as reflected by the peaks and falls. The boys' scores present greater approximation of normality than the girls' scores.

It may thus be concluded that though the girls appear to perform better on sight vocabulary test, yet there may not be much significant difference between the sight vocabulary of the two groups. This is supported by the means of the scores of the two groups. (The mean of the scores of below average boys is 41.35 whereas that of below average girls is 41.62).

Parental Support to Reading

Fig. 4.4 gives graphic presentation of data on PSRQ (Parental Support to Reading Questionnaire) for above-average boys and girls. As already stated, this category of students was formulated on the basis of students' scores on Raven's Standard Progressive Matrices Test. PSRQ

FIG. 4.3 : SIGHT VOCABULARY
(BELOW AVERAGE BOYS AND GIRLS)

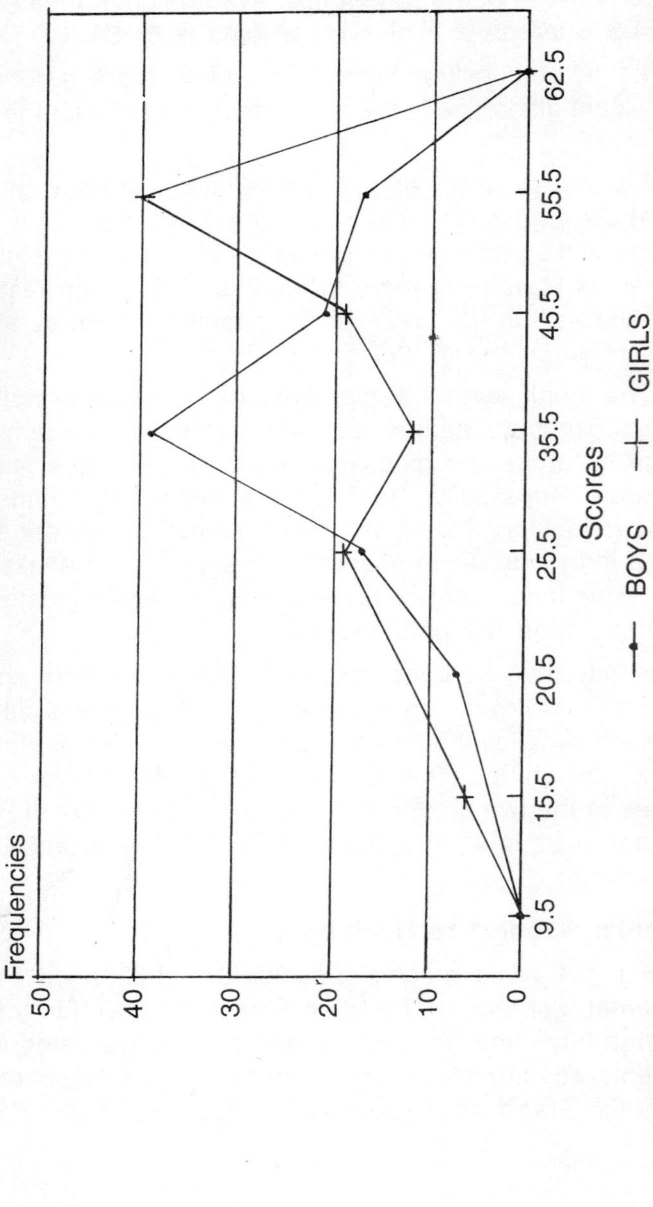

FIG. 4.4 : PARENTAL SUPPORT TO READING
(ABOVE AVERAGE BOYS AND GIRLS)

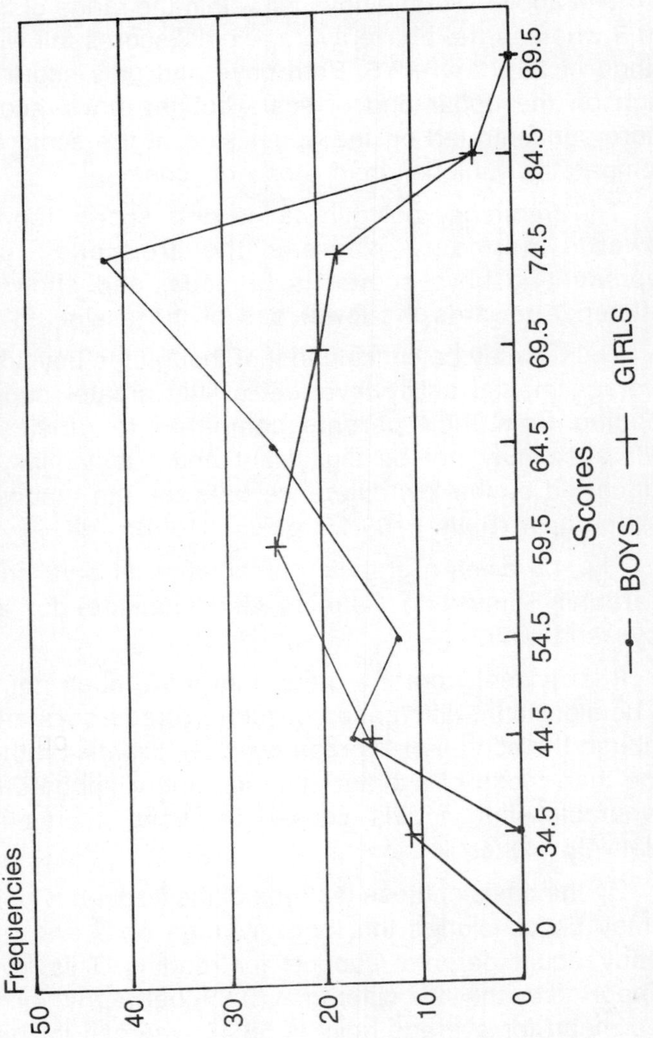

comprises a set of multiple answer type questions and was administered on the students in order to know the support they get from their parents for developing their reading skills.

The above average boys fall within the range of 39.5 and 89.5 whereas the above average girls' scores fall within the range of 29.5 and 89.5. Both boys and girls score equally high on the upper end of scale but the boys' scores are more concentrated on the upper side of the scale and are comparatively higher than those of girls.

The frequency polygon of the girls scores tends more towards normality whereas the frequency polygon representing boys scores is bi-modal and shows sharp difference towards the lower end of the scale.

Thus, it may be concluded that though the boys of above average mental ability level get a little greater support for reading from their parents compared to girls, yet this difference may not be significant and substantial. This is supported by the low difference between the means of the two groups. (Boys = 63.16; girls= 61.40).

Fig. 4.5 gives a graphic presentation of data on PSRQ (Parental Support to Reading Questionnaire) for average boys and girls.

It is evident from the graph that there does not appear to be significant difference between average boys and girls. Though the scores of average boys are slightly on the lower side than those of average girls and there appears to be a favourable shift in girls' scores, the boys' scores show a relatively higher range.

On the basis of these features of the frequency polygons, it may be concluded that both average boys and girls get nearly equal parental support for reading. This is further supported by the little difference (0.89) between their means. The mean for average boys is 58.49 whereas for girls it is 57.60.

Fig. 4.6 gives a graphic presentation of data on PSRQ (Parental Support to Reading Questionnaire) for below average boys and girls.

FIG. 4.5 : PARENTAL SUPPORT TO READING
(AVERAGE BOYS AND GIRLS)

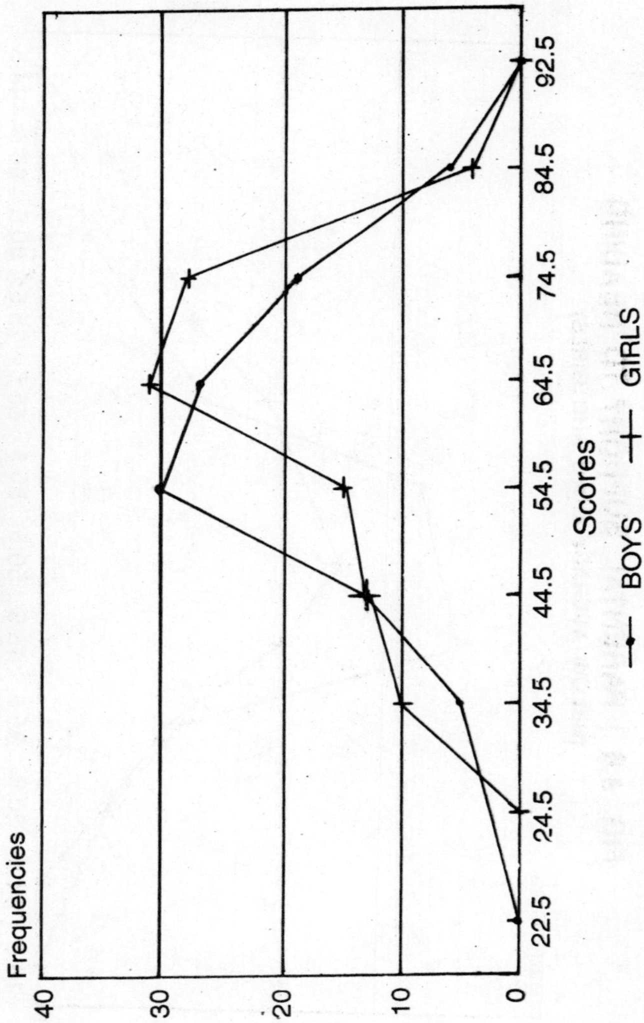

FIG. 4.6 : PARENTAL SUPPORT TO READING
(BELOW AVERAGE BOYS AND GIRLS)

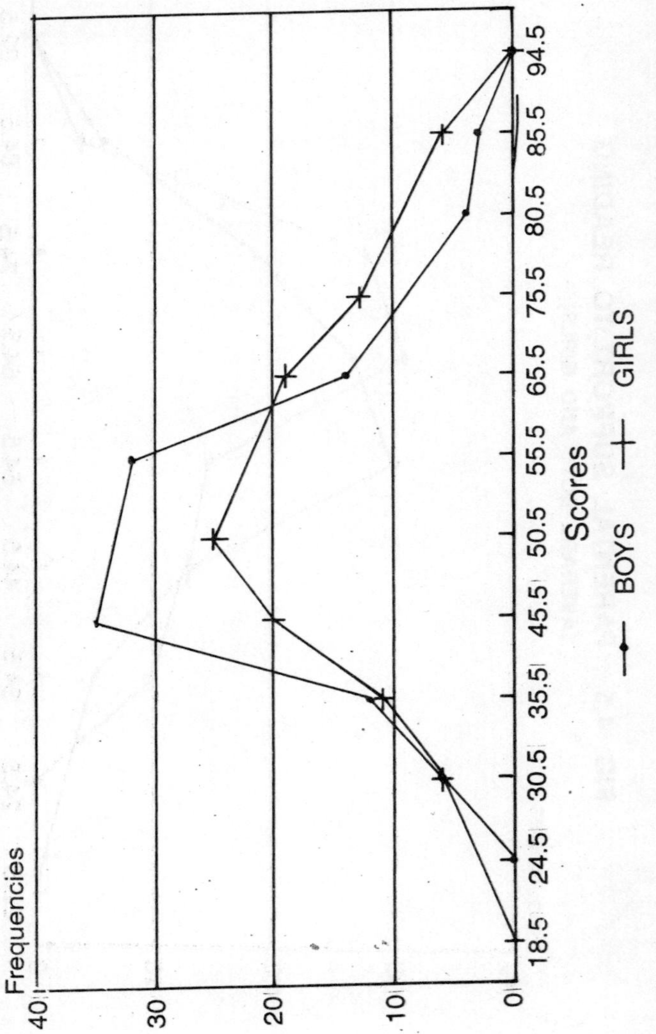

The frequency polygons indicate that more boys receive greater parental support for reading than the girls. The boys PSRQ scores are higher than those of girls on the middle part of the scale. On other parts of the scale, the two groups viz. boys and girls receive more or less equal parental support.

It may thus be concluded that below average boys and girls receive almost equal parental support for reading. The minor difference in the support provided by the parents may be attributed to the greater reliance of parents on their male children. However, the overall pattern of parental support does not appear to differ according to the gender of the child receiving this support.

Socio-Economic Status

Fig. 4.7 gives the graphic presentation of data on Socio-Economic Status Questionnaire for above average boys and girls.

It is obvious from the graph shown in Fig. 4.7 that there is not much significant difference reflected in the SES of above average boys and girls. Both above average boys and girls score between 50.5 and 90.5. The graph shows very negligible difference between the SES scores of above average boys and girls.

Thus, it may be concluded that there is no substantial and significant difference between the socio-economic status of above average boys and girls.

Fig. 4.8 gives graphic presentation of average boys and girls in terms of their scores obtained on Socio-Economic Status Questionnaire.

The graph indicates that more average girls have SES scores on the lower side of the graph as compared to average boys. The girls scores range between 9.5 and 89.5 whereas the boys scores range between 19.5 and 79.5.

It may be noted that girls' scores are widely spread on the graph both on the lower and the upper ends whereas

FIG. 4.7 : SOCIO-ECONOMIC STATUS
(ABOVE AVERAGE BOYS AND GIRLS)

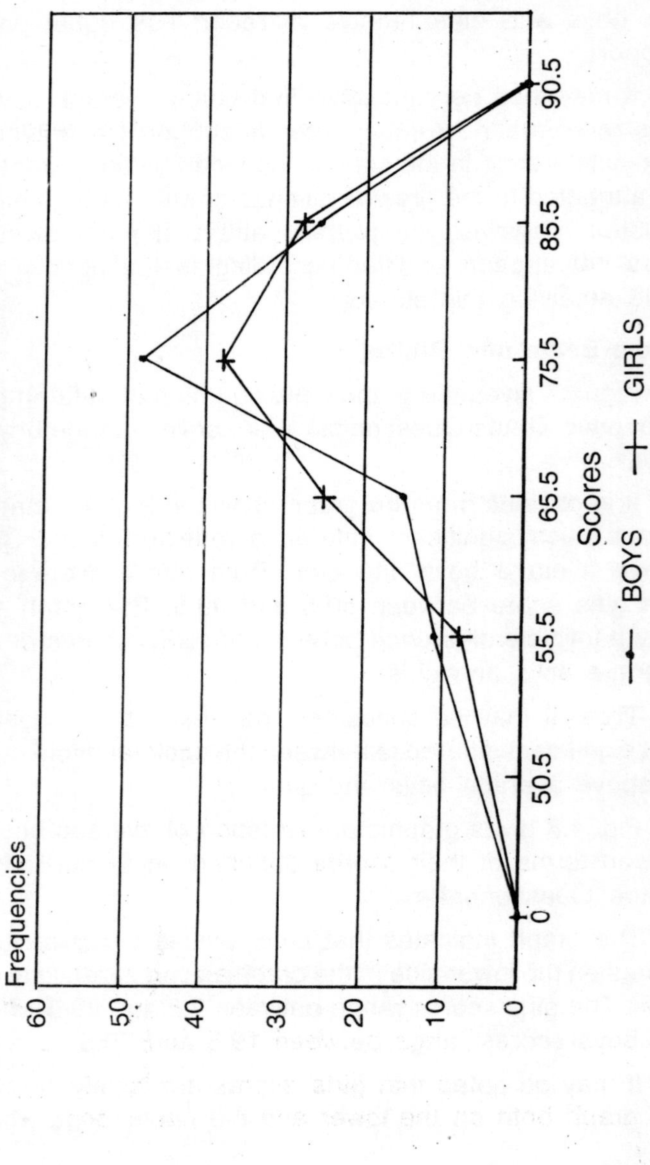

FIG. 4.8 : SOCIO-ECONOMIC STATUS
(AVERAGE BOYS AND GIRLS)

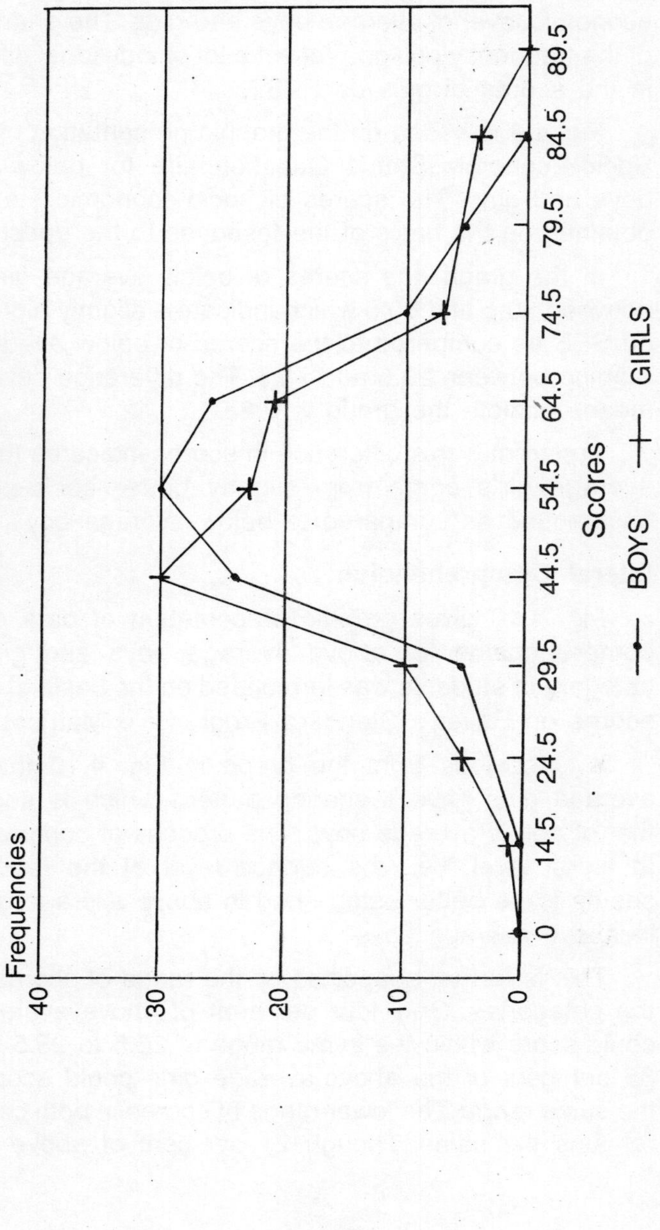

the boys scores are more concentrated towards the middle of the graph.

It may be thus concluded that there is not much substantial and significant difference between the socio-economic level of average boys and girls. The sharp modes of the frequency polygon reflect a lot of individual differences in the scores of girls on SES.

Fig. 4.9 is based on the graphic presentation of data on Socio-Economic Status Questionnaire for below average boys and girls. The scores of socio-economic status were obtained on the basis of the response to the questionnaire.

In the graph, the scores of below average girls range between 30.5 and 80.5 which indicate a slightly higher score on SES as compared to the scores of below average boys ranging between 20.5 and 70.5. The difference between the means of both the group is 2.83.

Apparently, this difference in scores indicates that below average girls come from slightly better socio-economic background as compared to below average boys.

Literal Comprehension

Fig. 4.10 gives graphic presentation of data on literal comprehension for above average boys and girls. This category of students was formulated on the basis of students scores on Raven's Standard Progressive Matrices Test.

It is obvious from the graph in Fig. 4.10 that above average girls have a scoring pattern which is superior to that of above average boys. The process of comprehending at literal level, i.e., the surface level of the reading text seems to be better established in above average girls than in above average boys.

This is further supported by the range of scores of both the categories. Only four per cent of above average boys could score within the same range of 20.5 to 28.5 whereas 35 per cent of the above-average girls could score within the same range. The lower range of scores in both categories remains the same. Though 21 per cent of above average

FIG. 4.9 : SOCIO-ECONOMIC STATUS
(BELOW AVERAGE BOYS AND GIRLS)

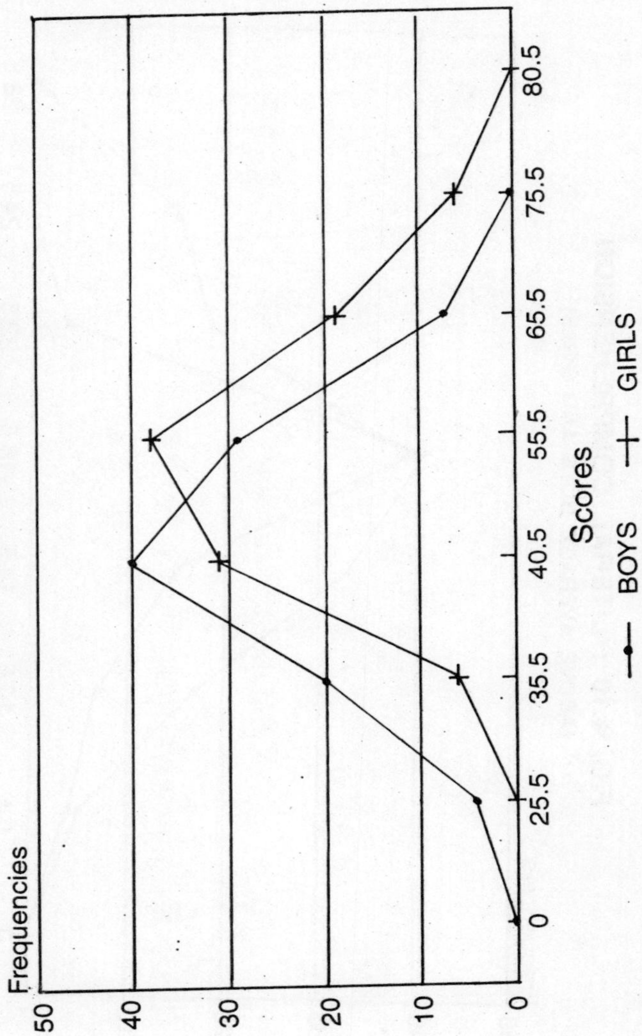

FIG. 4.10 : LITERAL COMPREHENSION
(ABOVE AVERAGE BOYS AND GIRLS)

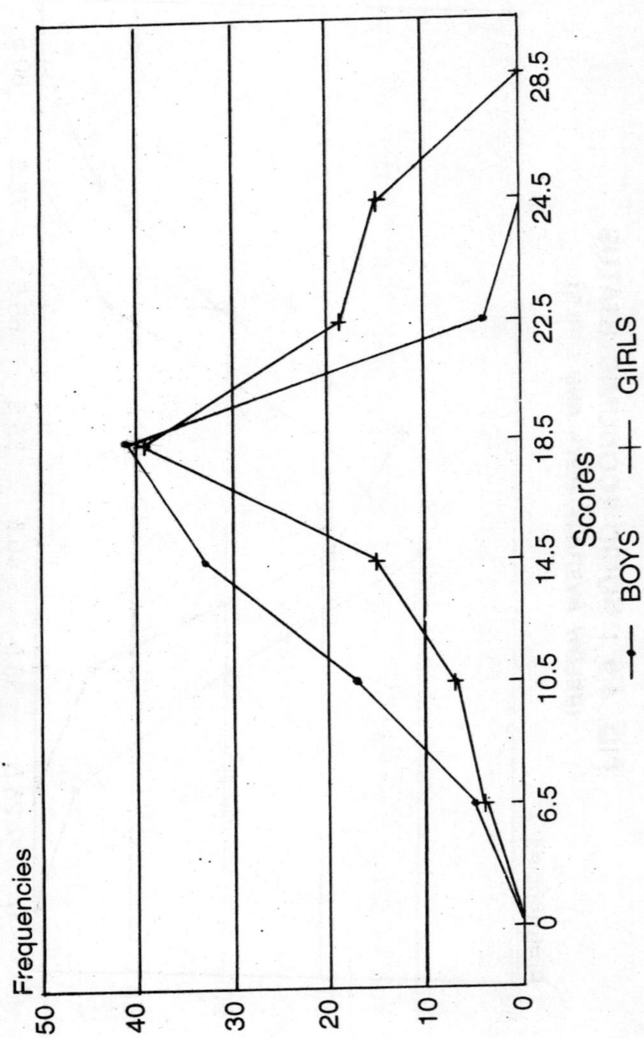

boys score within the range of 4.5 and 12.5, only 11 per cent of the above average girls fall within this range of scores.

One can conclude from the differences in frequency polygons in Fig. 4.10 that there appears to exist a significant difference in the literal comprehension of the students; i.e. boys and girls of this category and the girls definitely seem to score better. It may be said that the above average girls show better literal comprehension than above average boys. This is also supported by the difference in means of the two groups. Mean score of boys is 52.87 whereas that of girls is 59.03.

Fig. 4.11 gives a graphic presentation of data on literal comprehension for average boys and girls. This category of students was formulated on the basis of students scores on Raven's Standard Progressive Matrices Test. The ability of comprehending at literal level, i.e., the surface level of reading texts seems to have been acquired at a nearly same level in average boys and girls. The two frequency polygons establish it adequately.

This is also supported by the range of scores of both the categories of sample. The lower end scoring pattern is identical in both. There is not much difference even at the upper end scoring pattern except that the boys seem to have a little edge over girls. In the middle range the difference appears to be superficial as the frequency polygon of girls scores shows sharp fall and rise as compared to the smooth curve of boys scores.

One may conclude that the average boys and girls do not show any remarkable difference in their performance in comprehension at literal level.

Fig. 4.12 gives graphic presentation of data on literal comprehension for below average boys and girls. This category of students was formulated on the basis of the students score on Raven's Standard Progressive Matrices Test. It is obvious from the graph shown in Fig 4.12 that below average boys have a scoring pattern which is superior

FIG. 4.11 : LITERAL COMPREHENSION
(AVERAGE BOYS AND GIRLS)

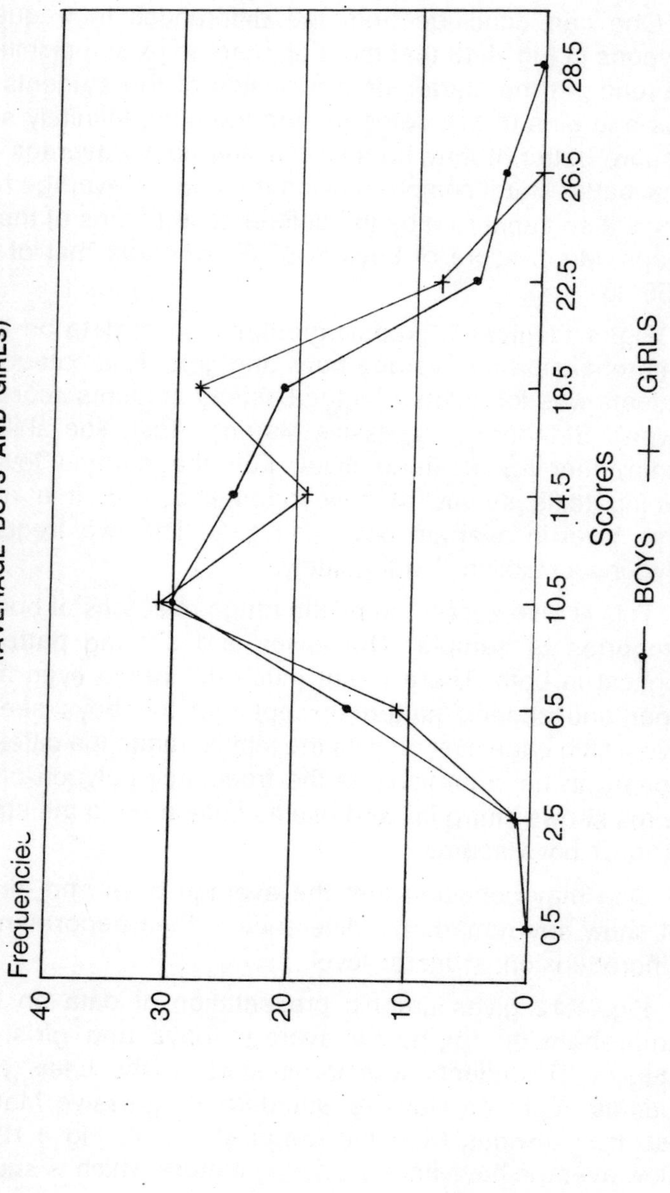

FIG. 4.12 : LITERAL COMPREHENSION
(BELOW AVERAGE BOYS AND GIRLS)

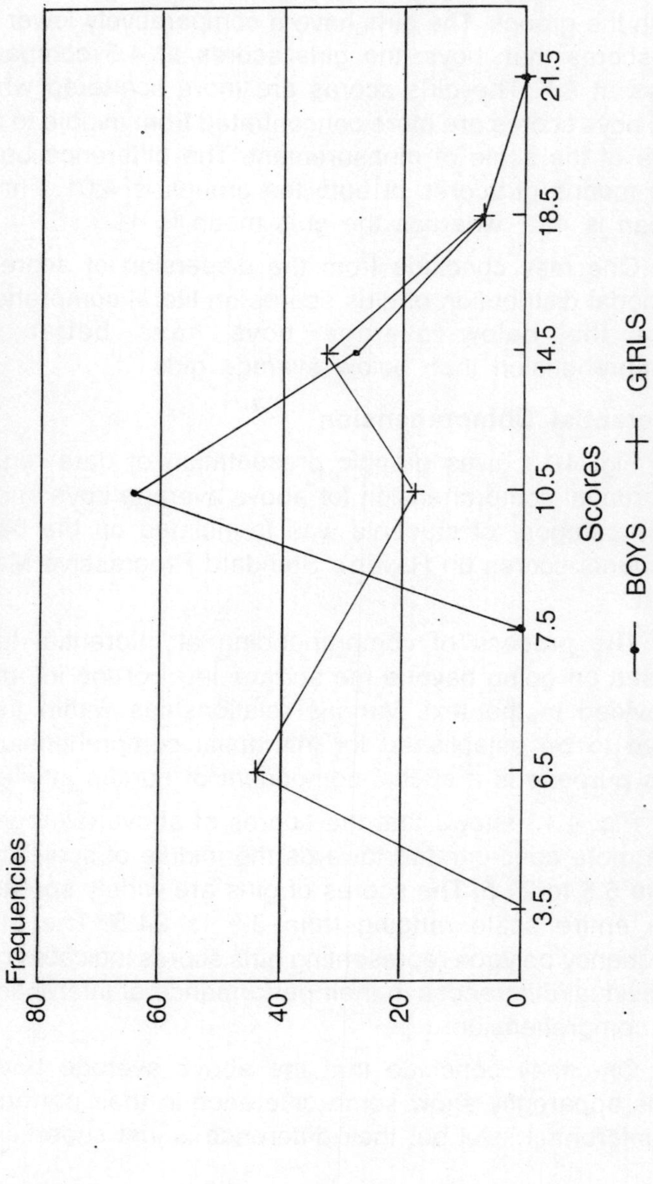

to that of below average girls, i.e., the surface level of the information seems to be better established in boys than in girls at below average level of mental ability.

This can be further supported by the range of scores of both the groups. The girls have a comparatively lower range of scores than boys; the girls scores at 4.5 compared to boys at 8.5. The girls scores are more scattered whereas the boys scores are more concentrated from middle to higher side of the scale of measurement. The difference between the means of scores of both the groups is 4.01. The boys mean is 45.7 whereas the girls mean is 41.7.

One may conclude from the dispersion of scores and bimodal distribution of girls scores on literal comprehension that the below average boys have better literal comprehension than below average girls.

Inferential Comprehension

Fig. 4.13 gives graphic presentation of data regarding inferential comprehension for above average boys and girls. This category of students was formulated on the basis of students scores on Raven's Standard Progressive Matrices Test.

The process of comprehending at inferential level is based on going beyond the surface level of the information provided in the text. Various relationships within the text have to be established for inferential comprehension and this purpose is a critical component of human intelligence.

Fig. 4.13 shows that the scores of above average boys are more concentrated towards the middle of scale ranging from 6.5 to 21.5. The scores of girls are widely spread over the entire scale ranging from 3.5 to 24.5. The bimodal frequency polygon representing girls scores indicates greater individual differences in their performance at inferential level of comprehension.

One may conclude that the above average boys and girls apparently show some difference in their performance at inferential level but their difference is just superficial and

FIG. 4.13 : INFERENTIAL COMPREHENSION
(ABOVE AVERAGE BOYS AND GIRLS)

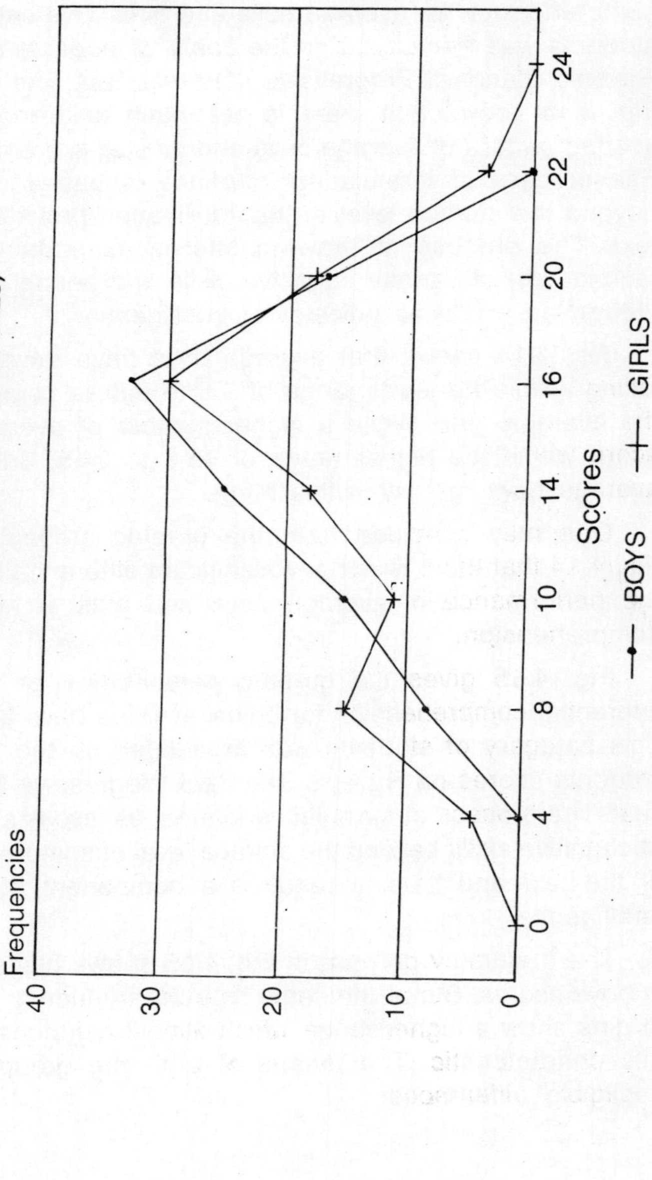

hence, not significant. This may be supported by the non-significant difference of 1.01 between their means.

Fig. 4.14 gives graphic presentation of data on inferential comprehension for average boys and girls. This category of students was formulated on the basis of students score on Raven's Standard Progressive Matrices Test. The graph in Fig. 4.14 shows that there is not much difference in the scoring pattern of average boys and girls at inferential level. The process of formulating inference is based on going beyond the surface level of the information provided in the text. The process of drawing inferences subsumes the rational use of various cognitive skills and hence it can be viewed as a critical indicator of intelligence.

Fig. 4.14 shows that average boys have fewer scores falling within the lower range of 0.5 to 6.5 as compared to the average girls. While a higher number of average girls score within the higher range of 15.5 to 24.5, only a few average boys fall within this range.

One may conclude from the graphic presentation in Fig. 4.14 that there is not any significant difference between the performance of average boys and girls in inferential comprehension.

Fig. 4.15 gives the graphic presentation of data on inferential comprehension for below average boys and girls. This category of students was formulated on the basis of students scores on Raven's Standard Progressive Matrices Test. The process of formulating inferences involves the use of cognitive skills beyond the surface level of comprehension of the text and thus, it requires a component of human intelligence.

The frequency polygon in Fig. 4.15 shows higher mode in boys scores. But at the same time the frequency polygon of girls show a higher range which almost compensates for this characteristic. The means of both the groups show negligible differences.

FIG. 4.14 : INFERENTIAL COMPREHENSION
(AVERAGE BOYS AND GIRLS)

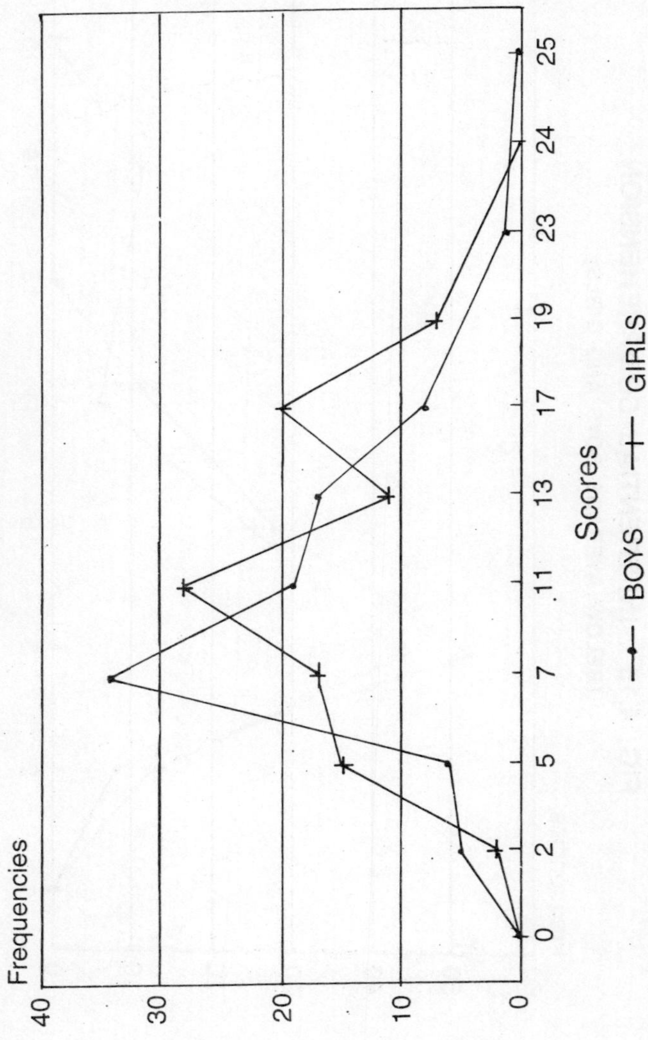

FIG. 4.15 : INFERENTIAL COMPREHENSION
(BELOW AVERAGE BOYS AND GIRLS)

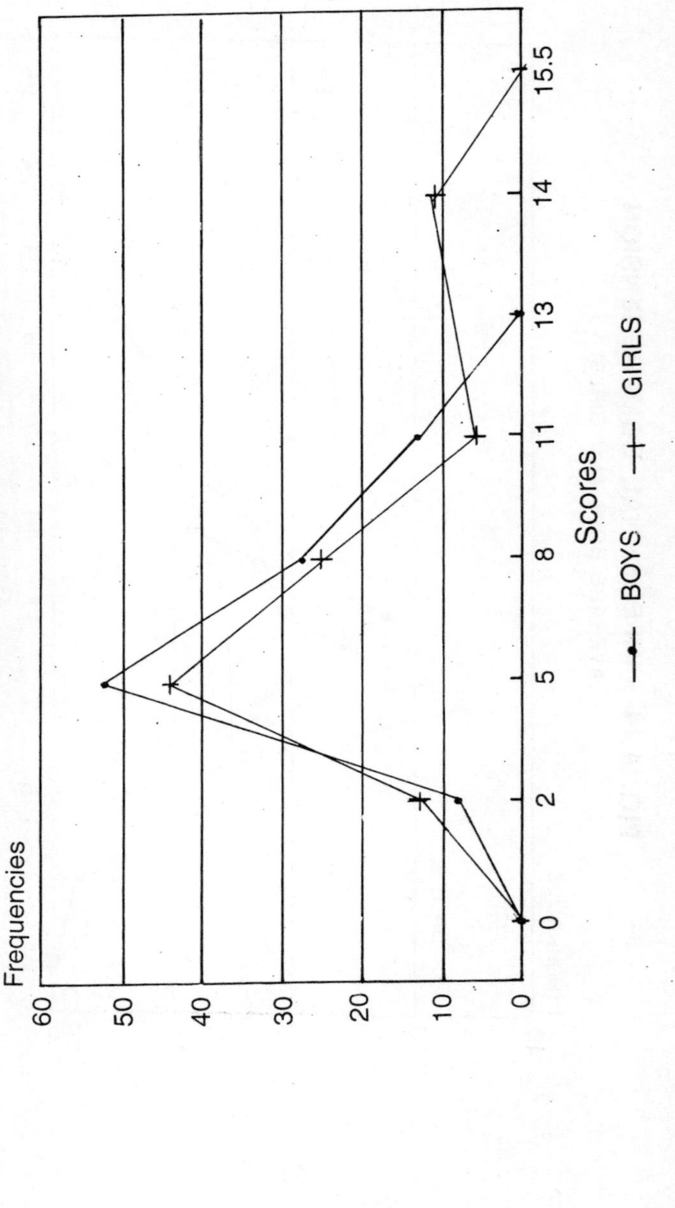

So it may be concluded that in spite of the superficial differences seen in Fig. 4.15 there is not much real difference in the performance of below average boys and girls on their inferential comprehension.

Total Reading Comprehension

Fig. 4.16 provides graphic presentation of data on total reading comprehension for above average boys and girls. This category of students was formulated on the basis of their scores on Raven's Standard Progressive Matrices Test.

The process of reading comprehension comprises both literal as well as inferential comprehension, i.e., seeking information at the surface level and going beyond the surface level.

Fig. 4.16 indicates that scores of above average boys fall within the range of 15.5 to 45.5 whereas the girls scores fall between 10.5 and 45.5. On the lower side of the scale, the boys perform better than the girls but on the upper part of the scale, the performance of girls seem to be slightly better than that of the boys in the region of the mode score.

The frequency polygon of boys scores show a lower homogeneous performance as compared to girls. There are sharper individual differences among girls than among boys in their total reading comprehension.

Thus, it may be concluded that there is not much real difference between the performance of above average girls and boys in their total reading comprehension.

Fig. 4.17 gives a graphic presentation of data on total reading comprehension for average boys and girls. This category of students was formed on the basis of their scores on Raven's Standard Progressive Matrices Test

The graph in Fig. 4.17 shows that the scores of average boys fall within the range of 5.5 to 45.5 whereas the girls scores range between 0.5 to 40.5. The frequency polygon for average girls is bimodal which reflects heterogeneity, whereas the frequency polygon of the boys scores is unimodal and approximates normality for more than that of

FIG. 4.16 : TOTAL READING COMPREHENSION
(ABOVE AVERAGE BOYS AND GIRLS)

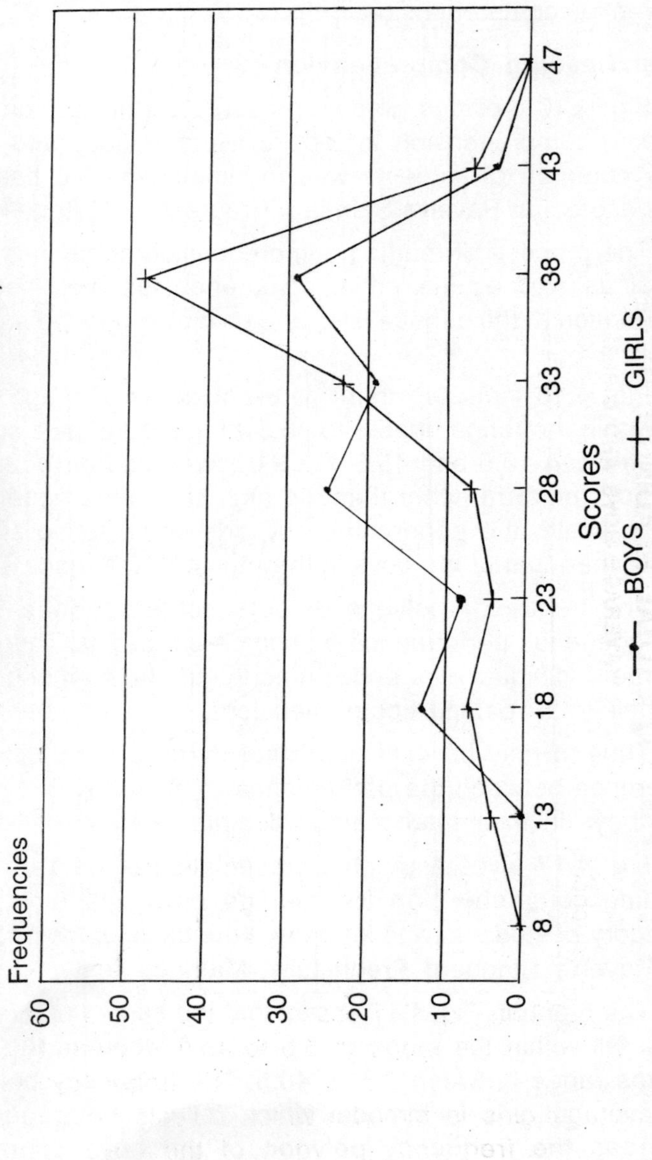

FIG. 4.17 : TOTAL READING COMPREHENSION
(AVERAGE BOYS AND GIRLS)

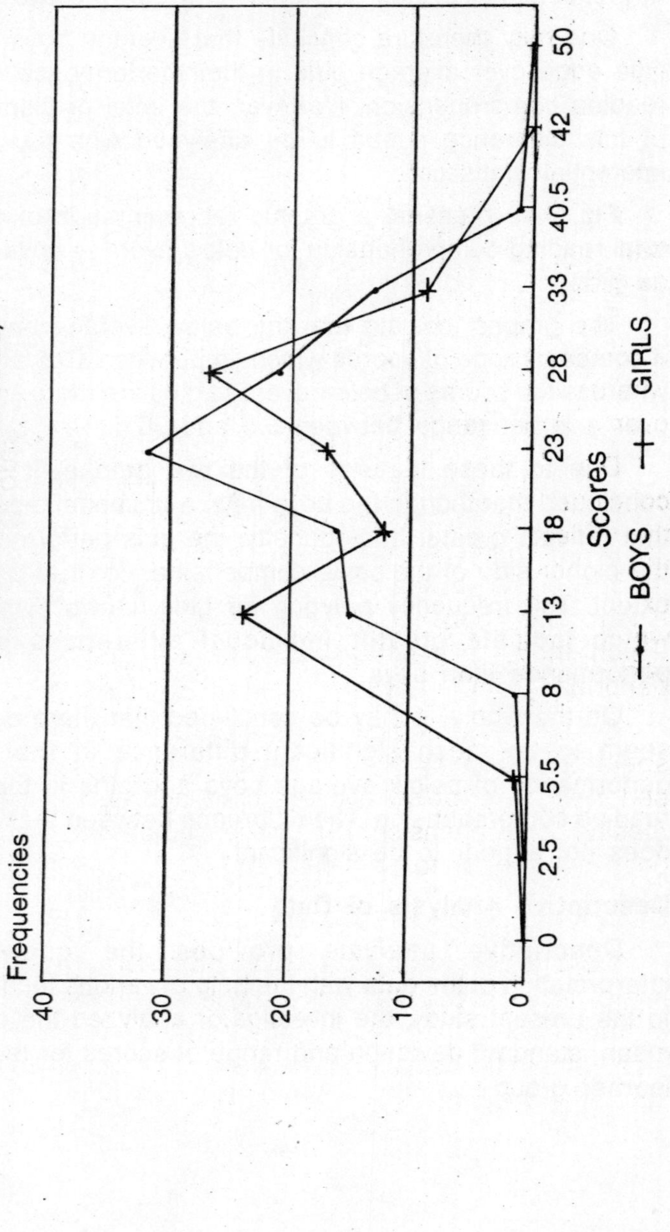

girls. The frequency polygons show wider differences between the performance of average girls and boys in total reading comprehension. But the mean scores do not show any substantial overall difference between the two groups.

One may therefore conclude that average boys show a little edge over average girls in their performance on total reading comprehension. However, the level of significance of this difference needs to be analysed with the help of inferential statistics.

Fig. 4.18 presents a graphic representation of data on total reading comprehension for below average boys as well as girls.

The graphs indicate that the below average boys have a compact range of scores which lie between 10.5 and 25.5, whereas the scores of below average girls are more scattered over a larger range between 5.5 and 30.5.

Due to these features of the two graphs, it may be concluded that though the boys have a unimodal distribution that reflects greater homogeneity, the girls performance on the higher side of the scale compensates for it to a greater extent. The frequency polygon for girls shows two modes which indicate greater individual differences in their performance than boys.

On the whole, it may be concluded that there does not seem to be much significant difference in the overall performance of below average boys and girls in their total reading comprehension. The difference between their means does not appear to be significant.

Descriptive Analysis of Data

Descriptive analysis provides the quantitative interpretation of the data with the help of various techniques. In the present study, the investigator analyzed the data for mean, standard deviation and range of scores for the entire learner group.

FIG. 4.18 : TOTAL READING COMPREHENSION
(BELOW AVERAGE BOYS AND GIRLS)

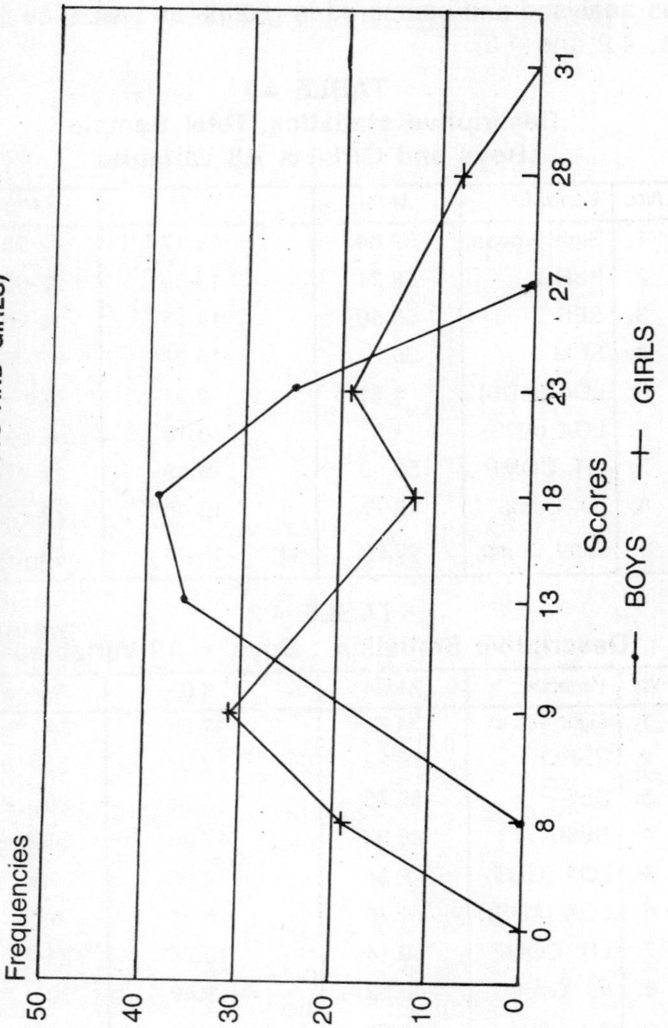

Descriptive Statistics

The entire data was analysed for mean, standard deviation, range of scores and correlation values. The data was analysed and compared in groups as well. (see Tables 4.1, 4.2 and 4.3).

TABLE 4.1
Descriptive statistics: Total Sample (Boys and Girls) X All Variables

S.No.	*Variable*	*Mean*	*S.D.*	*Range*
1.	Sight Vocab.	55.84	19.17	12-98
2.	PSRQ	58.31	13.39	22-90
3.	SES	55.86	14.45	18-90
4.	SPM	30.77	16.07	6.7-52
5.	LOA (GDS)	1.81	2.97	-5.5-+3.2
6.	LOA (ADS)	1.5	6.10	-6.9-+2.0
7.	LIT. COMP.	50.09	9.86	25-77
8.	Inf. Comp.	48.77	10.98	21-77
9.	Total Comp.	49.98	10.06	22-77

TABLE 4.2
Descriptive Statistics : Boys X All Variables

S.No.	*Variable*	*Mean*	*S.D.*	*Range*
1.	Sight Vocab.	54.72	17.53	14 - 98
2.	PSRQ	58.22	12.98	30 - 88
3.	SES	55.23	13.15	26 - 88
4.	SPM	28.37	17.29	6.7 - 50
5.	LOA (GDS)	2.34	2.05	-1.9 - +7.9
6.	LOA (ADS)	1.76	6.51	-6.0 - +2.0
7.	LIT. COMP.	50.14	10.76	21-77
8.	Inf. Comp.	46.52	9.48	30 - 75
9.	Total Reading Comp.	50.56	11.21	22 - 77

TABLE 4.3
Descriptive Statistics : Girls X All Variables

S. No.	Variable	Mean	S.D.	Range
1.	Sight Vocab.	57.05	20.70	12 - 98
2.	PSRQ	58.40	13.89	22 - 90
3.	SES	56.50	15.67	18 - 90
4.	SPM	33.19	14.43	1.8 - 52
5.	LOA (GDS)	1.28	3.60	-5.5 - +3.2
6.	LOA (ADS)	1.42	5.60	-6.9 - +2.0
7.	LIT. COMP.	51.02	10.75	21 - 77
8.	Inf. Comp.	50.04	10.26	25 - 75
9.	Total Reading Comp.	50.56	11.21	22 - 77

The different values of Table 4.1 indicate that the sample of 250 students of the whole comprised average students. It is evident from the mean values on different tests such as sight vocabulary, parental support to reading, socio-economic status, literal comprehension, inferential comprehension and total reading comprehension which approximates to the mean average intelligence giving mean value of 30.77 but a low level of aspiration. It is indicated by the low mean value of level of aspiration (Goal discrepancy score) of 1.81 and again low mean value of level of aspiration (Attainment discrepancy score) of 1.5.

A comparative analysis of the different values of Tables 4.2 and 4.3 reveals that the mean value, the standard deviation and the range of scores of girls are slightly higher than that of boys in case of certain variables such as sight vocabulary, parental support to reading, socio-economic status and mental ability scores. However as far as level of aspiration is concerned, boys seem to have a slightly higher mean value, standard deviation and range of scores than girls at goal discrepancy as well as attainment discrepancy level. Girls appear to have an edge over boys on inferential comprehension as reflected by the mean values of boys and girls 46.52 and 50.04 respectively. Both the groups, otherwise seem to have nearly same level of literal comprehension.

Comparing the different values of mean, standard deviation and also the range of obtained scores of boys with girls, there seems to be not much difference in the groups on all these variables.

Once these values were obtained, the investigator thought it imperative to study correlation between the scores of reading comprehension of the students at all the levels with the scores of students obtained on the tests based on various variables. The three levels of comprehension are:

1. Literal comprehension (LC)
2. Inferential comprehension. (IC)
3. Total reading comprehension (TRC).

Correlation at Various Levels

The Product-Moment correlation was determined at various levels. It was assumed that a correlation does exist between the reading comprehension skills of the learner and other indicators, both psychological as well as social.

TABLE 4.4
Coefficient of Correlations: Levels of Reading Comprehension X Correlates.

S.No.	Variables	S.V.	PSRQ	SES	SPM	LOA (GDS)	LOA (ADS)
1.	LC	0.65**	0.42**	0.50**	0.36**	0.07	0.16*
2.	IC	0.75**	0.47**	0.70**	0.47**	0.19**	0.33**
3.	TRC	0.86**	0.57**	0.72**	0.57**	0.17*	0.34**

*for significance at 0.05 level.

**for significance at 0.05 level and 0.01 level.

As can be seen from Table 4.4 which gives the correlation between reading comprehension and other variables, there is a high degree of correlation between reading comprehension at all levels with the sight-vocabulary and socio-economic status of the students. A positive correlation exists between total reading comprehension, parental support to reading and the mental abilities of the students.

The table also indicates that the correlation between the literal comprehension and the other variables seem to be positive but not as high as compared to the correlation between total reading comprehension and other variables.

In order to extend the analysis little further, the entire learner group was classified into three major groups on the basis of their scores on the mental ability tests (see Table 4.5).

TABLE 4.5
Classification of Sample in Groups

Group	Score Range	N.	
1. Above average boys	43 - 52	27	51
2. Above average girls	43 - 52	24	
3. Average boys	20 - 42	73	155
4. Average girls	20 - 42	82	
5. Below average boys	5 - 19	28	44
6. Below average girls	5 - 19	16	

Besides this, the variables were also grouped under three main heads.

1. Psychological Variables

(a) Visual Perception (through sight vocabulary);

(b) Level of Aspiration; and

(c) Sex of the Child.

2. Social Variables

(a) Socio-economic status of family; and

(b) Parental support to reading.

3. Cognitive Variable

(a) General Mental Ability.

4. Linguistic Competency

(a) Literal Comprehension;

(b) Inferential Comprehension; and

(c) Total Reading Comprehension.

TABLE 4.6
Correlation Analysis : Above Average Boys and Girls; Levels of Comprehension X Other Variables

Group	*Variable*	*S.V.*	*PSRQ*	*SES*	*SPM*	*LOA (GDS)*	*LOA (ADS)*
Above average Boys	LC	0.79**	0.44*	0.48*	0.45*	0.21	0.27
	IC	0.71**	0.55**	0.41	0.28	0.03	0.005
	TRC	0.62**	0.71**	0.63**	0.56	0.05	0.03
Above average Girls	LC	0.46*	0.62**	0.56**	0.30	0.16	0.42*
	IC	0.63**	0.24	0.45*	0.22	0.16	0.13
	TRC	0.65**	0.43*	0.55**	0.47*	0.20	0.32

* for significance at .05 level.

** for significance at 0.1 level as well as .05 level.

Table 4.6 gives a comparative picture of correlation between the reading comprehension of above average boys and girls at various levels, literal, inferential and total reading comprehension with various variables. It can be seen from the table that the boys show a high correlation between reading with sight vocabulary at all the three levels of comprehension. Level of aspiration of the boys appear to have low correlation with reading at literal and inferential level as well as total reading comprehension. The same trend is seen in case of above average girls.

The social variables, both parental support to reading and socio-economic status show a high positive correlation with total reading comprehension and mild positive correlation with reading at literal comprehension as well as inferential comprehension level for above average boys. In the case of above average girls, a high positive correlation is seen between literal comprehension and parental support to reading as well as socio-economic status but a substantial positive correlation is observed between the inferential comprehension and parental support to reading and their socio-economic status of the family. The same trend is maintained in case of total reading comprehension and other variables.

Table 4.7 shows that the average boys reading scores at various levels of comprehension have comparatively low correlation with the scores of other correlates as compared to average girls. Average girls seem to have a high positive correlation of reading comprehension on all the 3 levels with sight vocabulary, parental support to reading and socio-economic status of the family. Average boys show comparatively mild/substantial correlation of reading comprehension at all the three levels with the above-stated variables. Both average boys and girls show no/negligible correlation of reading comprehension with level of aspiration scores (both goal discrepancy and attainment discrepancy scores).

TABLE 4.7

Correlation Analysis: Average Boys and Girls: Levels of Reading Comprehension X other variables

Group	*N*	*Variable*	*S.V.*	*PSRQ*	*SES*	*SPM*	*LOA (GDS)*	*LOA (ADS)*
Average		LC	0.46**	0.30*	0.14	0.34**	0.03	0.09
	73	IC	0.49**	0.42**	0.59**	0.08	0.24	0.35**
Boys		TRC	0.65**	0.55**	0.61**	0.29*	0.15	0.19
Average		LC	0.79**	0.56**	0.65**	0.46**	0.04	0.005
	82	IC	0.83**	0.61**	0.72**	0.42**	0.02	0.01
Girls		TRC	0.88**	0.64**	0.74**	0.48**	0.03	0.009

*for significance at 0.05 level.

**for significance at 0.01 level as well as 0.05 level.

Table 4.8 reflects that below average boys have comparatively low correlation between reading comprehension at all the levels and other correlates as compared to the correlation that exists in case of below average girls. Below average girls show high positive correlation between scores of reading comprehension at all the three levels and sight vocabulary scores. The below average boys show a substantial positive correlation of their reading comprehension with sight vocabulary and very low, non-significant correlation of reading comprehension and parental support to reading, socio-economic status and mental ability.

At the same time, below average girls seem to have substantial positive correlation of their reading comprehension scores with parental support to reading, socio-economic status and mental ability.

There is no marked difference between the correlation values of reading comprehension and level of aspiration (both at goal discrepancy and attainment discrepancy scores) between below average boys and girls as the values are negligible/non-significantly low sharing no correlation.

TABLE 4.8

Correlation Analysis: Below Average Boys and Girls : Levels of Comprehension X Other Variables.

Group	*N*	*Variable*	*S.V.*	*PSRQ*	*SES*	*SPM*	*LOA (GDS)*	*LOA (ADS)*
Below Average Boys	28	LC	0.52**	0.03	0.03	0.01	0.08	0.25
		IC	0.43*	0.05	0.05	0.04	0.06	0.01
		TRC	0.57**	0.01	0.06	0.11	0.17	0.11
Below Average Boys	16	LC	0.72**	0.39	0.70**	0.30	0.05	0.006
		IC	0.71**	0.50*	0.69**	0.37	0.08	0.16
		TRC	0.76**	0.45	0.66**	0.31	0.04	0.03

*for significance at 0.05 level.

**for significance at 0.01 level as well as 0.05 level.

Table 4.9 gives a comparative picture of correlation values of the scores of total boys and girls. Both the groups show high positive correlation between reading scores at all levels and sight vocabulary, girls show comparatively higher correlation of reading comprehension scores with scores on sight vocabulary and socio-economic status as compared to boys. There appears to be some difference between the correlation coefficient for boys and girls on reading comprehension scores and mental ability test scores and level of aspiration. The boys show negligible correlation between reading comprehension at all levels and level of aspiration whereas girls show low positive correlation value for the same.

More detailed analysis at inferential level will reflect the significance of these correlation values.

TABLE 4.9
Correlation Analysis: Total Boys and Girls : Levels of Comprehension X Other Variables

Group	*N*	*Variable*	*S.V.*	*PSRQ*	*SES*	*SPM*	*LOA (GDS)*	*LOA ADS)*
		LC	0.51**	0.32**	0.30**	0.19*	0.03	0.04
Boys	73	IC	0.66**	0.44**	0.65**	0.49**	0.13	0.40**
		TRC	0.74**	0.54**	0.69**	0.50**	0.11	0.36**
		LC	0.78**	0.53**	0.69**	0.53**	0.20*	0.33**
Girls	125	IC	0.83**	0.49**	0.75**	0.47**	0.23**	0.26**
		TRC	0.87**	0.53**	0.76**	0.54**	0.24**	0.33**

* for significance at .05 level

** for significance at .01 level as well as .05 level

Analysis of Responses of Parental Support to Reading Questionnaire—Diagrammatic Presentation

After the coefficient of correlation was computed, the investigator thought it worthwhile to illustrate the responses of parental support to Reading Questionnaire with the help of a Pie-diagram. The investigator obtained the parental opinion in the form of responses to the questionnaire under five major heads, such as:

(i) Amount of time given to the child;

(ii) Availability of reading material for the child;

(iii) Guidance to the child;

(iv) Motivation to the child; and

(v) Incuicating good reading habits.

(i) Amount of time given to the child

This comprised question numbers 7, 20 and 21 regarding the amount of time parents usually give to the children for improving their reading. The data reveal that 54.7 per cent of the parents spend one to two hours daily with their children helping them out in studies. Besides that, they also ensure

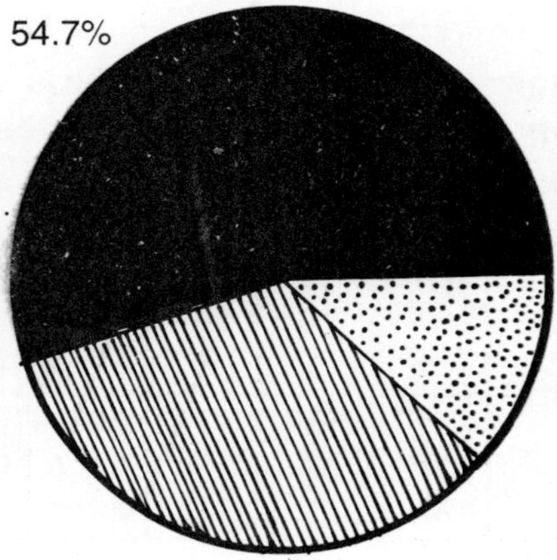

Fig. 4.19. Percentage of Parents - Giving Time to Children.

that the child should devote only a limited time for leisure reading and utilize some time for extra reading other than homework. There were 33.3 per cent parents who tried to devote about one hour to their wards' studies and encouraged them for extra reading. Only 12 per cent of the parents felt that they had no time for their children. They neither spent time with them nor they encouraged them for reading.

Availability of reading material

This comprises question numbers 1, 2 and 3 regarding the availability of newspapers and magazines, their number, frequency and regularity and also the type of magazines. Whereas 39 per cent of the parents claimed that they regularly bought newspapers and magazines particularly children's magazines to enhance reading habits in their children; 29 per cent of the parents admitted that they bought newspapers and magazines but not with so much regularity

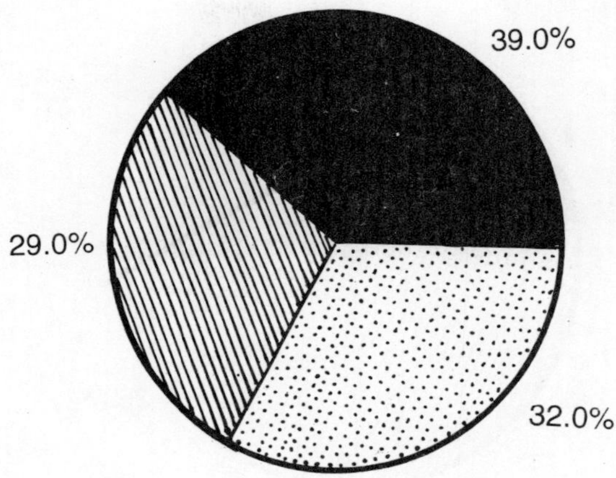

Fig. 4.20. Percentage of Parents making Reading Material Available to Children.

and consciousness of buying children's magazines and 32 per cent of the parents still don't pay any attention towards the availability of any reading material in the form of newspapers or magazines.

Guidance to the Children

Question numbers 4, 5, 6, 9, 10 and 24 belong to this category. These questions are related to the availability of parents at the time of study, their needful help, guidance for the selection of right type of reading material, etc. Fig. 4.21 shows the percentage of parents providing guidance to their children. 40.7 per cent of the parents claimed that whenever the children required their help, they helped them in development of their personality. Not only that, they guided the children for leisure time reading and suggested good books to them and took them to good libraries. 32.7 per cent parents ensured help to the children through tutions, and tried to discuss good books and reading materials depending upon the availability of time. Though they did'nt take the

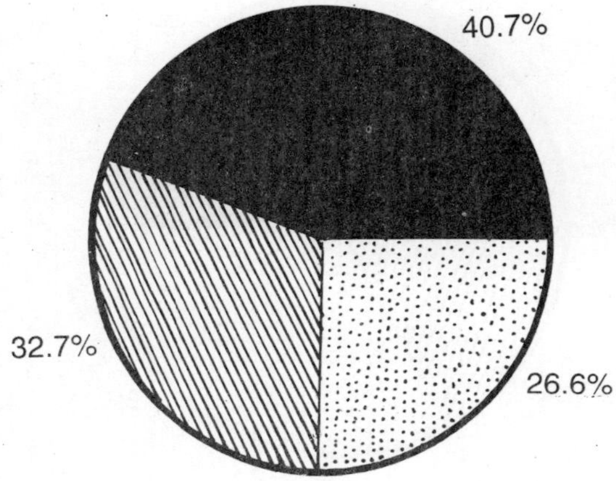

Fig. 4.21. Percentage of parents providing guidance in reading.

children to libraries frequently, they helped them out in selection of good books once in a while. 26.6 per cent of the parents still neglected their children and were unable to provide any guidance. Probably the reasons being low SES of the family or no educational background of parents.

Motivation to the children

This comprises question nos. 11, 12, 13, 14 and 15 regarding parents own reading interest, motivation to the children by asking them to read from magazines and the visits to exhibitions and book fairs. The data analysis revealed that only 21.6 per cent of the parents really motivated their children for reading by making extra efforts such as: visiting book exhibitions and fairs and by encouraging their children to read the books and magazines regularly.

Thirty-six of the parents occasionally took their children to book exhibitions, fairs and libraries but 42.4 per cent of the parents did not make any efforts in this direction.

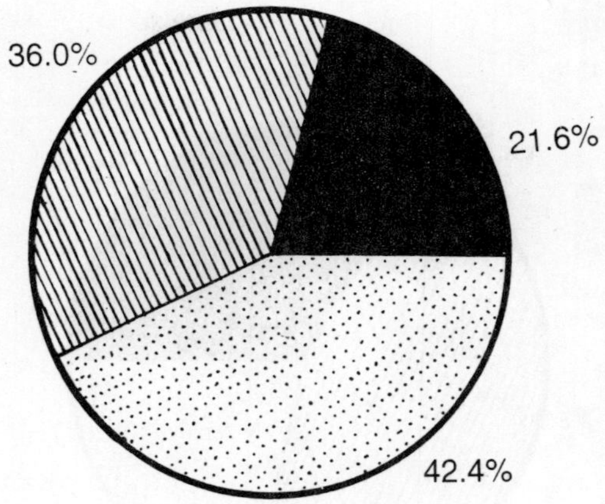

Fig. 4.22. Percentage of parents providing motivation for reading.

Inculcating Good Reading Habits

This major area comprises many questions (Q.Nos. 8, 16-19, 22, 23, 25) regarding parents awareness about good reading habits, reading posture, consulting dictionary while reading, etc. Fig 4.23 shows that 33.5 per cent of the parents put in efforts to inculcate good reading habits in their children by directing them to sit in correct posture, checking them off and on for their reading habits. 45 per cent of the parents were partially aware and occasionally tried to develop good reading habits amongst their children. 21.5 per cent of the parents do not pay any attention towards their children's reading.

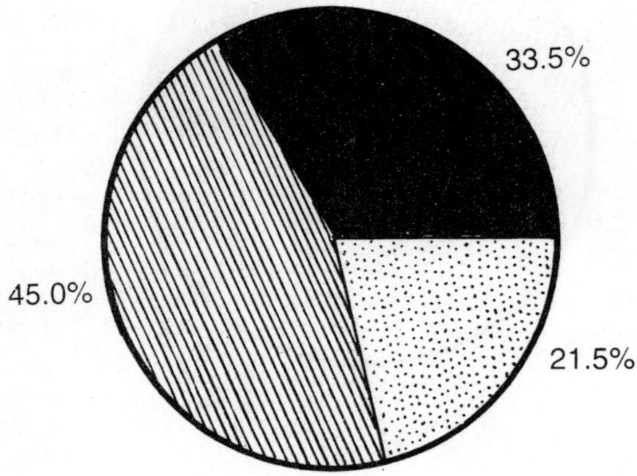

Fig. 4.23. Percentage of parents inculcating good reading habits.

With the help of descriptive analysis, the investigator has been able to get some results apparently. These results would be further studied with the help of inferential statistics.

Inferential Statistical Analysis

The primary objective of statistical inference is to enable the researcher to generalize from a sample. This involves inductive reasoning and probability theory.

In the present study, the researcher used:

(A) Significance of difference between means through:

(i) t ratio

(ii) f ratio.

The groups were made on the basis of two main criteria:

(A) Sex of the child

(B) Mental ability of the child

The inferential analysis of the data has been done for eight psycho-social variables only. As the sample was classified into sub-groups on the basis of their scores on RSPM, the cognitive factor though mentioned in each table has not been referred to for analysis.

The analysis has been done and the results are presented in tabular form as follows:

Group I : Above Average Boys and Girls

Table 4.10 presents data related to eight variables of the study and their analysis leading to statistical inferences.

As seen from Table 4.10 the mean difference is highest in respect of sight vocabulary test (dm= 4.41) and lowest in respect of LOA-ADS (dm=0.02). The t-ratios range between 0.42 (for inferential comprehension) and 2.48 (for inferential comprehension) and 2.48 (for literal comprehension).

Above average boys and girls do not show any significant difference in their scores obtained on tests related to psychological correlates viz. sight vocabulary and level of aspiration. The same trend is seen for the cognitive and social variables also. As far as the performance on different levels of reading comprehension is concerned, no significant difference appears between the performance of above average boys and girls.

Group II : Average Boys and Girls

Table 4.11 presents data related to 8 variables of the study and their analysis leading to statistical inferences. As seen from Table 4.11, the mean difference is highest in respect of LOA (GDS), i.e., dm=1.61 and lowest in respect of total reading comprehension, i.e., dm= 0.13. The t-ratios range between 0.11 (Total Reading Comprehension) and 4.74 (LOA-GDS).

On the basis of the data analysis, it can be concluded that average boys and girls differ significantly in terms of their level of aspiration (both GDS and ADS). So far as the performance of these groups on various level, of comprehension is concerned, the groups do not differ significantly. Besides, they exhibit more or less comparable performance on other correlates also.

TABLE 4.10

Inferential Analysis of Above Average Boys and Girls

Variable	Score / Variable	M_1	M_2	SD_1	SD_2	dn	SED	F-ratio	t-ratio	P-value
Psycho-logical	SV Test	74.37	69.96	16.65	16.56	4.41	4.66	0.90	0.95	>0.01
	LOA	2.29	2.61	1.26	1.43	0.32	0.38	0.71	0.84	>0.01
	GSD LOA ADS	1.54	1.52	1.07	1.01	0.02	0.29	0.48	0.69	>0.01
Cognitive	SPM	46.25	47.22	1.96	2.83	0.97	0.69	1.99	1.41	>0.01
Social	PSRQ	63.17	61.41	11.28	14.16	1.76	3.62	0.24	0.49	>0.01
	SES	71.92	75.04	8.60	9.18	3.12	2.50	1.56	1.25	>0.01
Level of Reading Comprehension	Lit. Comp.	15.67	18.67	3.86	4.66	3.00	1.21	6.15	2.48	>0.01
	Inf. Comp.	15.04	14.52	3.85	4.81	0.52	1.23	0.18	0.42	>0.01
	Total Comp.	30.71	33.19	7.09	7.69	2.48	2.08	1.48	1.19	>0.01

M_1 and SD_1 relate to boys.
M_2 and SD_2 relate to girls.

No. of Boys = 24 | 51
No. of Girls = 27 |

TABLE 4.11

Inferential Analysis of Average Boys and Girls

Variable	Score / Variable	M_1	M_2	SD_1	SD_2	dm	SED	F-ratio	t-ratio	P-value
Psychological	SV Test	54.84	54.38	16.03	19.32	0.46	2.87	0.025	0.16	>0.01
	LOA GDS	2.45	0.84	1.72	2.36	1.61	0.34	22.47	4.74	<0.01
	LOA ADS	1.50	0.12	1.53	2.55	1.38	0.34	16.48	4.06	<0.01
Cognitive	SPM	33.86	34.85	5.64	6.46	0.99	0.98	1.02	-1.01	>0.01
Social	PSRQ	58.49	57.61	13.65	13.50	0.88	2.18	0.16	0.40	>0.01
	SES	52.48	51.48	11.20	13.62	1.00	2.02	0.25	0.50	>0.01
Level of Reading Comprehension	LIT. Comp.	13.73	14.26	5.15	4.78	0.53	0.79	0.45	0.67	>0.01
	INF. Comp.	9.52	8.94	4.18	4.18	0.58	0.67	0.76	0.87	>0.01
	Total Comp.	23.11	23.24	6.86	8.24	0.13	1.23	0.01	0.11	>0.01

M_1 and SD_1 relate to boys.
M_2 and SD_2 relate to girls.

No. of Boys = 73
No. of Girls = 82 | 155

It is necessary to point out here that the average boys are more aspirant (both at GDS and ADS level) as compared to girls (refer Table 4.6). But this difference does not contribute to their 'r' values with reading comprehensions at various levels. Average boys and girls show non-significant difference in their performance on cognitive as well as social correlates.

Group III: Below Average Boys and Girls

Table 4.12 presents data related to 8 variables of the study and their analysis leading to statistical analysis.

As seen from Table 4.12 the mean difference is highest in respect of parental support to reading, i.e., dm=4.09 and lowest in respect of total comprehension, i.e., dm=0.04. The t-ratio ranges between 0.02 for total comprehension and 2.96 (for LOA-ADS).

Below average boys and girls do not show any significant difference in their performance on sight vocabulary test, (one of the psychological correlates) but boys have significantly higher mean than girls in their level of aspiration (attainment discrepancy score). Though this difference seems to be significant but it does not affect their 'r' value for reading comprehension. As far as other cognitive and social variables are concerned, below average boys and girls do not exhibit significant difference in their means on different test scores.

Therefore, it is established that below average boys and girls do not differ from each other in terms of their reading comprehension skills as highlighted in respect of average boys and girls. The level of aspiration does not seem to have any substantial relationship with reading comprehension.

Group IV: Above Average Boys and Average Boys

Table 4.13 presents data related to all 8 variables of the study and their analysis leading to statistical inferences.

TABLE 4.12

Inferential Analysis of Below Average Boys and Girls.

Variables	Score / Variable	M_1	M_2	SD_1	SD_2	*dm*	*SED*	*F-ratio*	*t-ratio*	*P-value*
Psycho-logical	SV Test	41.36	41.63	10.04	14.50	0.27	3.71	0.005	0.07	>0.01
	LOA GDS	1.17	0.93	2.89	1.84	0.24	0.80	6.86	2.62	>0.01
	LOA ADS	2.09	0.46	3.15	1.84	1.53	0.86	0.76	2.96	<0.01
Cognitive	SPM	13.07	14.50	4.05	4.30	1.43	1.30	1.21	1.10	>0.01
Social	PSRQ	53.28	57.37	11.05	15.19	4.09	3.97	1.06	1.03	>0.01
	SES	48.10	50.93	8.74	9.53	2.83	2.83	1.00	1.00	>0.01
Level of Reading Comprehension	Lit. Comp.	11.64	10.56	2.36	4.53	1.08	1.04	1.09	1.04	>0.01
	Inf. Comp.	6.46	6.75	2.64	3.57	0.29	0.94	0.10	0.30	>0.01
	Total Comp	17.46	17.50	3.90	7.57	0.04	1.72	0.0004	0.02	>0.01

M_1 and SD_1 relate to boys.
M_2 and SD_2 relate to girls.

No. of Bab = 28
No. of Bag = 16 | 44

As seen from Table 4.13 the mean difference is highest in respect of socio-economic status, i.e., dm=19.44. The t-ratio ranges between 7.70 (for SES) and 0.13 (for LOA-ADS).

Above average boys and average boys do not show any significant difference as far as psychological correlates are concerned. This reflects that there isn't much difference between the sight vocabulary and level of aspiration of the two groups and also its effect on language acquisition. The factors related to cognitive aspect certainly show a significant difference. The two correlates, parental support to reading and socio-economic status show a variation also. There isn't much difference between the parental support to reading available to the above average and average boys. In spite of significant difference reflected in their socio-economic status, the two groups do not show any significant difference in their performance at various levels of comprehension.

Group V: Above Average Boys and Below Average Boys

Table 4.14 presents data related to 8 variables of the study and their analysis leading to statistical inferences.

As seen from Table 4.14, besides the high difference shown on cognitive abilities, the mean difference is highest in respect of sight vocabulary, i.e., dm=28.60 and lowest in respect of level of aspiration goal discrepancy score, i.e., dm= 3.46. The t-ratio ranges between 9.88 (for socio-economic status) and 31.9 (for parental support to reading).

The probability of obtaining this data for various variables is more than 0.01. The two groups differ significantly in terms of sight vocabulary. Besides, the means of level of aspiration for the two groups also reveal significant difference. The same trend is seen for other variables also.

It may be concluded that the two groups differ from each other and can not be taken to belong to the same parent population.

The results of Table 4.14 when compared with that of Table 4.13, have meaningful messages. If a child has below

TABLE 4.13

Inferential Analysis of Above Average and Average Boys

Variables	Score / Variable	M_1	M_2	SD_1	SD_2	*dm*	*SED*	*F-ratio*	*t-ratio*	*P-value*
Psycho-logical	SV Test	69.96	60.83	16.56	16.03	9.13	3.80	5.76	2.40	>0.01
	LOA GDS	2.29	2.45	1.26	1.72	0.16	0.38	0.18	0.42	>0.01
	LOA ADS	1.54	1.50	1.07	1.53	0.04	0.34	0.01	0.13	>0.01
Cognitrive	SPM	46.25	33.86	1.96	5.64	12.39	1.18	110.66	10.52	>0.01
Social	PSRQ	63.17	58.50	11.28	13.65	4.67	3.09	2.29	1.51	>0.01
	SES	71.92	52.48	8.59	11.20	19.44	2.50	60.43	7.77	<0.01
Level of Reading Comprehension	Lit. Comp.	15.67	13.73	3.86	5.15	1.94	1.74	3.09	1.76	>0.01
	Inf. Comp.	13.73	11.78	3.57	4.29	1.95	0.97	4.02	2.01	>0.01
	Total Comp	30.71	27.11	7.09	6.86	3.60	1.43	6.35	2.52	>0.01

M_1 and SD_1 relate to above average boys.
M_2 and SD_2 relate to average boys.

No. of AAB = 24
No. of AB = 73
97

TABLE 4.14

Inferential Analysis of Above Average Boys and Below Average Boys.

Variables	Score / Variable	M_1	M_2	SD_1	SD_2	*dm*	*SED*	*F-ratio*	*t-ratio*	*P-value*
Psycho-logical	SV Test	69.96	41.36	16.56	10.04	28.60	3.74	58.22	7.65	<0.01
	LOA GDS	2.29	1.17	1.26	2.88	3.46	0.64	29.26	5.41	>0.01
	LOA ADS	1.54	2.09	1.07	3.15	3.63	0.67	29.38	5.42	<0.01
Cognitive	SPM	46.25	13.07	1.96	4.05	22.18	0.91	1329.33	36.46	<0.01
Social	PSRQ	63.17	53.29	11.28	11.05	9.88	3.10	10.18	3.19	<0.01
	SES	71.92	48.11	8.60	8.74	23.81	2.41	97.61	9.88	<0.01
Level of Reading Comprehension	Lit. Comp.	15.67	11.64	3.86	2.36	4.02	0.87	21.34	4.62	<0.01
	Inf. Comp.	15.04	6.46	3.85	2.64	8.58	0.91	88.92	9.43	<0.01
	Total Comp.	30.71	17.46	7.09	3.90	13.25	1.56	72.25	8.50	<0.01

M_1 and SD_1 relate to above average boys.
M_2 and SD_2 relate to below average boys.

No. of AAB = 24
No. of BAB = 28 | 52

average mental ability, the influence of correlates in terms of their effect on performance on the dependent variables works as a disadvantage.

However, for the average and above average mental ability students, the correlate seizes to be a disadvantage. Thus, a certain minimum level of mental ability appears to be a prerequisite for satisfactory performance in terms of reading comprehension skills.

Group VI : Average Boys and Below Average Boys

Table 4.15 presents data related to 8 variables of the study and their analysis leading to statistical inference.

As seen from Table 4.15, the mean difference is highest in respect of sight vocabulary, i.e., dm=13.481 and lowest in respect of Inferential comprehension, i.e., dm=3.06.

The t-ratios are between 1.81 (for parental support to reading) and 7.70 (for level of aspiration-goal discrepancy score).

The probability of obtaining this data for various correlates is more than 0.01 for all except parental support to reading and socio-economic status. As can be seen from Table 4.14 the below average boys receive low parental support for reading and they come from a relatively poorer socio-economic background. However, the difference between these two groups is substantial but not significant. The two groups differ significantly on psychological correlates having high differences in their means on sight vocabulary as well as level of aspiration. The same trend holds true in case of cognitive correlates and achievement on level of comprehension.

The result of data analysis of Table 4.15 indicates that mental abilities between certain critical level and poor performance on faculties related to various psycho-social correlates act as a compounded disadvantage for developing reading skills. This is cross validated by the data from Table 4.18 because of the same mental ability level of girls there.

TABLE 4.15

Inferential Analysis of Average Boys and Below Average Boys

Variables	*Score* / *Variable*	M_1	M_2	SD_1	SD_2	*dm*	*SED*	*F-ratio*	*t-ratio*	*P-value*
Psycho-logical	SV Test	54.84	41.36	16.03	10.03	13.48	3.25	17.22	4.15	<0.01
	LOA GDS	2.45	-1.17	1.72	2.89	3.62	0.47	59.29	7.70	<0.01
	LOA ADS	-1.49	2.09	1.53	3.15	3.58	0.47	58.10	7.62	<0.01
Cognitive	SPM	33.86	13.07	5.64	4.05	20.79	1.17	315.77	17.77	<0.01
Social	PSRQ	58.49	53.28	13.65	11.05	5.21	2.88	3.28	1.81	>0.01
	SES	52.46	48.11	11.20	8.74	4.37	2.35	3.46	1.86	>0.01
Level of Reading Comprehension	Lit. Comp.	13.73	10.64	5.15	2.36	3.09	1.01	9.36	3.06	<0.01
	Inf. Comp.	9.52	6.46	4.18	2.64	3.06	0.85	12.96	3.60	<0.01
	Total Comp.	23.11	17.46	6.86	3.90	5.65	1.38	16.81	4.10	<0.01

M_1 and SD_1 relate to average boys.
M_2 and SD_2 relate to below average boys.

No. of AB = 73
No. of BAB = 28
(Total) 101

Group VII : Above Average Girls and Average Girls

Table 4.16 presents data related to 8 variables of the study and their analysis leading to statistical analysis.

As seen from Table 4.16, the mean difference is highest in respect of socio-economic status (dm=23.56) and lowest in respect of level of aspiration ADS (dm=1.39). The t-ratios range between 1.25 (for parental support to reading) and 8.38 (for socio-economic status). The probability of obtaining this data is more than 0.01 for all the correlates except for parental support to reading.

Comparing above average girls with average girls for their psychological correlates, the groups differ significantly in their sight vocabulary as well as level of aspiration. Besides their differences in mental abilities, they also differ in level of comprehension on all levels and socio-economic status of the family.

The only factor that does not affect significantly, is the amount of parental support to reading, the two groups receive. The possible reason for this may be the increasing general awareness of the parents for education.

When we juxtapose the result of Table 4.16 with that of 4.13, we find some interesting differences. Unlike the two groups in Table 4.16, the above average boys and average boys do not appear to be different significantly on almost all the variables. One possible reason for this could be the skewed distribution of scores for average groups. It can be inferred that characteristics of average girls do not match with that of average boys in terms of the various variables.

Group VIII : Above Average Girls and Below Average Girls

Table 4.17 presents data related to 8 variables of the study and their analysis leading to statistical inferences.

As seen from Table 4.17 the mean difference is highest in respect of sight vocabulary (dm=32.75) and lowest in respect of level of aspiration - attainment discrepancy score (dm=1.05). The t-ratios range between 0.38 (for parental

TABLE 4.16

Inferential Analysis of Above Average and Average Girls

Variables	Score / Variable	M_1	M_2	SD_1	SD_2	dm	SED	F-ratio	t-ratio	P-value
Psycho-logical	SV Test	74.37	54.37	16.65	19.32	20.00	4.15	23.22	4.82	<0.01
	LOA GDS	2.61	0.84	1.43	2.36	1.77	0.48	13.61	3.69	<0.01
	LOA ADS	1.52	0.13	1.01	2.55	1.39	0.50	7.72	2.78	<0.01
Cognitive	SPM	47.22	34.85	2.83	6.46	12.37	1.28	93.31	9.66	<0.01
Social	PSRQ	61.41	57.61	14.61	13.50	3.80	3.03	1.57	1.25	>0.01
	SES	75.03	51.47	9.18	13.62	23.56	2.81	70.22	8.38	<0.01
Level of Reading Comprehension	Lit. Comp.	18.67	14.26	4.66	4.77	4.41	1.05	17.64	4.20	<0.01
	Inf. Comp.	14.52	8.94	4.81	4.18	5.58	0.96	33.77	5.81	<0.01
	Total Comp	33.18	23.14	7.69	8.24	9.94	1.80	30.47	5.52	<0.01

M_1 and SD_1 relate to above average girls.
M_2 and SD_2 relate to average girls.

No. of AAG = 27 | 109
No. of AG = 82 |

TABLE 4.17

Inferential Analysis of Above Average Girls and Below Average Girls

Variables	Score / Variable	M_1	M_2	SD_1	SD_2	*dm*	*SED*	*F-ratio*	*t-ratio*	*P-value*
Psycho-logical	SV Test	74.37	41.62	16.65	14.50	32.75	5.01	42.64	6.53	<0.01
	LOA GDS	2.61	0.93	1.42	1.84	1.68	0.50	11.29	3.36	<0.01
	LOA ADS	-1.51	-0.46	1.02	1.84	1.05	0.43	5.95	2.44	>0.01
Cognitive	SPM	47.22	14.50	2.83	4.30	32.72	1.09	900.60	30.01	<0.01
Social	PSRQ	61.41	57.37	14.16	15.19	4.04	4.58	0.77	0.88	>0.01
	SES	75.04	50.93	9.18	9.53	24.11	2.93	67.73	8.23	<0.01
Level of Reading Comprehension	Lit. Comp.	18.67	10.56	4.67	4.53	8.10	1.46	30.80	5.55	<0.01
	Inf. Comp.	14.51	6.75	4.81	3.57	7.76	1.39	31.13	5.58	<0.01
	Total Comp.	33.18	17.50	7.69	7.57	15.68	2.41	42.25	6.50	<0.01

M_1 and SD_1 relate to above average girls.
M_2 and SD_2 relate to below average girls.

No. of AAG = 27
No. of BAG = 16 | 43

support to reading) and 8.23 (for socio-economic status). The probability of obtaining this data is more than 0.01 for all variables except for parental support to reading and level of aspiration (attainment discrepancy score).

The two groups differ significantly on the psychological correlates (both sight vocabulary and level of aspiration), cognitive correlates and on levels of comprehension. The groups also reveal significant difference in their socio-economic status but no significant difference appears between the parental support, the two groups get for reading.

When we compare the results of Table 4.17 with that of Table 4.14, many interesting facts emerge out. Above average boys get more parental support to reading than below average boys and there the difference is substantial and significant. In case of above average and below average girls, the difference in parental support to reading remains non-significant.

It can be thus concluded that in case of girls, the parental support for developing reading skills seizes to cause its influence on their performance at all levels of reading comprehension, whereas in case of boys it remains a significant correlate.

Group IX : Average Girls and Below Average Girls

Table 4.18 presents data related to 8 variables of the study and their analysis leading to statistical inferences.

As seen from the Table 4.18, the mean difference is highest in respect of sight vocabulary (dm= 12.75) and lowest in respect of level of aspiration-goal discrepancy score (dm=0.09). The t-ratios range between 0.06 (for parental support to reading) and 2.85 (for literal comprehension). The probability of getting this data is more than 0.1 for one of the dependent variables and is less than 0.01 for other correlates.

No significant difference appears between the two groups on the psychological correlates viz. sight vocabulary and level of aspiration. The same trend is indicated for the social

TABLE 4.18

Inferential Analysis of Average Girls and Below Average Girls

Variables	Score / Variable	M_1	M_2	SD_1	SD_2	dm	SED	F-ratio	t-ratio	P-value
Psycho-logical	SV Test	54.38	41.63	19.32	14.50	12.75	5.09	6.25	2.50	>0.01
	LOA GDS	0.84	0.93	2.36	1.84	-0.09	0.63	0.02	0.14	>0.01
	LOA ADS	-0.13	0.46	2.55	1.84	-0.33	0.67	0.24	0.49	>0.01
Cognitive	SPM	34.85	14.50	6.46	4.30	20.35	1.69	144.96	12.04	<0.01
Social	PSRQ	57.61	57.38	13.50	15.19	0.23	3.76	0.004	0.06	<0.01
	SES	51.48	50.94	13.62	9.53	0.54	3.57	0.02	0.15	>0.01
Level of Reading Comprehension	Lit. Comp.	14.26	10.56	4.78	4.53	3.70	1.30	8.12	2.85	<0.01
	Inf. Comp.	8.94	6.75	4.18	3.57	2.19	1.11	3.88	1.97	>0.01
	Total Comp.	23.24	17.50	8.24	7.57	5.74	2.22	6.66	2.58	>0.01

M_1 and SD_1 relate to average girls.
M_2 and SD_2 relate to below average girls.

No. of AG = 82 | 98
No. of Bag = 16 |

correlates viz. parental support to reading and socio-economic status.

This indicates that despite their differences in mental abilities, the groups do no differ significantly on most of the correlates. The difference in the scores of the two groups on literal comprehension appears to be significant. This might be because of the high difference in the sight vocabulary of the two groups.

When we compare Table 4.18 with Table 4.15, we find that mental ability below a certain level influences the development of reading skills. The below average girls, despite having not much difference in their means on parental support to reading and socio-economic level show a substantial difference in the performance on literal comprehension.

On the basis of this analysis, the investigator has reached at certain conclusions, which are discussed in the next chapter.

Qualitative Analysis of Data

In addition to the analysis of data on quantitative terms, the investigator was guided to study the parents' attitude through interview. Hence, the interviews of the parents of the sample group were conducted in an informal manner. The interviews were held generally in the respective schools of their children on parent-teacher meeting day.

The interviews were recorded, analysed and interpreted later on. The findings have been summarized as:

(a) with the ever increasing awareness of education, the attitude of parents regarding the studies of their children is highly positive. 52.5 per cent of the parents show their concern towards reading and language development. 27.5 per cent of the parents do realize the importance but they do not find time to guide their children but they try to arrange coaching. 20 per cent of the parents are still there who feel that they have performed their duty once they have sent their children to school. These parents neither make any effort in this direction nor do they arrange any coaching.

(b) Regarding availability of the reading material, 41 per cent of the parents are aware of good reading material and they provide that to their children. 15 per cent of the parents are aware, but they can not afford to provide reading material. 46 per cent of the parents are not at all conscious in this direction. The reading material available at their home is generally of their interest and level and not of their children.

(c) The motivation given by the parents is usually examination-oriented by nearly 82 per cent of the parents. Only 18 per cent of the parents really motivate their children for extra reading and take the children to book fairs and exhibitions. Children's temptation for reading comics remained a common complaint of all the parents. Perhaps it is due to the lack of guidance and non-availability of good reading material, the children are left with the only option of reading comics.

(d) As far as inculcation of good reading habits is concerned, only 33 per cent of the parents show concern in this direction as also confirmed by the quantitative analysis. Most of the parents are themselves ignorant in this regard.

(e) On the basis of the interview conducted, the investigator feels that most of the parental support is directed to the high achievement in school examination especially in subjects like mathematics and science. Parents from all the socio-economic status have higher level of aspiration than their children. This was further supported on the basis of the following findings of the study:

- average boys have higher level of aspiration as compared to average girls.
- above average girls have a higher level of aspiration, better sight-vocabulary and a higher level of comprehension than average girls.

Conclusion

On the basis of the quantitative as well as qualitative analysis, certain facts have emerged:

(a) On the whole, reading of the child, irrespective of the sex, is positively related to his/her sight vocabulary, one of the psychological correlates;

(b) Level of aspiration of the child seems to have almost negligible, non-significant correlation with reading. Perhaps it is due to the conscious inclination and higher aspiration of the students towards the subject like mathematics and science;

(c) Sex of the child does not seem to affect his performance on various correlates of reading; and

(d) Social factors like parental support to reading and socio-economic level contribute to the acquisition of reading skills of the child.

These results will be further elaborated and discussed in the following chapter.

5

Major Findings and Discussions

Introduction

Reading is a complex skill and a number of factors influence the reading ability of an individual. Reading in general implies inferring meaning from the graphic symbols that one reads and this process of inferring includes biological, psychological and cultural aspects which constitute the foundation of reading. Reading is an essential aid to personal development and social progress. Directly or indirectly, it serves as the means for intellectual equipment, for development of advanced knowledge, for pursuit of excellence, for scientific, social, economic and even political growth and welfare of the country. To develop effective reading comprehension skills, is a prized individual asset. Hence, it is also imperative to study the effects of the various factors on reading.

This chapter presents the essence of the present study in terms of various findings and conclusions regarding the research work. The usefulness of the findings is reflected in their implications. Moreover this chapter briefly describes the constraints under which the study was carried out and the findings arrived at. Lastly the chapter provides suggestions for further research, which the present investigator considers quite important and useful for further research in this area.

The present study was carried out with 250 students in grade VI at five Kendriya Vidyalayas of Delhi, selected randomly. The sample comprised 125 boys and 125 girls. These students were further classified into three groups, namely above average, average and below average on the basis of their performance on a non-verbal mental ability test (RSPM). The relationships among various correlates was studied comparatively on these three groups in view of the problem under study: "A Study of Psycho Social Factors Affecting Reading Skills in English".

Objectives Restated

The various objectives of the present study are :

1. To investigate the various psycho-social factors affecting reading comprehension;
2. To examine the influence of socio-economic level of the learner's family on his reading comprehension at both literal and inferential levels;
3. To study the role of parental support to reading on the learner's reading comprehension skills at various levels;
4. To examine whether the learner's sex affects his/her reading comprehension;
5. To examine the contribution of the learner's sight vocabulary towards reading comprehension;
6. To assess the learner's level of aspiration and its correlation with reading comprehension; and
7. To study the contribution of general mental ability towards reading omprehension at various levels.

Hypotheses Restated

The present study had the following hypotheses:

1. Various psychological and social factors affect a learner's reading comprehension individually as well as collectively;
2. Socio-economic status of the family the learner comes from and reading comprehension skills of the learner are positively correlated;

3. Parents support in reading reinforces the learner's reading comprehension skills;
4. The learner's reading comprehension skills are independent of learner's sex;
5. More developed sight vocabulary of the learner promotes reading comprehension;
6. The level of aspiration of the child is positively related to his acquisition of reading comprehension skills;
7. There exists a positive correlation between the general mental ability and reading comprehension skills of the learner; and
8. Various levels of reading comprehension have a hierarchical relationship.

Major Findings

The present study was conducted keeping in mind the above stated objectives and the hypotheses were tested through the data collected through a set of tools.

Hypothesis No. 1

It was revealed that various psychological as well as social factors affect individually as well as collectively the students reading comprehension skills. This hypothesis was verified and accepted. A high positive correlation is seen between the learners reading comprehension skills at both the levels viz. literal and inferential with sight vocabulary in all the groups viz. above average, average and below average boys and girls. Besides, a high correlation is seen between sight-vocabulary scores and socio-economic status of the learners at all levels. This implies that if a learner has better facilities at home with a better standard of living, the child has access to better reading material. This contributes to his sight-vocabulary. On the contrary, if a learner is from a lower socio-economic background and has below average mental ability, then these two factors affect negatively his reading comprehension skills individually as well as collectively.

Hypothesis No. 2

The second hypothesis was that the socio-economic status of the child does influence his reading comprehension skills. The hypothesis was verified and accepted. The above average boys and girls exhibit comparatively low positive correlation between SES and reading comprehension skills both at literal and inferential level. Below average boys and girls show comparatively high and significant correlation between SES and reading comprehension skills.

This indicates that a certain level of mental ability is essential for the child. A child may have good socio-economic status, but if he/she is a below average child, then this correlate will not help to acquire good reading comprehension skills. But on the other hand, seeing the high value of 'r' between SES and comprehension skills in above average and average learners, one may infer that if the child has a certain required level of mental abilities then this social factor has a positive effect on acquiring reading skills.

Hypothesis No. 3

The third hypothesis was that the parental support in reading reinforces the learner's reading comprehension skills. This hypothesis was verified and accepted. The analysis shows the high positive correlation between reading skills at various levels of comprehension and the parental support to reading. The value of 'r' is comparatively high for the above average group of both boys and girls as compared to the average group and the below average group. In the below average group, particularly the boys group show a low significant correlation between parental support to reading and acquisition of reading comprehension skill.

Hypothesis No. 4

The fourth hypothesis framed was that the learner's reading comprehension skills are independent of his/her sex. The hypothesis was verified by the results and was accepted. Data analysis revealed that no significant difference exists between the performance of learners at various levels of comprehension and their achievement in relation to their sex. Reading comprehension and sight vocabulary are highly and positively correlated in case of both boys and girls. On the other hand, there exists low correlation between reading comprehension and level of aspiration for both boys as well as girls. Only in the case of average boys and girls, there seems to be a significant difference in the level of aspiration. Since this correlate has a very low value of 'r' with reading comprehension, it may not contribute substantially to reading comprehension of both groups.

Hypothesis No. 5

The fifth hypothesis states that more developed sight vocabulary promotes reading comprehension skills. This was substantiated by the present study and accepted. A high positive correlation between reading comprehension and sight vocabulary supports this hypothesis. If the learner has more developed sight vocabulary, then his performance at various levels of reading comprehension is better.

Hypothesis No. 6

The sixth hypothesis states that the level of aspiration of the child is positively related to the acquisition of his reading comprehension skills. This hypothesis has not been confirmed by the present study.

This study reveals that there exists a very low and non-significant correlation between level of aspiration and reading skills. The investigator tried to probe the reasons. Due to cut-throat competition at every level of achievement, the learners and their parents are more worried about the achievement level of the child in the so-called high scoring subjects like mathematics and science. Therefore; the level of aspiration of the child as well as his parents high expectations remain confined to these subjects only and usually do not concern English. The English language has comparatively less scope of high scores as compared to science subjects and mathematics. This might be the reason for very low correlation between the level of aspiration of the child and his/her reading comprehension skills.

Hypothesis No. 7

This hypothesis states that there exists a positive correlation between the general mental ability and reading comprehension skills of the child. This hypothesis has been confirmed and accepted. The study reveals that above average boys and girls score high on reading comprehension skills. On the other hand, the below average boys and girls have comparatively low scores on total reading comprehension also.

Inferential analysis of the data reveals that there is a significant high difference between the performance of above average groups and below average groups (both boys and girls) in the acquisition of reading skills. An interesting fact emerged from the study is that the difference between the performance of the above average learners and average learners on reading comprehension is found to be low but this difference is comparatively high and significant between the other two groups viz. above average and below average group as well as average and below average group.

It may be pointed out here that a certain minimum level of mental ability is a prerequisite for acquisition of reading comprehension skills. Once that minimum level of mental ability is there, then there may not be any significant difference between the acquisition of reading comprehension skills of average and above average learner. A positive correlation has been found between the scores obtained on Standard Progressive Matrices Test and those on reading comprehension at various levels viz. literal and inferential.

Hypothesis No. 8

This hypothesis states that various levels of comprehension viz. literal as well as inferential comprehension have a hierarchical relationship. This hypothesis has been accepted. According to this hypothesis, literal comprehension skills are simpler and thus can be mastered to a higher degree whereas inferential comprehension skills are complex and can not be easily mastered. It has been further observed in the present study that the learners scores on literal comprehension are higher than on inferential comprehension. The same trend is seen in all groups. Boys as well as girls of all mental ability groups viz. above average, average and below average show the same trend. The scores of each group on literal comprehension are higher as compared to the scores on inferential comprehension. Students of younger age can easily master those skills of reading comprehension that are related to factual information. Drawing inference, being a highly complex skill can be attained only on a little mature level. Perhaps this might be the reason for the comparatively high scores obtained by the group on literal comprehension as compared to the scores obtained on inferential comprehension. Thus, it may be concluded that there is a hierarchical relationship between these two levels of reading comprehension.

Certain other facts that have emerged from the present study are:

(a) Average and below average boys have higher level of aspiration as compared to the girls of both the groups but it does not influence the reading comprehension skills in any way because of the low non-significant correlation between level of aspiration and reading comprehension skills.

(b) Above average boys get more parental support to reading than below average boys which has significant effect on acquisition of their reading skills. At the same time above average girls and below average girls do not differ much in getting the parental support to reading. In case of girls, parental support to reading seizes to cause its effect on reading comprehension whereas in boys it remains a significant correlate.

Discussion on Findings

A research study has its genesis in the background of the area in which it is located and the research findings of the earlier studies which justify its conception as well as its implications. Therefore it is natural that after completion of research study, its findings should be reviewed against the perspective of the cumulative research evidence in the concerned area. It is because of this that the investigator thought it proper to juxtapoze the findings of the present research with the findings of the research already conducted in this area.

Since other already conducted research studies in the area in which the present research is rooted, deal only partly and tangentially with the variables of this study, the possibility of empirical evidence wholly in support of or opposed to it, does not exist. Consequently, an attempt has been made here to cite such findings which corroborate or refute the findings of the present study.

The findings of the present study have already been summed up in the preceding section. The fact that there are various psychological and social factors that affect a learner's reading comprehension individually as well as collectively, has been supported by numerous studies, main among the Indian studies are Shah (1979), Joshi (1984), Alavander (1992) and Sankarappan (1992). As far as the studies abroad are concerned Jimmy Chan (1986), Elliott and Hewison (1991) and Hickman, Greenwood and Miller (1994) found research evidence that supports the findings of the present study. These studies established that various psychological factors such as anxiety, aspiration, reading-rate and meaning-vocabulary are positively related to the language ability. Social factors like family background, family physical resources, parental involvement, parent-child interaction and parents educational level have a positive correlation with acquisition of reading skills of the learner.

Amongst these factors, the one most discussed is the socio-economic status of the child. The present study reveals that the socio-economic status of the family does influence the learner's reading ability. Socio-economic status includes parental occupation, parental education, family income and physical resources available at home. Several studies have been conducted on this social variable and the findings of most of these support the present study. The relatively more notable among these are Bhishikar (1980), Agrawal (1981), Das (1984), Srivastava (1984), Joshi (1984), Singh (1989), Alavandar (1992) and Hashway, Duke and Farmer (1993). All these studies support the present hypothesis that socio-economic status of the family the child comes from, affects his reading ability.

Another factor which has been studied by many researchers earlier concerned differences due to the sex of the child on his acquisition of reading comprehension skills. The present study revealed that the sex of the child does not influence his acquisition of reading comprehension skills. No substantial differences were noticed in the performance of boys and girls of various mental ability levels in respect of reading comprehension, factual, inferential or total. It was further observed that the performance of boys and girls remained comparable on all other variables viz. sight vocabulary, SES, parental attitude towards reading and level of aspiration. This finding has been supported by sizable studies on reading research in the past decades. Notable among these are Shah (1979), Neuman, Susan and Prowda (1979), Bhishikar (1980), Agrawal (1981) and Grover (1991). These studies have shown that sex has no correlation with the language achievement of the child as well as the acquisition of reading comprehension skills of the child.

Parental support to reading, parental involvement in the child's acquisition of reading skills and parental attitude towards child's reading are some of the aspects worth mentioning under the social factors influencing reading skills. In the present study the researcher studied the parental support to reading through a questionnaire. The study reveals that parental support to reading has a positive relationship with acquisition of reading skills. The parental support includes the amount of time given to the child, help or guidance made available to the child and inculcation of good reading habits through parental help. Various studies conducted in the last decades also support the present finding. Jimmy Çhan's (1986) study also supports the present finding that favourable parent-child relationship is positively correlated with the reading ability of the child. Parents' motivation or parents' attitude affects language acquisition by children, was established by Shashi Mohan (1991). Hickman, Greenwood and Miller (1994) established that there was a high positive correlation between parents involvement and scholastic achievement of the child.

The present study also led to the conclusion that there is a positive correlation between the mental ability of the child and his acquisition of reading skills at various levels of comprehension. This factor has been investigated in many studies and their findings support the conclusion arrived at here e.g., Shah (1979), Agrawal (1981), Srivastava (1984), Joshi (1984), Manju Singh (1989) and Sabharwal (1989).

Yet another psychological factor that has been investigated through the present study deals with the level of aspiration of the child and its relationship with the acquisition of reading skills. The present study reveals a low and non-significant relationship between the level of aspiration of the child and his reading ability. Pal (1984) concluded that sex of the child has significant impact on level of aspiration. Pal's study does not directly mention the impact of level of aspiration on acquisition of reading skills. The researcher feels that due to the ever-increasing competition in admissions in higher studies, the relatively higher level of aspiration of the children has been restricted to high scoring subjects like Science and Mathematics rather than languages.

Educational Implications

The present study is related to two areas viz. reading skills and social as well as psychological factors affecting the acquisition of the reading skills. It tries to bring out the influence of these factors on reading skills of young learners. The findings of this study have a message for the educationists, teachers and parents. Even though there is a message for individuals too, but these individuals being relatively immature, its relevance is much higher for the teachers and parents because they are more intimately concerned with the acquisition of reading skills of children and their language proficiency. The implications of the findings of this study have, therefore, been listed separately for teachers as well as parents.

Most people think that reading is a purely knowledge-based activity. In fact, reading is a process of acquisition of certain skills with the help of which one is able to comprehend the meaning of the printed text. A child's reading comprehension is related to his mental abilities. So, firstly the teacher should know that all the learners can not be expected to read and comprehend equally well and equally efficiently. Reading instructions should be individualized as far as possible. The teacher should try to give a number of reading passages to the learners according to their comprehension level. All the learners may not be expected to complete reading at the same time.The teacher should allow the students to work on their own pace.

Secondly, acquisition of reading skills is related to the sight vocabulary of the learner. More opportunities should be provided to the students to interact with the written texts. The teacher should try to expose the students to a variety of texts. A good number of small passages along with glossary may be provided to the students.

So far as the implications of the findings of this study for parents are concerned, these are indeed very significant.

Firstly, the parents would do well to remember that parental help is a must for the child. So, the parents should try to devote more time to their children to help them in reading.

Secondly, reading interest can be nurtured by providing a good range of reading material to the child at home. So, the parents should try to provide a good variety of printed texts including books and magazines to the children according to their interests and level of comprehension.

Thirdly, the parents should remember that there is no substitute available to replace the positive and supportive psycho-social effects that are provided to the child by their company and their interaction with him. Therefore, parents would do well to find time to discuss good reading texts with the child, help him in reading and provide guidance in selecting a good reading text. Besides these, it is the parents who can correct the posture of the child while reading or help him in gaining speed while reading.

Fourthly, as the study reveals, reading comprehension of the child is not significantly related to his level of aspiration. But parents should make an effort in this direction also. Instead of over-emphasizing on the subjects like mathematics and science, the parents should motivate the child for reading also. They need not pressurize children to attain extraordinary achievement but try to develop a natural inclination towards reading. Parents should encourage genuine diversity in reading. They should inculcate good reading habits in the children. Parents should try to build up a good reading atmosphere for the child by providing healthy, informative as well as entertaining reading material to the children at home.

Lastly, the parents should realize that an exposure to various media these days is a must for the child for creating an interest for reading. Hence, parents should provide better facilities for the child to develop his reading interest.

Limitations of the Study

After the completion of the research study, every investigator should address himself to the question "How far the findings of my study can be generalized or extended to other groups or situations?" In the context of this question, the investigator feels that like any other study, the findings of this study also have a few limitations which are given below:

1. The present study was conducted in a particular area viz. Delhi region. In Delhi region also, only five schools were randomly selected. The only criterion kept in mind was that these five schools should be from north, west, east, south and central Delhi. Delhi has a variety of schools. These comprise government schools, public schools, schools run by certain missionaries and societies and Kendriya Vidyalayas. The study may be useful to all schools because the age group of the children remain more or less same. Most of the government schools have also adopted a new pattern and being converted into Sarvodaya Vidyalayas where English is taught as a school subject from class I. The findings of the present study would certainly be helpful in these schools also.
2. The study was conducted on a sample of 250 students. This sample belonged to urban population. The investigator did not include those school students who belonged to rural environment. As a result only a particular section of the society can be benefited by the findings.
3. The investigator confined the study to the students of Kendriya Vidyalayas only. Government schools of NCT Delhi, public schools and other aided schools were not included in the sample.
4. The sample comprised those students only who have acquired the basic skills of English. These children have read English up to class V. The study did not include either the beginners or the more mature and proficient learners.
5. The investigator selected class VI students as the study sample. These students were of the age group of 11-12 years. The study sample did not include very young learners as well as adolescent learners who have more psychological problems otherwise.

Suggestion for Further Research

No research work is complete in itself. It is a part of a long process in which one string joins another to form a chain. Hence, the present study also provides considerable scope for further research in this area. Some of the suggestion for further research are given below:

1. A similar study may be undertaken in the schools of other regions of Kendriya Vidyalaya Sangatnan.
2. A comparative study of the acquisition of reading skills may be carried out at various levels of school viz. primary, secondary and senior secondary school levels.
3. A longitudinal study of psycho-social factors affecting reading skills may be carried out at various levels of school viz. primary, secondary and senior secondary school levels.
4. A comparative study of the psycho-social factors affecting reading skills of students of urban schools and rural schools may be conducted.

Appendix—A

Holding up the Sky

Once there was a great, Greek hero, Hercules. On his shoulder, he carried a club and a bow in his hand. He wore lion's skin as armour and lion's head as helmet. Hercules served a king who was afraid of him. So he sent him frequently on difficult errands, the so called 'Labours of Hercules.'

One morning the king asked him to fetch three golden apples from the garden of singing maidens. Hercules said, "where is the garden?"

"Nobody knows that, so go and find it yourself," said the king smilingly.

Hercules walked for months but couldn't find that garden. One morning he saw a giant holding the sky on his shoulders. Hercules recognized him and said, "Atlas, do you know the way to the garden of singing maidens? I have to fetch golden apples for the king from there." Atlas said, "I have been holding the sky for centuries. Only strong men can do that. Hold the sky while I fetch golden apples for you."

Hercules, being proud, shouldered the sky. Atlas flew and after a long time came back with apples. Hercules shouted, "Thanks for apples, come and hold the sky. It weighs heavy." Atlas said laughingly, "Go on holding it for ever. I'll take the apples to the king." Hercules understood the trick. He said, "All right, hold it for a minute while I make cushion of my lion's skin." Atlas believed him and putting the apples aside, he held the sky. Hercules snatched the apples and ran back to the palace.

The king was horrified to learn that he had held the sky. He gave Hercules those apples and asked him to go away forever.

277 words

By Freda Saxey

Q. No. 1. Match the words given under column A with the phrases given under column B and write their numbers in the space provided.

Column A	*Column B*
(i) hero	(a) a female servant
(ii) armour	(b) a very big and strong man
(iii) giant	(c) hundreds of years
(iv) centuries	(d) a young beautiful unmarried girl
(v) maiden	(e) a covering dress to protect against enemies
	(f) a number of years
	(g) one who can perform difficult tasks easily.

Ans. (i)__________ (ii)__________

(iii)__________ (iv)__________

(v)__________

Q. No. 2. Choose and tick (✓) the most appropriate statement to complete the given sentences:

(i) The king asked Hercules to fetch three golden apples from the garden of singing maidens because__________

(a) he loved apples very much.

(b) the king was proud of Hercules' powers and wanted to prove it to the people.

(c) Hercules wanted to go to the garden of singing maidens.

(d) the king feared Hercules and he wanted to get rid of him.

(ii) Hercules agreed to hold up the sky while Atlas went to fetch apples because______________________

(a) Atlas put this condition before him for bringing apples.

(b) Hercules had already held up the sky many times and so he agreed readily.

(c) Hercules wanted to show his strength to Atlas.

(d) Hercules was courteous and he agreed to Atlas' request.

Q. No. 3. Choose and write the words that describe each of the following characters. You may use a word more than once.

(1) Strong, (2) Big-statured, (3) Astonished, (4) Proud, (5) Timid, (6) Horrified, (7) Clever, (8) Helpful, (9) Simple-hearted, (10) Intelligent.

Hercules : _________, _________, _________, _________,

Atlas : _________, _________, _________, _________,

King : _________, _________, _________, _________,

Q. No. 4.

(a) Choose and write 4 words/phrases that describe the appearence of Hercules from the lines 1 to 4 from the given passage.

(i) ______________________, (ii) ______________________,

(iii) ______________________, (iv) ______________________,

(b) Which word/phrase in the story tells you that Hercules knew Atlas before?

Ans. ______________________________

Q.No. 5. Choose and tick (✓) to the most appropriate answer to each question:

(i) 'Hercules understood the trick'. What was the trick?

(a) that Atlas wanted Hercules to hold the sky for ever.

(b) that Atlas was making fun of him.

(c) that Atlas wanted to go to King's palace.

(d) that Atlas didn't want to give him the apples.

(ii) 'Hercules snatched the apples'. In this sentence the word 'snatched' means :-

(a) to take away forcibly

(b) to hold firmly

(c) to grab quickly.

(iii) The phrase 'Labours of Hercules' means :-

(a) the usual routine work

(b) Hercules' duties as a servant

(c) the difficult task

(d) King's orders.

Q.No. 6. Rearrange the following sentences in the order in which they actually occur in the story and write their numbers below:-

(i) Hercules ran back to the palace.

(ii) The king asked Hercules to bring apples.

(iii) The king gave away the apples to Hercules.

(iv) Atlas agreed to help Hercules.

(v) Hercules saw Atlas and shouted with joy.

Ans. ________, ________, ________, ________, ________,

Q. No. 7. Suggest any suitable title to the story other than the given one, 'Holding up the sky.'

Ans.

Appendix B

The Lotus Temple—Bahai House of Worship

New Delhi, the capital of India, has always been an attraction for tourists from all over the world. One of the main attractions of this city is the Bahai House of worship — The Lotus Temple. It is situated in the south part of Delhi near Nehru Place. The building has a very distinctive design of lotus flower set amidst green lawns and large pools. The temple shaped like a lotus flower has 27 petals made of white concrete. The stairs surrounding the pools are made of white marble. The temple symbolises the beauty and purity of a lotus flower in true sense. The temple has a main prayer hall, a reception room, a library and an office. There are nine pools that surround the temple. These pools keep the temple cool even in summer. The construction of this temple started in 1980 and was completed in 1986. This magnificent building has nine sides. Number nine is the highest single digit and it signifies oneness, fullness and unity. This temple has 9 sides, 9 pools and 27 petals. People of all faiths are welcome to visit the temple and pray there in silence. Perfect silence is maintained in the prayer hall. The temple is closed to visitors on Mondays. Outside the prayer hall, it is written 'God is one and we are all one'. This is the main principle of the Bahai religion. Unlike other temples, this temple does not support idol-worship. The temple has no idol of any God at all. The Lotus Temple is certainly a beautiful place to visit.

265 words

22 sentences

Developed By : Kusum Sharma

Q. No. 1. Match the words given under column A with the phrases given under column B and write their letter/ Code (a,b, c.............etc), in the space provided:

Column A	*Column B*
(i) amidst	(a) a mixture of sand and cement
(ii) Magnificent	(b) image of an object of worship
(iii) idol	(c) in the middle of
(iv) concrete	(d) different
(v) distinctive	(e) grand/unusually good
	(f) solid

Ans : (i)_______ (ii)_______ (iii)_______ (iv)_____(v)_______

Q. No. 2. Choose and tick (✓) the most appropriate statement to complete the given sentences:-

1. The Lotus Temple is very distinctive because __________
   (a) It is made of white marble and concrete.
   (b) It has big lawns and pools surrounding the temple.
   (c) Unlike other temples, its shape resembles a flower.
   (d) People of all faiths are welcome here.
2. The nine pools that surround the temple keep the place __
   (a) cool
   (b) peaceful
   (c) clean
   (d) full of sunlight.
3. The main teaching of the Bahai religion is that___________
   (a) We should pray in silence
   (b) God is one and we are all one

(c) We should not worship idols

(d) We should worship the lotus flower.

Q. No. 3. (i) Which word in line 9 in the passage means 'represents'?

Ans.____________________

(ii) Which word in line 12 in the passage means 'cover from all sides'?

Ans.____________________

(iii) Which word in line 4 in the passage means 'places'?

Ans.______________________________

Q. No. 4. Number nine is reflected in the temple through various things. Choose and tick (✓) the appropriate ones from the list.

(a) number of pools surrounding the temple

(b) number of lawns in the temple

(c) number of petals of the lotus flower

(d) number of stairs that lead to the pools

(e) number of the sides of the temple.

Q.No. 5. Select and tick (✓) the most appropriate statement.

The passage tells us about:-

(i) the Bahai religion and its principles

(ii) the touring places in Delhi

(iii) a new tourist spot in Delhi

(iv) the construction of the Lotus Temple.

Appendix C

Kapil Dev—The Hero of Indian Cricket

Just two decades ago, a young, 16-year old boy from Chandigarh joined the Indian Cricket team. Kapil Dev, son of Shri Ramlal Nikhanj and Smt. Lajwanti Nikhanj belonged to a middle class family. The family moved to Chandigarh from Jhang, Pakistan during 1947. Kapil started his Cricket career with the first test match played in Oct. 1978 in Faisalabad against Pakistan. He could take only one wicket in that match. Within a year his tally of wickets rose to 50. He took his fifteeth wicket during his 16th test match played against Australia in Kanpur on 17th Oct. 1979. That one year proved the talent in the young bowler. Today the number of wickets that Kapil has taken is 432. This is the highest score ever made. It was on Feb. 8, 1994 that Kapil took the 432nd wicket in Ahmadabad playing against Sri Lanka. In today's cricket world, two figures emerge much larger than other.........Allen Border of Australia and India's own Kapil Dev. Border has scored more runs than any other batsman in test cricket. Kapil has emerged as the all-time great wicket-taker. As an all-rounder, Kapil is a man for all seasons. He has excelled with the bat also and has scored 5226 runs including 8 centuries with the highest score of 163.

It was a moment of great pride and happiness for the whole nation when Kapil took his 432nd wicket. People from all walks of life sent him their messages of congratulations. The spectators in the stadium came running to embrace him. Kapil dedicated his success to his late father who encouraged him to play cricket but couldn't see his son bringing laurels to his country. India's leading musicians composed a song in praise of Kapil. Today Kapil Dev has become a superstar in cricket.

282 words

Developed By: Kusum Sharma

Q. No. 1. Match the words given under column A with the phrases given under column B and write their letter/ Code (a,b, c.............etc.) in the space provided:

Column A	*Column B*
(i) decade	(a) honour
(ii) pride	(b) to feel shy
(iii) embrace	(c) a high opinion about self/ self respect
(iv) spectators	(d) to hold closely in arms
(v) laurels	(e) viewers
	(f) a period of ten years

Ans. (i)________ (ii)________ (iii)________ (iv)______(v)________

Q. No. 2. Choose and tick (✓) the most appropriate statement to complete the given sentences:-

(i) Today Kapil Dev is compared with Allen Border because ________

(a) both of them play cricket

(b) both of them have highest scores of making runs in the test matches

(c) both of them are fast bowlers

(d) both of them have highest scores, Allen Border as a batsman and Kapil Dev as wicket-taker

(ii) Feb. 8, 1994 was an important date in Kapil's Cricket career because ________

(a) on this day Kapil took his 432nd wicket

(b) on this day Kapil played very well

(c) that day was his birthday

(d) nothing special happened on that day

(iii) The viewers sitting in the stadium came running to Kapil because____________

(a) they wanted to thank him

(b) they wanted to talk to him

(c) they wanted to express their happiness at his achievement

(d) they wanted to play cricket with him.

(iv) Kapil dedicated his success to his father because____________

(a) his father is no more alive to share the happiness

(b) he made a promise to his father

(c) he learned cricket from his father

(d) he loved his father more than any one else

Q. No. 3. Choose and tick (✓) the most appropriate answer to each question:-

(i) Kapil has emerged as a man for all seasons. What does the phrase 'a man for all seasons' mean?

(a) a man who can play in all seasons

(b) a man who can play equally good as a batsman, a bowler and a fielder

(c) that he can play better than any one else

(d) that he can play any game.

(ii) People from all walks of life sent messages of congratulations. What does the phrase 'all walks of life' mean?

(a) people belonging to different religions

(b) people belonging to different states of India

(c) people belonging to different sections of society

(d) people belonging to different age groups.

Q. No. 4. (i) Which word in line 28 in the passage means 'famous'?

Ans.____________________

(ii) Which word in line 15 in the passage means 'rise above'?

Ans.____________________

Q. No. 5. Choose and tick (✓) the most appropriate statement to complete the sentence:-

The passage tells us about______________

(i) Kapil Dev's family background

(ii) Kapil Dev's greatest achievement in cricket

(iii) The Indian cricket team

(iv) Kapil Dev's advice to young cricketers.

Appendix D

(Letter sent to Middle School English Teachers along with enclosed passages/questionnaires)

To Dated :..............

____

____

____

Dear

As an expert in the field of English language, you might have had varied experiences while teaching English to various levels of students. I am sure you would agree to the opinion that it requires much efforts on the part of a language teacher to make language learning an interesting and challenging experience for the students. For this it is imperative that the students should be well-equipped with the skills of learning English. Therefore, more emphasis should be laid on learning of skills. Reading, no doubt is a very important skill as it widens the horizon of knowledge of the learner.

Hence, the investigator has decided to work in the area of 'Reading comprehension'. The topic of research is 'The study of Psycho-Social Factors affecting Readings Skills in English'.

The investigator has decided to conduct the study on the students of class VI who have already mastered the basic structures and skills for five years, i.e. class I to V. The reason for selection of this age group was that a class VI student of age-group 11-12 years can be tested for psychological factors in a more reliable manner than a student of class VIII or IX who might try to deceive the true picture. Children less than 11 years

The investigator has selected 3 passages (one of each type, (Narrative, Descriptive and Expository) of nearly same length and difficulty level. Initially 5 passages of nearly 270 words each were selected and the questions were framed on each passage to test the reading-comprehension skills of the students. The passages along with questions and answer key and the identified skills were sent to the different teachers of Kendriya Vidyalayas who have been teaching/have taught English to class VI students. Besides these passages, a questionnaire was also sent to be filled up by the teacher, giving her/his opinion on the passage.

On the basis of the suggestions received from the teachers; three passages (the enclosed ones) were selected keeping in view the interest and the difficulty level of the students. These passages along with their questions have been tried out on a small sample of students of class VI (2 above-average, 4 average and 2 below-average) of Kendriya Vidyalayas to ascertain the time an average student would take to complete the whole exercise. The two passages rejected by the teachers were, 'Some facts about Asia' and 'Value of sports and games'. The teachers were of the opinion that the passages were lengthy, a little higher in level for class VI and not interesting.

Sir, I am sending you these three passages and it is my request to you to kindly give your valuable suggestion/comments on these passages keeping in view the following points:-

(a) suitability of the topic

(b) length of the passage

(c) difficulty level

(d) questions framed on the passage

(e) suitability of the answers

(f) assumed reading skills identified on the basis of the passage.

I hope you would certainly spare some time from your busy schedule to do this favour to me. I am sure that with your rich and valuable suggestions, I will be greatly benefitted.

I hope you would certainly spare some time from your busy schedule to do this favour to me. I am sure that with your rich and valuable suggestions, I will be greatlv benefitted.

With sincere regards,

Kusum Sharma

List of enclosures :

1. (i) Passage I 'Holding up the sky'

   (ii) Questions on the passage along with the answers marked on it.

2. (i) Passage II 'The Lotus Temple— Bahai House of Worship'

   (ii) Questions on the passage along with the answers marked on it.

3. (i) Passage III 'Kapil Dev— The Hero of Indian Cricket'.

   (ii) Questions on the passage along with the answers marked on it.

4. Assumed reading skills to be acquired on the basis of these passages.

5. Teachers' questionnaire for reference.

Expected Reading Skills involved in Text I

Q.No. 1. (a) To understand the meaning of the words in their contextual usage.

Q. No. 2. (a) To understand the main idea of the text.

(b) To understand the relation within sentences and between the different parts of the text.

Q. No. 3. (a) To infer explicitly stated information in conceptual meaning.

(b) To appreciate text by identifying characters.

Q. No. 4. (a) To present factual view in support of something.

(b) To appreciate text by identifying the characters.

Q. No. 5. (a) To understand the explicitly-stated information from the text.

Q. No. 7. (a) To understand and appreciate the text.

Expected Reading Skills involved in Text- 2&3

Q. No. 1. To understand the meaning of the words of the text in their contextual usage.

Q. No. 2. To understand and infer explicitly-stated information of the text in its conceptual meaning.

Q. No. 3. (a) Sequencing and reordering the parts of the text.

(b) To understand the relation between the parts of the text.

Q. No. 4. (a) To locate the specific information in the text.

(b) To understand the vocabulary items used in the text.

Q. No. 5. To understand, infer and appreciate the main idea of the text.

Q. No. 6. To appreciate the text with its global comprehension.

Appendix E

Scoring Scheme For Passage I : Holding up the Sky

Passage I - (Holding up the sky) Narrative Text

Max. Marks : 25

Time : 25 minutes

Q. No 1. Reading skill - To identify the contextual meaning of words.

Ans. Marks allotted 5 (unit score for each)

(i)	-	g
(ii)	-	e
(iii)	-	b
(iv)	-	c
(v)	-	d

Q. No. 2. Reading skill (i) to indicate the main idea of the text. (ii) to indicate the relation within sentences and between different parts of the text.

Ans. Marks allotted - 2 (unit score) (i) - d (ii) - c

Q. No. 3. Reading skill (i) to infer explicitly stated conceptual meaning. (ii) to appreciate by identifying characters

Marks allotted - 6 (½ mark for each)

Ans.

Hercules	-	1, 3, 4, 8, 9, 10
Atlas	-	1, 2, 7, 8
King	-	5, 6.

Q. No. 4. Reading skill to present necessary supportive factual information.

Marks allotted - a - 2 Marks (½x 4)

b - 1 Mark

Ans. (a) (i) club on shoulder

(ii) bow in hand

(iii) Lion's skin as armour

(iv) Lion's head as helmet.

(b) recognised.

For Q. 4 (a) marks will be given if the child uses the first word in every answer instead of the complete phrase.

Q. No. 5. Reading skill - To infer the main idea and details given in the text.

Marks allotted - 3

Ans. (i) c (ii) c (iii) b.

Q. No. 6. Reading skill to sequence and reorder parts of the text.

Marks allotted - 5 (unit score)

Ans. Correct sequence

(ii), (v), (iv), (i), (iii).

Q. No. 7. Reading skill - To choose/give a suitable alternative title

Marks allotted - 1

Ans. (i) Hercules, The Hero

Or

(ii) The Heroic Act of Hercules

Or

(iii) any other suitable title.

Appendix F

Scoring Scheme For Passage II : The Lotus Temple - Bahai House of Worship

Passage II - Descriptive Text (The Lotus Temple - Bahai House of Worship)

Max. Marks : 15

Time allotted : 25 minutes.

Q. No. 1. Reading skill - To identify the contextual word meaning

Marks allotted : 5 (unit score)

Ans. (i) c (ii) e (iii) b (iv) a (v) d.

Q. No. 2. Reading skill - To understand and infer conceptual meaning.

Marks allotted : 3 (unit score).

Ans (i) c (ii) a (iii) b.

Q. No. 3. Reading skill - To locate the specific information in the text.

Marks allotted = 3 (unit score)

Ans. (i) symbolises

(ii) surround

(iii) situated

Q. No. 4. Reading skill - To choose the main idea as well as details.

Marks allotted - 3 (unit score)

Ans. Statements a, c, and e reflect number nine in the temple.

Q. No. 5. Reading skill - To infer and appreciate the text.

Marks allotted - 1

Ans. (iii) is the correct answer.

Appendix G

Scoring Scheme For Passage III : Kapil Dev - The Hero of Indian Cricket

Passage III - Expository Test (Kapil Dev - The Hero of Indian Cricket)

Max. Marks - 15

Time allotted - 25 minutes.

Q. No 1. Reading skill - To identify contextual meaning.

Marks allotted - 5 (unit score)

Ans.

(i)	-	f
(ii)	-	c
(iii)	-	d
(iv)	-	e
(v)	-	a

Q. No. 2. Reading skill - To choose/indicate the main idea of the text and infer.

Marks allotted - 4 (unit score)

Ans. (i) d (ii) a (iii) c (iv) a.

Q. No. 3. Reading skill - To infer and analyse the text.

Marks allotted - 2 (unit score)

Ans. (i) b (ii) c.

Q. No. 4. Reading skill - To locate specific information in the text.

Marks allotted - 2 (unit score).

Ans. (i) Leading

(ii) Emerge

Q. No. 5. Reading skill - To appreciate the text by suggesting/selecting title.

Mark allotted - 1

Ans. (ii).

Appendix—H

Sight-Vocabulary Test

(Student is to be asked to read the words 1-50 given below)

Name :____________________Age:____________________

Class :____

School :_______________________________________

Time Limit : 2 mts.

Sl.N.	*Word*	*Student's Response*	*Sl.N.*	*Word*	*Student's Response*
1.	Rule		26.	Hatred	
2.	Sigh		27.	Traffic	
3.	Proud		28.	Signal	
4.	Ocean		29.	Pleasure	
5.	Wheel		30.	Furniture	
6.	Chance		31.	University	
7.	Growth		32.	Dictionary	
8.	Funny		33.	Definite	
9.	Honour		34.	Champion	
10.	Tourist		35.	Emperor	
11.	Current		36.	Computer	
12.	Notice		37.	Photograph	
13.	Poison		38.	Period	
14.	Private		39.	Magician	
15.	Purpose		40.	Engineer	

16.	Polite		41.	Dependent	
17.	Worship		42.	Poverty	
18.	Medicine		43.	Popular	
19.	Agreement		44.	Encourage	
20.	Challenge		45.	Calculator	
21.	Insult		46.	Electricity	
22.	Cruel		47.	Agriculture	
23.	Camera		48.	Advertise-ment	
24.	Valuable		49.	Artificial	
25.	Treasure		50.	Satisfaction	

Total No. of Words read correctly =

No. of words couldn't be read =

Developed by : Kusum Sharma
Prof. V.K. Sabharwal

Appendix I (i)

सामाजिक-आर्थिक स्तर मापने हेतु प्रश्नावली (शहरी)

प्रो. वी. के. सभरवाल व कुसुम शर्मा

नाम ——————————कक्षा——————आयु————————

घर का पता————————————————————————————

स्कूल का पता——————————————————————————

निर्देश :-

यह फार्म आपके (छात्र) द्वारा भरा जाना है जिसमें आप अपने परिवार से सम्बन्धित जानकारी देंगे। नीचे लिखे प्रश्नों को ध्यान से पढ़कर अधिक से अधिक प्रश्नों का सही उत्तर दीजिए। अगर आप अपने माता–पिता के साथ नहीं रहते हैं तो यह जानकारी अपने अभिभावक व उसके परिवार के बारे में दीजिये। हर प्रश्न के सामने कुछ सम्भावित उत्तर दिये गये हैं। सबसे उपयुक्त उत्तर के सामने सही का निशान (✓) लगाइये। केवल प्रश्न 10 के लिए निर्देश प्रश्न के संलग्न दिये गये हैं।

1. आपके पिता की शिक्षा किस स्तर तक हुई है?

   अ. रिसर्च अथवा पी.एच.डी. ——————————————————

   ब. एम.ए. अथवा एम.एस.सी. ——————————————————

   स. बी.ए. अथवा बी.एस.सी. ——————————————————

   ङ. इन्टर ——————————————————————————

   ए. ग्यारहवीं कक्षा ————————————————————

   एफ. आठवीं कक्षा ————————————————————

ग. पाँचवी कक्षा ————————————————————

ह. बिल्कुल नहीं ————————————————————

2. आपके पिता किस पद पर काम करते हैं?

अ. गैज़ेटिड आफिसर, प्रोफेसर, रीडर, सीनियर लेक्चरार, सीनियर साइंटिस्ट, जनरल मैनेजर (बैंक या कम्पनी), उद्योगपति, आर्मी या नेवी या एयरफोर्स में उच्च पदाधिकारी, राजनैतिक नेता।

ब. बैंक आफिसर, लेक्चरार, साइंटिस्ट, प्रिंसीपल, डॉक्टर, वकील, इन्जीनियर, समाचार–पत्र के पत्रकार, संपादक, कम्पनी के मालिक, राजनैतिक नेता (एम.एल.ए./एम.पी.)।

स. आफिसर, सीनियर सैकेंडरी स्कूल/इन्टर कॉलेज में अध्यापक, रिसर्च असिस्टेंट, जूनियर इंजीनियर, दुकानदार, बिजनेसमैन।

ङ. क्लर्क, टाइपिस्ट, अकाउन्टेंट, लैब–असिस्टेंट, प्राइमरी/मिडिल स्कूल में अध्यापक, स्टेशन मास्टर, सुपरवाइजर, टेलीफोन ऑपरेटर, किसान।

ए. मोटर ड्राइवर, पेन्टर, बढ़ई, मैकेनिक।

फ. चपरासी, फैक्टरी में कर्मचारी, चलता–फिरता दुकानदार।

ग. बेरोजगार अथवा दूसरों पर आश्रित।

3. आपकी माता की शिक्षा किस स्तर की हुई है?

अ. रिसर्च अथवा पी.एच.डी. ————————————————————

ब. एम.ए./एम.एस.सी ————————————————————

स. बी.ए./बी.एस.सी. ————————————————————

ङ इन्टर/बारहवीं कक्षा ————————————————————

ए. ग्यारवीं कक्षा ————————————————————

फ. आठवीं कक्षा ————————————————————

ज. प्राथमिक कक्षा (पाँचवीं कक्षा) ————————————————————

ह. बिल्कुल नहीं ————————————————————

4. आपकी माता किस पद पर कार्य करती हैं?

अ. गैज़ेटिड आफिसर, प्रोफेसर, रीडर, सीनियर लेक्चरार, सीनियर साइंटिस्ट, जनरल मैनेजर (बैंक या कम्पनी), उद्योगपति, आर्मी या नेवी या एयरफोर्स में उच्च पदाधिकारी, राजनैतिक नेता।

ब. बैंक आफिसर, लेक्चरार, साइंटिस्ट, प्रिंसीपल, डॉक्टर, वकील, इन्जीनियर, समाचार–पत्र की पत्रकार, संपादक, कम्पनी की मालिक, राजनैतिक नेता (एम.एल.ए./एम.पी.)।

स. आफिसर, सीनियर सैकेंडरी स्कूल/इन्टर कॉलेज में अध्यापक, रिसर्च असिस्टेंट, जूनियर इंजीनियर, दुकानदार, बिजनेसमैन।

ङ. क्लर्क, टाइपिस्ट, अकाउन्टेंट, लैब–असिस्टेंट, प्राइमरी/मिडिल स्कूल में अध्यापिका, टेलीफोन ऑपरेटर।

ए. सेल्स वूमेन, दुकानदार (छोटी दुकान)।

फ. चपरासी, मजदूर।

ग. सिर्फ गृहिणी।

5. नीचे बनी तालिका में अपने भाई–बहनों के बारे में जानकारी दीजिए। सबसे बड़े भाई/बहन से शुरू करें व अपने बारे में नहीं लिखें।

क्रमांक	नाम	आयु	अगर पढ़ता/पढ़ती है तो कक्षा लिखो	शिक्षा	पद	ऑफिस का नाम

6. आपके परिवार की औसत मासिक आय क्या है? (सभी प्रकार की आमदनी जोड़कर बतायें)

अ. 20,000 रु. से अधिक ————————————————

ब. 15,000 रु. और 20,000 रु. के बीच में ——————————

स. 10,000 रु. और 15,000 रु. के बीच में ——————————

ङ 5,000 रु. और 10,000 रु. के बीच में ——————————

ए. 1,000 रु. और 5,000 रु. के बीच में ——————————

फ. 1,000 रु. से कम ————————————————

7. क्या आपका परिवार कोई समाचार पत्र खरीदता है?

अ. रोज़ाना ———————— कौन–सा (नाम लिखिए) ——————

ब. कभी–कभी——————————कौन–सा (नाम लिखिए) ——————

स. नहीं ——————————————————————————

8. क्या आपका परिवार कोई पत्रिका खरीदता है?

अ. महीने में चार या उससे अधिक ———————————————

कौन–कौन सी? ——————————————————————

ब. महीने में दो या तीन —————————————————

कौन–कौन सी? 1 ——————————————————

2. ——————————————————

3. ——————————————————

स. महीने में एक ————————————————————

कौन–सी? ——————————————————————

ङ कभी–कभी ——————————————————————

कौन–सी? ——————————————————————

ए. कोई नहीं ——————————————————————

9. आप किस तरह के घर में रहते हैं

अ. कोठी, दो मंजिला/तीन मंजिला घर, 250 गज या उससे बड़ा घर

——————————————————————————————

ब. 100 गज से 250 गज का एक मंजिला ———————————

स. एच.आई.जी. फ्लैट ————————————————————

ङ. एम.आई.जी. फ्लैट ————————————————————

ए. एल.आई.जी. फ्लैट

फ. सरकारी क्वाटर ——————————————————————

जी. किराये का मकान ————————————————————

10. आपके घर में निम्नलिखित वस्तुओं में कौन–कौन सी वस्तुएँ हैं? कृपया संख्या भी लिखें।

अ. कार —————, मोटरसाइकिल —————, स्कूटर —————

साइकिल —————, कोई भी नहीं ——————————————

ब. एयरकण्डीशनर ————————, कूलर ————————

पँखे ————————, कोई नहीं ————————

स. वी.सी.आर. ————————, रंगीन टी.वी. सेट ————————

सादा टी.वी. सेट ————————, टेप रिकार्डर ————————

ङ ट्राजिस्टर ————————, कोई नहीं ————————

ए. कुकिंग रेंज ————————, गैस स्टोव ————————

तेल वाला स्टोव ————————, कोई भी नहीं ————————

11. क्या तुम रोज स्कूल में नाश्ता/खाना लाते हो?

अ. यदि हाँ ————————

आज तुम नाश्ते में क्या लाये हो? ————————

ब. नहीं ————————

12. क्या आपको हर महीने जेब खर्च मिलता है?

अ. हाँ ————————

तो, कितना ————————

ब. नहीं ————————

13. क्या आपके पिता किसी क्लब के सदस्य हैं?

अ. यदि हाँ ————————

तो क्लब का नाम लिखिये ————————

ब. नहीं ————————

14. क्या आपके पिता किसी सामाजिक/राजनैतिक/धार्मिक संस्था के कार्यों में भाग लेते हैं?

अ. यदि हाँ ————————

तो संस्था का नाम लिखो ————————

(i) क्या आपके पिता संस्था के प्रधान हैं ————————

(ii) क्या आपके पिता संस्था में किसी पद पर हैं? ————————

(iii) क्या आपके पिता संस्था के सदस्य हैं? ————————

ब. नहीं ————————

Appendix—I (ii)

Socio-economic Status Scale Questionnaire (Urban)

Prof. V.K. Sabharwal and Kusum Sharma

Name :________________________Age:______________________

Address (Home):________________Class:__________________

____

Address (School) : ________________________

____

Instructions: This proforma is to be filled by you (i.e. students) regarding your family. Please read carefully the following questions and answer them as correctly as you can. If you don't live with your father/mother, write about the family which supports you. There are several possible answers to each question. You have to choose only one (the most appropriate) answer and put a tick (✓) against that answer. Note that only one tick (✓) is to be put against each question except for question No. 10. Separate instructions have been given for question No. 10.

1. What is the highest level of education of your father?

(a) Research or Doctorate degree ....

(b) Post-Graduate degree ....

(c) Graduate degree ....

(d) Intermediate ....

(e) Higher Secondary/Matric etc. ....

(f) Upto Middle School ....

(g) Upto Primary School ....

(h) No Education ....

2. What is the occupation of your father?

(a) High Administrative (gazetted) officer, Professor, Reader, Senior Lecturer, Senior Scientist, General Manager (Bank/ Company), Industrialist, High official in army/navy/airforce, Political leader..

(b) Bank-officer, Lecturer, Scientist, Principal, Doctor, Lawyer, Engineer, Editor, Owner of a big firm, Political leader (M.L.A./M.P.)..

(c) Non-Gazetted Officer, Teacher in Sr. Sec. School/ Intermediate College, Research Assistant, Junior-Engineer, A big Shopkeeper, Businessman ....

(d) Clerk, Typist, Accountant, Lab Assistant, Primary-Teacher/ Middle School Teacher, Station Master, Supervisor, Telephone operator, Agriculturist..

(e) Motor Driver, Painter, Carpenter, Mechanic ....

(f) Peon, Factory Labourer, Mobile Shopkeeper..

(g) Unemployed or dependent on others..

3. What is the highest level of education of your mother?

(a) Research or Doctorate degree ....

(b) Post-Graduate degree ....

(c) Graduate degree ....

(d) Intermediate ....

(e) Higher Secondary/Matric etc. ....

(f) Upto Middle School ....

(g) Upto Primary School ....

(h) No Education ....

4. What is the occupation of your mother?

(a) High Administration (gazetted) officer, Professor, Reader, Senior Lecturer, Senior Scientist, General/Deputy Manager in a Bank/Company, Industrialist, High official in Civil Services, Political leader..

(b) Bank Officer, Lecturer, Scientist, Principal, Doctor, Lawyer, Engineer, Editor, Owner of a big firm, Political leader (M.L.A./M.P.)...

(c) Non-Gazetted Officer, Teacher in Sr. Sec. School/ Intermediate College, Research Assistant, Junior Engineer, A big Shopkeeper, Business woman ....

(d) Clerk, Typist, Accountant, Lab Assistant, Primary Teacher/ Middle School Teacher, Telephone operator.......................

(e) Sales Woman, Shopkeeper ....

(f) Peon, Unskilled Labourer..

(g) Non-working, house wife...

5. Write the names of your Brothers/Sisters and furnish the following information in the table. (Begin with the eldest and don't include yourself).

Sl.No.	*Name*	*Age*	*If student, then mention class*	*Studies upto*	*If working, working as*	*Name of Office*

6. What is the average monthly income of your family? (This includes income from all sources).

(a) Above Rs. 20,000/- ....

(b) Between Rs. 15,000/- and Rs. 20,000/- ....

(c) Between Rs. 10,000/- and Rs. 15,000/- ....

(d) Between Rs. 5,000/- and Rs. 10,000/- ....

(e) Between Rs. 1,000/- and Rs. 5,000/- ....

(f) Below Rs. 1,000/- ....

7. Does your family purchase any newspaper ?

(a) Daily .... Which one (s) ? Write Name ....

(b) Sometimes .... Which one(s)? Write Name ....

(c) No. ....

8. Does your family buy any magazine?

(a) Four or more in a month ....

(b) Between two and three in a month ....
Which ones?

(c) Once a month ....
Which one?

(d) Occasionally ....Which one? ....

(e) No. ....

9. What type of house do you live in?

(a) Privately owned Bungalow, Two/Three Storey house of more than 250 Sq. Yards ....

(b) Privately owned single storey house (between 100 Sq. Yards and 250 Sq. Yards)..............................

(c) Privately owned flat (H.I.G.)..............................

(d) Privately owned flat (M.I.G.)..............................

(e) Privately owned flat (L.I.G.) ....

(f) Govt./leased Accommodation ....

(g) Rented Accommodation ....

10. Which one(s) of the following items does your family own? Write number against each.

(a) Car........, Motor cycle ...., Scooter..........,Cycle ....
None of these ....

(b) Airconditioner........,Air Cooler.......,Electric Fan..................
None of these ....

(c) V.C.R................,Coloured T.V. set ....Black & White T.V. set ...., Tape recorder......................, Transistor....................None of these.................................

11. Do you get food and refreshment to bring to school daily?

(a) Yes ....

What food & refreshment did you bring with you today?

....

(b) No. ....

12. Do you get a monthly pocket money?

(a) Yes ....

How much per month? ....

(b) No. ....

13. Is your father a member of any club? Yes/No

(a) If yes, write the name of the club

....

14. Does your father participate in the activities of any social, political or religious organisation? Yes/No

(a) If yes, then write the name of organisation........................

....

(i) He works as president of the organisation..................

(ii) He works as an office bearer of the organisation ....

(iii) He works as a member of the organisation ....

No. ....

Appendix J(i)

बालकों में पठन-कौशल विकसित करने में अभिभावकों का योगदान जानने हेतु प्रश्नावली

प्रो. वी. के. सभरवाल व कुसुम शर्मा

मुख्य क्षेत्र : अभिभावक द्वारा बालक को–

1. दिया गया समय
2. पठन–सामग्री उपलब्ध कराना
3. मार्गदर्शन
4. अभिप्रेरणा
5. पठन सम्बन्धी अच्छी आदतों पर बल।

नाम——————————————आयु ——————

कक्षा ——————————————————————

पिता का नाम ————————————————————

पिता की शिक्षा ———————————————————

पिता का पद व कार्यालय का पता ——————————————

——————————————

निर्देश :

1. ऊपर लिखी सभी जानकारी दीजिये।
2. सभी प्रश्नों को ध्यानपूर्वक पढ़ें।
3. सबसे उपयुक्त उत्तर पर सही का निशान (✓) लगा दें।
4. कृपया एक प्रश्न के लिए एक से अधिक उत्तरों पर निशान न लगाएँ।

5. सभी प्रश्नों के उत्तर सही– सही तथा साफ–साफ लिखें।
6. सभी प्रश्नों के उत्तर निर्धारित समय (25 मिनट) में ही देने का प्रयास करें।

1. क्या आप नियमित रूप से समाचार–पत्र खरीदते हैं?

क. हाँ ————————————————

ख. कभी–कभी ————————————————

ग. नहीं ————————————————

यदि आपका उत्तर क/ख है तो समाचार–पत्र का नाम लिखिये–

1. ————————————————हिन्दी/अंग्रेजी

2. ————————————————हिन्दी/अंग्रेजी

2. क्या आप कोई पत्रिका भी खरीदते हैं?

क. हाँ, नियमित रूप से ————————————————

ख. हाँ, कभी–कभी ————————————————

ग. कभी–कभी ————————————————

पत्रिकाओं के नाम व भाषा : 1. ————————————————

2. ————————————————

3. ————————————————

3. क्या आपके माता–पिता कोई बाल–पत्रिका भी खरीदते हैं?

क. नियमित रूप से ————————————————

ख. हाँ, कभी–कभी ————————————————

ग. कभी नहीं ————————————————

यदि हाँ, तो नाम लिखिये : 1. ————————————————

2. ————————————————

3. ————————————————

4. जब आप पढ़ते हैं, तो क्या आपके माता–पिता आपके साथ बैठते हैं?

क. हमेशा ————————————————

ख. कभी–कभी ————————————————

ग. कभी नहीं ————————————————

5. क्या आपके माता–पिता आपकी पढ़ाई में सहायता करते हैं?

क. हमेशा———————————————————

ख. जब भी जरूरत हो ——————————————

ग. कभी नहीं ———————————————————

6. जब कभी आप अपने माता–पिता से पढ़ाई में मदद माँगते हैं, तो वे क्या करते हैं?

क. स्वयं आपकी मदद करते हैं।——————————

ख. नियमित ट्यूशन का प्रबन्ध करते हैं।————————

ग. कोई बहाना बनाकर टाल देते हैं।——————————

7. आपके माता–पिता आपको पढ़ाई में सहायता देने के लिए कितना समय देते हैं?

क. एक से दो घण्टे ——————————————————

ख. एक घण्टा या कम ——————————————————

ग. बिल्कुल नहीं ———————————————————

8. पिछले वर्ष आपके जन्मदिन पर आपके माता–पिता ने आपको क्या उपहार दिया था?

क. आपकी मन–पसन्द कोई पुस्तक ——————————

ख. आपका मन–पसन्द खेल ——————————————

ग. एक सुन्दर पोशाक ———————————————————

9. पिछले वर्ष छुट्टियों में आपके माता–पिता ने आपको क्या राय दी थी?

क. किसी अच्छी लायब्रेरी का सदस्य बनना ————————

ख. खेल–कूद क्लब का सदस्य बनना ——————————

ग. किसी मनोरंजन क्लब का सदस्य बनना ————————

10. क्या आषके माता–पिता आपसे कभी अच्छी पुस्तकों की चर्चा करते हैं?

क. कई बार ———————————————————————

ख. कभी–कभी ——————————————————————

ग. कभी नहीं ——————————————————————

11. क्या आपके माता–पिता आपको राष्ट्रीय पुस्तक मेले में लेकर गये हैं?
    - क. हमेशा/हर बार————————————————
    - ख. कभी–कभी————————————————
    - ग. कभी नहीं ————————————————

12. क्या आप अपने परिवार के साथ इस वर्ष फरवरी 1994 में प्रगति मैदान में आयोजित पुस्तक मेले में गये थे?
    - क. हाँ————————————————
    - ख. योजना बनाई थी परन्तु जा नहीं सके ————————————
    - ग. योजना ही नहीं बनाई ————————————————

13. क्या आपके माता–पिता पुस्तकें/पत्रिकायें पढ़ते हैं?
    - क. नियमित रूप से————————————————
    - ख. कभी–कभी————————————————
    - ग. एक–आध बार ————————————————

14. क्या आपके माता–पिता आपको पुस्तक/पत्रिका में से पढ़कर सुनाते हैं?
    - क. नियमित रूप से ————————————————
    - ख. कभी–कभी ————————————————
    - ग. कभी नहीं ————————————————

15. क्या आपके माता–पिता आपको पुस्तक/पत्रिका में से पढ़कर सुनाने को कहते हैं?
    - क. नियमित रूप से ————————————————
    - ख. कभी–कभी ————————————————
    - ग. कभी नहीं ————————————————

16. आपके माता–पिता आपको किस अवस्था में बैठकर पढ़ने के लिए प्रोत्साहित करते हें?
    - क. कुर्सी/मेज पर बैठकर ————————————————
    - ख. आरामदायक स्थिति में कहीं भी बैठकर ————————————
    - ग. लेटकर ————————————————

17. क्या आपके माता–पिता आपको पढ़ते समय शब्दकोष साथ रखने के लिए जोर देते हैं?

क. हमेशा————————————————————

ख. कभी–कभी ——————————————————

ग. कभी नहीं ——————————————————

18. क्या आपके माता–पिता आपको कभी ऐसे समय ऊँचे स्वर में पढ़ने को टोकते हैं जबकि आपको मौन–वाचन करना हो?

क. हाँ, हमेशा ————————————————

ख. हाँ, कभी–कभी ——————————————

ग. कभी नहीं ——————————————————

19. क्या आपके माता–पिता ने कभी आपकी पढ़ने की गति का निरीक्षण किया है?

क. हमेशा ——————————————————

ख. कभी–कभी ——————————————————

ग. कभी नहीं ——————————————————

यदि आप उत्तर क या ख से सहमत हैं तो कृपया यह लिखिये कि यह निरीक्षण आपके माता–पिता ने यह किस प्रकार किया?

————————————————————————

————————————————————————

————————————————————————

20. आपके माता–पिता के अनुसार आपको प्रतिदिन पत्रिकायें/कॉमिक्स/कहानियाँ आदि पढ़ने में कितना समय देना चाहिए?

क. एक घण्टा ——————————————————

ख. एक से दो घण्टे ——————————————

ग. इच्छानुसार समय ——————————————

21. आपके माता–पिता के अनुसार आपको गृहकार्य के अतिरिक्त पढ़ाई में कितना समय देना चाहिए?

क. आवश्यकता अनुसार समय ——————————————

ख. एक से दो घण्टे ————————————————

ग. कम से कम एक घण्टा ————————————————

22. क्या आपके माता–पिता आपको समाचार–पत्र पढ़ने के लिए जोर देते हैं?

क. हाँ, प्रतिदिन ————————————————

ख. कभी–कभी ————————————————

ग. कभी नहीं ————————————————

23. जब आप समाचार–पत्र पढ़ते हैं, तो आपके माता–पिता क्या अपेक्षा करते हैं?

क. विस्तार में समाचार पढ़ना ————————————————

ख. अपनी रुचि के समाचार पढ़ना ————————————————

ग. केवल मुख्य समाचार पढ़ना ————————————————

24. क्या आपके माता–पिता कभी आपके साथ पुस्तकालय गये हैं?

क. अक्सर जाते हैं।————————————————

ख. कभी–कभी जाते हैं।————————————————

ग. कभी नहीं गये।————————————————

25. क्या कभी आपके माता–पिता ने आपको मौन–बाचन के समय फुसफसाने या होंठ हिलाने से रोका है?

क. हमेशा ————————————————

ख. कभी–कभी ————————————————

ग. कभी नहीं ————————————————

Appendix J (ii)

Questionnaire Regarding Parental Support to Reading of Class VI Students

Prof. V.K. Sabharwal and Kusum Sharma

Major Areas:

1. Amount of time given to the child.
2. Availability of reading material for the child.
3. Guidance to the child.
4. Motivation to the child.
5. Inculcating good reading habits.

Name : .... Date : ....

Class : .... Age : ....

School : .... Male/Female : ....

Father's Name : ....

Father's Qualification: ....

Father's present post: ....

& official address : ....

Instructions:

1. Please fill in the above-mentioned information.
2. Read all the questions carefully.
3. Put a tick mark (✓) on the most appropriate answer to each question.
4. Please don't put more than one tick mark (✓) for one question.

5. Please try to reply honestly and neatly.
6. Try to complete all the questions within 25 minutes.

---

1. Do you buy newspaper regularly?

    A-Yes, daily

    B-Sometimes

    C-Never

In support of answer A/B, write their names.

1. ....
2. ....
3. ....

2. Do you buy any magazines also?

    A - Yes, regularly

    B - Sometimes

    C - Never

In support of answer A/B, write their names.

1. ....
2. ....
3. ....

3. Do you buy any children's magazine also?

    A - Yes, regularly

    B - Sometimes

    C - Never

In support of answer A/B write their names.

1. ....
2. ....
3. ....

4. Do your parents sit with you when you study?

    A - Yes, always

    B - Sometimes

    C - Never.

5. Do your parents help you in your studies?

   A - Always

   B - Whenever required

   C - Never.

6. Whenever you request your parents to help you in studies, what do they do?

   A - help you personally

   B - engage tuition instead

   C - refuse you by giving some excuse.

7. How much time do your parents spend daily to help you in studies?

   A - one to two hours

   B - one hour or less

   C - no time at all.

8. What present did you get from your parents last year on your birthday?

   A - a good book of your choice

   B - a game of your choice

   C - a beautiful dress

9. During last summer vacation, what did your parents advise you?

   A - to join a good library

   B - to join a sports club

   C - to join any recreational club

10. Have your parents ever discussed good books/suggested the names of good books to you?

    A - yes, many times

    B - sometimes

    C - never

11. Have your parents ever taken you to the National Book Fair?

    A - always

    B - sometimes

    C - never

12. Did you visit with your family the book fair held at Pragati Maidan this year in February 1994?

    A - yes

    B - planned but couldn't go

    C - didn't plan to go at all

13. Do your parents read books/magazines?

    A - regularly

    B - sometimes

    C - never

14. Do your parents read out to you from books/magazines?

    A - Yes, regularly

    B - sometimes

    C - never

15. Do your parents ask you to read out to them from books and magazines?

    A - yes, regularly

    B - sometimes

    C - never

16. Which posture do your parents encourage/approve of when you are reading?

    A - sit at the table and read

    B - sit in a relaxed manner and read

    C - lie down and read

17. Do your parents insist that you should keep a dictionary with you while reading/studying?

    A - yes, many times

B - sometimes

C - never

18. Do your parents check your habit of reading aloud when you should be reading silently?

    A - yes, always

    B - sometimes

    C - never

19. Have your parents ever checked your speed of reading?

    A - yes, always

    B - sometimes

    C - never

    In case of A/B write how ....

    ....

20. How much time do your parents think that you should spend on reading magazines/comics/story books?

    A - not more than one hour

    B - one to two hours

    C - as much as you want

21. How much time do your parents think that you should spend for your studies besides your home work?

    A - as much as required

    B - one to two hours

    C - at least one hour

22. How often do your parents insist you on reading newspaper?

    A - daily

    B - sometimes

    C - never

23. What do your parents expect you to read from the newspaper?

    A - news in detail

B - news of your interest

C - news in headlines

24. Do your parents ever take you to a library?

A - quite frequently

B - sometimes

C - never

25. Have your parents ever checked you for whispering or moving your lips while reading silently?

A - Always/everytime whenever

B - sometimes

C - never.

Appendix K

Standard Progressive Matrice

Sets A,B,C,D, & E

Name .... Class ....

School .... Date ....

Age .... Birthday ....

Test begun .... Test ended ....

	A			B			C			D			E	
1			1			1			1			1		
2			2			2			2			2		
3			3			3			3			3		
4			4			4			4			4		
5			5			5			5			5		
6			6			6			6			6		
7			7			7			7			7		
8			8			8			8			8		
9			9			9			9			9		
10			10			10			10			10		
11			11			11			11			11		
12			12			12			12			12		

Time	Total	Grade

Notes

Tested by ....

Published by Manasayan, New Delhi
by special arrangements with the
original published H.K. Lewis & Co.
Ltd., London.

Appendix L

Revised Scoring Key for RSPM Test

		A		B		C		D		E
1	->	4	-	2	-	8	-	3	-	7
2	->	5	-	6	-	2	-	4	-	6
3	->	1	-	1	-	3	-	3	-	8
4	->	2	-	2	-	8	-	7	-	2
5	->	6	-	1	-	7	-	8	-	1
6	->	3	-	3	-	4	-	6	-	5
7	->	6	-	5	-	5	-	5	-	1
8	->	2	-	6	-	1	-	4	-	6
9	->	1	-	4	-	7	-	1	-	3
10	->	3	-	3	-	6	-	2	-	2
11	->	4	-	4	-	1	-	5	-	4
12	->	5	-	5	-	2	-	6	-	5

Appendix M

डॉ. एम.ए. शाह एवम् डॉ. महेश भार्गव

निम्न सूचनाऐं भरिये :

नाम (Name)____________ लिंग (Sex)____________ आयु (Age) ____________

जाति (Caste) ____________ ग्रामीण/शहरी (Rural/Urban)____________ कक्षा (Class)________

पिता का व्यवहार एवं आय (Parents Occupation & Income)____________ विद्यालय (School)____________

निर्देश

'तुम एक सरल कार्य करने जा रहे हो। तुम्हारे सामने एक 50 वृत्तों (circles) वाला पृष्ठ है तुम्हें इन वृत्तों में चार लाइने एक व्यवस्थित क्रम में इस प्रकार लगानी है कि एक मानव शक्ल (human face) के समान बन जावें। व्यवस्थित शक्ल इस क्रम में बननी चाहिए – दायीं आंख, बायीं आंख, नाक, मुंह। पंक्तियों में बायीं से दायीं ओर तथा फिर अगली पंक्ति में इसी प्रकार से काम करें।

प्रत्येक प्रयास के लिए तुम्हें 30 सैकण्ड का समय दिया जाएगा तथा इस समय के समाप्त होते ही तुम्हें काम रोक देना है तथा पूर्ण शक्लों की संख्या गिनकर उन्हें नीचे के खानों में प्रविष्ट करने को कहा जावेगा। यह तुम्हारा पहला अभ्यास प्रयास होगा। अगले प्रयासों में इसी प्रकार कार्य करना होगा तथा ऊपर वाले खाने में इस संख्या को लिखना होगा जितना कि तुम पिछले, कार्य के आधार पर करने की सोच रहे हो। इस प्रकार वास्तविक कार्य करने के लिए तुम्हें दस प्रयास करने होंगे'।

INSTRUCTIONS

'You are going to do a simple task, you have a page containing 50 circles in front of you and have to draw four lines in these circles, so that they may appear like a human face. You must draw lines in a sequence - right eye, left eye, nose and mouth. Work from left to right across the rows and then proceed to the next line.

For each trial 30 seconds are allotted for work and at the end of this time duration you will be asked to stop the performance and count the number of completed faces and enter it in lower box. This trial will be treated as Practice Trial. In the next trials you have to do the same things including writing the total number of faces in the upper box which you intend to complete within 30 seconds time duration on the basis of last actual performance. Thus, you have to complete 10 trials for actual work.'

Scoring Table

Trial No.	G.D.S.	A.D.S.	N.T.R
1			
2			
3			
4			
5			
6			
7			
8			
9			
10			
+ Score=			
-Score=			
Mean=			

(This questionnaire is to be presented / filled by English Teachers of Middle School)

Name : Name of School :

Designation: Residential Address:

Teaching experience:

Questionnaire Passage No.....................

For Researcher Use only

Read the given questions and answer them by ticking (✓) to the most appropriate option

Q. 1. Do you think that the passage is suitable as a test for reading comprehension exercise for class VI students?	Most suitable	Suitable	Not Suitable
Q. 2. Do you find the passage interesting for class VI students?	Very Interesting	Interesting	Boring
Q. 3. Comment on the level of the passage in terms of			
(a) Language used in passage	easy	average	difficult
(b) Vocabulary used in passage	easy	average	difficult
(c) Sentence structures in passage	easy	average	difficult
Q. 4. What you think about the length of the passage?	lengthy	average	short

Q. 5. Do you think that the instruction given for each question are: (Q. 1 to...) (Please mention Q.No. in the columns also)	Clear	Not very clear	Not at all clear
Q. 6. Do you think that the questions are relevant to the passage?	Very relevant	relevant	irrelevant
Q. 7. In your option, how much time will an average student of class VI take to complete the exercise?	10-12 mts.	15-20 mts	25-30 mts.

Q. 8. Please mention if any of the questions is ambiguous or a defective test item.

Q. 9. Please write your suggestions for further improvement.

Q 10. Please write your overall comments on this type of exercise on reading comprehension.

Appendix N

Table Showing Percentile Ranks of Raw Scores on Level of Aspiration Test

Percentiles	*GDS*	*ADS*	*Category*
95	7.9	-6.7	
90	6.5	-5.4	> High Aspirant
80	5.3	-3.8	
75	4.7	-3.2	
70	4.3	-2.7	
60	3.7	-1.9	
50	2.8	-1.1	> Average
40	1.9	0.5	
30	1.1	0.2	
25	-0.7	0.4	
20	-0.1	0.7	
10	-2.1	2.2	> Low Asprint
5	-2.7	3.3	
Mean	-2.62	1.42	
Median	-2.78	-1.11	
S.D.	-3.08	2.52	
N	-6.00	6.00	

Passage 1

Kanyakumari

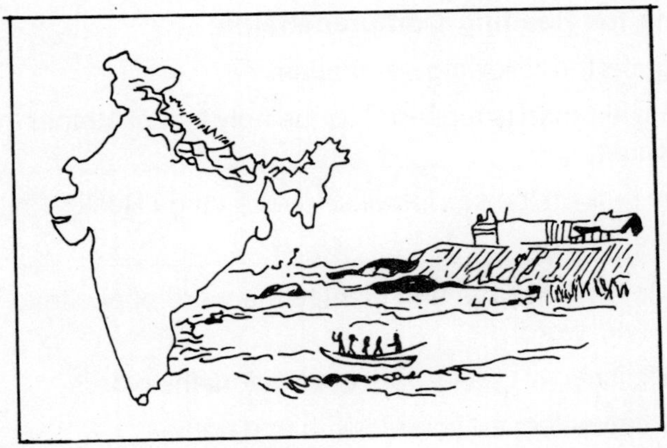

Have you heard of a place called Kanyakumari? It is a cape at the southernmost end of India. We sometimes say that the Himalayas are the crown of Mother India, so we can regard Kanyakumari as her holy feet surrounded by sea on three sides, it is a real beauty spot. At Kanyakumari, there is a famous old temple, it stands on the southernmost point of land, very near the sea. Pilgrims bathe in the sea and go up to the temple for worship. In the temple, there stands a praying figure of a girl goddess, she stands facing the Bay of Bengal to the east. The goddess is called Kanyakumari. The place is called Kanyakumari after her. In foreign countries, it is generally known by the name Cape Comorin, but its Indian name, Kanyakumari is now becoming popular.

At Kanyakumari, there is an old church and a Gandhi Mandap. A few hundred metres to the south of Cape, there is a rock in the sea called the Vivekananda Rock. Swami Vivekananda was a great patriot and saint who is still loved and respected all over India and also abroad. Before he started his public work, he went all over India as a pilgrim and visited Kanyakumari. From the Cape, he swam to the rock, sat there and meditated. People say that he meditated on the great past and the great future of India and offered himself for the service of the motherland.

Questions for Reading Comprehension:

1. Complete the following sentences:-
   (i) Kanyakumari is regarded as the holy feet of Mother India because____________________
   ii) The rock on the sea is called Vivekananda Rock because ____________________
2. Refer to the passage and identify the word opposite to the underlined word.
   (i) He <u>finished</u> his homework even before the others______.
   (ii) We can select <u>artificial</u> flowers and not the__________ as they will last forever.
3. Name the three sight seeing places of Kanyakumari that you suggest to visit and give their details in one sentence each.

   You may begin as:

   If you visit Kanyakumari, do not forget to go to:

   (i) ____________________ as ____________________
   (ii) ____________________ as ____________________
   (iii) ____________________ as ____________________
4. Which word in the passage means as:
   (i) Prayer ____________________

(ii) One who loves his country ________________ and serves for it.

(iii) Travellers on religious ________________ mission.

5. Four options are given for each statement, put a (✓) mark on the most suitable one.

(i) Swami Vivekananda was very popular all over India and abroad because

(a) he travelled far and wide.

(b) he swam across and meditated

(c) he served his nation and humanity

(d) he was a national leader.

(ii) Kanyakumari is a beauty spot because

(a) It has many temples

(b) It is surrounded by sea on three sides

(c) It has many attractive places for visitors

(d) Good looking visitors are seen in Kanyakumari

(iii) Meditation means:

(a) a prayer or offering to God

(b) a physical exercise

(c) a deep philosophical thinking process

(d) taking long rest

Passage 2

Bhopal

Suresh is six. He sits in the compound of a temporary orphanage in Bhopal. "Where will you live now?" asks a visitor. "I'll go home when my father comes to take me." No one tells him that his father will never come.

"I looked everywhere for my brother", said eight year old Hamida, "but I could not find him. Then they put up the photos and he was there. I knew it was him because he was so handsome." Her brother was dead.

On December 3rd 1984, 11 year old Salim Khan was fast asleep, stretched out on the floor beside his sister, mother and father, in the one-roomed *jhuggi* just across the road from the Union Carbide factory on the outskirts of Bhopal. Salim's sleepy dreams were rudely interrupted by the raucous sounds of his father coughing... Salim opened his eyes to see and blinked. It was as though someone had thrown a fistful of chillies into his eyes. And now his mother and sister, too, were clutching at their throats, rubbing their eyes and sputtering. The night outside was shattered with similar noises, footsteps running past the door and shouts of *Bhago, Bhago.* In blind panic, Salim and his family joined the fleeing crowds outside—barefoot, unkempt, lungs aching and hearts panting with fear of the yellowish gas they could see licking its ways through Jayaprakash Nagar—the colony of shacks which was their home. Many fell by the roadside. In the darkness, pain and confusion of the cold night Salim lost track of his family. He was never to see them again.

Question for reading comprehension:

1. Complete the following statement after reading the passage: The passage is mainly related to a tragedy that took place in______________on____________. This incident took place at ____________where all were ____________. The only thing they could see was __________leaking through the city.
2. (a) Select and write 3 words from the passage that support that there was a tragedy.

   Ans. (i) ____________________

   (ii) ____________________

   (iii) ____________________

   (b) Give one line description of the 3 characters being named in this passage.

   (i) ____________________

   (ii) ____________________

   (iii) ____________________
3. Complete the following statement giving suitable reasons:

   (i) Salim lost track of his family because ______________

   (ii) Suresh lives in an orphanage because______________
4. Which word in the passage means the same as given:

   (i) Impolitely ____________________

   (ii) Having sound sleep ____________________

   (iii) Paining ____________________
5. Four options are given to complete each statement. Put (✓) the most appropriate one.

   (a) Orphanage is a place where

   (i) old people live

(ii) people who are mentally disturbed, live

(iii) small infants are kept

(iv) children having no parents are kept.

(b) The yellow gas was creating a fear because of

(i) Its strange colour

(ii) Its suffocating effect

(iii) Its harmful and painful effect

(iv) Its large leakage in air

Passage 3

Letter from a Parent to a Teacher

(Letter from the famous American President Abraham Lincoln, which he wrote as a parent, to his son's teacher)

He will have to learn, I know, that all men are not just, all men are not true. But teach him also that for every scoundrel, there is a hero, that for every selfish politician there is a dedicated leader. Teach him that for every enemy there is a friend. Teach him that a dollar earned is of far more value than five pounds. Teach him to learn to lose and also to enjoy winning. Steer him away from envy, if you can. Teach him the secret of quiet laughter. Teach him the wonder of books, but also give him quiet time to ponder the eternal mystery of birds in the sky, bees in the sun, and flowers on a green hillside.

In school teach him it is far more honourable to fail than to cheat. Teach him to have faith in his own ideas, even if everyone is getting on the band wagon. Teach him to listern to all men, but teach him also to filter all he hears on a screen of truth, and take only the good that comes through. Teach him how to laugh when he is sad. Teach him there is no shame in tears. Teach him to close his ears to howling mob, and to stand and fight if he thinks he's right. Teach him gently, but do not cuddle him, because only the test of the fire makes fine steel.

Let him have the courage to be impatient, let him have the patience to be brave. Teach him always to have sublime faith in his creator and faith in himself too because then he will always have faith in mankind. This is a big order, but please see what you can do. He is such a fine little fellow, my son.

Answer the following questions:

1. (a) Which line indicates that the child should learn to have faith in goodness that exists even though the world may appear to be a terrible place to live.

   ____

   (b) When the child learns "that a dollar earned is of far more value than five pounds", he realises____________________

   (c) Winning is a wonderful feeling, yet one must learn________

   (d) Lines ___ to ___ indicate that apart from realising the value of the treasure that books contain, it is equally important that the child must ________________________________

   ____

   (e) In lines ___ to ____ Abraham Lincoln expresses his child's teacher to teach him that even though the majority may

   ____

2. Given below is a summary of the parent's expectations as stated from lines ____ to _____. Fill in the gaps with the words in the bubbles to complete the summary.

   Lincoln expects the teacher to teach his child to fight for ____ and to be very careful of ____ by the mob.

His child should be taught in a clear and polite way to ____ to all but take only the ____. The child should be treated _____ but he should be made ____ to face _________ of life.

3. Write 3 things that the parent wants his child to learn to accept and other 3 things which he should not do.

   (i) the child should

   (a) ______________________

   (b) ______________________

   (c) ______________________

   (ii) The child should not

   (a) ______________________

   (b) ______________________

   (c) ______________________

4. Explain the following lines in one sentence each:

   (a) Test of fire make fine steel means ________________

   (b) In every enemy there is a friend means ______________

5. Which word in the poem means the same to the word given below:

   (i) Jealousy ______________________

   (ii) Think deeply ______________________

   (iii) Respectable ______________________

Passage 4

Save the Trees

In the government reserve park
I found a man cutting a tree,
I felt like shouting at him to set it free,
But all that was left was just a small stump
And in my throat formed a lump,
I could not speak, I was too taken aback,

But the tree, he continued to hack,
At last I spoke, for the sake of our environment
As man has started to behave like a tyrant
I asked him, "Why are you cutting down this tree?"
To which he replied. "I am buying it, It's not for free."
I stood there, shocked, thinking that,
Was Mother Nature being sold off plant by plant?
How can man be so cruel?
To think about only his gruel?
Only the flora could prevent soil erosion
In addition, it makes our world free of pollution.
The air we breathe is purified by them,
So, we should not spoil nature's rhythm
Ecological balance is what they maintain
Without them, there will be no rain.
Here's a message which you ought to undertake
Contribute to environmental conservation
Don't Wait or It will be Too Late.

Achint Sandhu

Questions :

1. Complete the following summary of the poem.

   The poet found a man _________ a tree in a park and it greatly _____________her. She felt ________and found it ______to speak. The man _______to cut down the tree. At last she spoke so that our _____could be saved. She asked the man the reason for his _____ the tree. He replied that he had _____it. She wondered whether Mother Nature was being ______off gradually. The poet questioned herself why man is so cruel and ______. The man did not ______that trees made the environment _________free and the most important thing was to ______the environment before it was too late.

2. Find the words in the poem which mean the same as the following.

   (a) Surroundings ________

   (b) Cut ________

   (c) Cruel and powerful man ________

   (d) Liquid food of oatmeal, etc. ________

   (e) Washing away of fertile soil ________

   (f) Preservation ________

3. Write 3 pair of words from the poem that give similar ending sounds.

   Ans. Example Stump Lump

   (a) ________ ________

   (b) ________ ________

   (c) ________ ________

4. Reply in one sentence only

   a) Why was nature called "mother nature?"

   Ans. ________________

   b) What is meant by "Environmental conservation?"

   Ans. ________________

   c) How are trees helpful to us? (Give the reason)

   Ans. ________________

5. Give some other title to the poem?

   Ans. The other title to this poem is ________________

Passage 5

Memories

I went on holiday last week,
I had a lovely time.
The sea and sand were clear and clean,
And the weather was so fine
You need children on a holiday,
If you want to have some fun.
Mine have grown and gone now,
So I went and borrowed some.
We flew a kite on windy days
Built cruises made of sand
With a windmill for our steering wheel,
We sailed to far-off lands,
At night we went off to the fair,
Had lots of scary rides
Ate doughnut rings and candy-floss,
And chips all crisp and fried.
I used my camera,
Took photos of it all.
Then put them in a picture frame,
And hung them on my wall.
So when the days are cold and gray,
Or if I'm feeling sad.

I'll see my photos on the wall
And recall the fun I had!

Questions:

1. On the basis of your reading of the poem answer the following questions as briefly as possible. Write your answers in the space provided.

   (a) The poet feels that in order to enjoy a holiday, it is necessary to ______________________________

   ____

   (b) The poet feels that he had a lovely time last week because ______________________________

   ____

2. Use the pair of words in sentences giving different meaning.

   (a) Fair : ______________________________

   Fair : ______________________________

   (b) Fine : ______________________________

   Fine : ______________________________

3. List 5 activities that the poet enjoyed doing when he was on a holiday.

Ans. The poet enjoyed:

   (a) ______________________________

   (b) ______________________________

   (c) ______________________________

   (d) ______________________________

   (e) ______________________________

4. (a) Refer to the line 8 and explain what does the poet mean by saying "I went and borrowed some."

Ans. The poet means ______________________________

   (b) Refer to the line 21 and explain "the days are cold and gray!"

Ans. The poet means ______________________________

5. Find out two words from the poem with the suffix 'Y'

   (a) ___ ______________________________

   (b) ___ ______________________________

Passage 6

Obesity

It would be safer to remain obese than to jump from one diet fad to another; lose pounds now, and gain them back later. Research shows that this yo-yo effect gradually depletes important body tissues such as muscle and bones. Eventually it weakens the body so that it becomes more susceptible to disease and less able to shed excess fat.

Being fat isn't healthy. Excess weight impairs health and shortens life. As little as 10 to 15 pounds of extra weight produces measurable changes that can lay the foundation for degenerative disease. And for every 10 pounds of over-weight, a lifespan can be shortened by as much as a year.

Managing obesity is much more than a dietary problem. Like diabetes, hypertension, alcoholism, or smoking, obesity requires a comprehensive approach to lifestyle changes.

Firstly, you have to have a long-term commitment, that does not change when binges or other serious lapses occur.

Second, you need to identify and change habits that cause obesity. This may be as simple as eliminating soft drinks or cutting back of fats and oils. Or it may require you to completely restructure your eating patterns and lifestyle.

Changing life-long habits is about the most difficult things a person can do, and the process is very threatening. Faithfully regular meetings with a support group really increase changes of success. This kind of team effort is for those more than 20 pounds over-weight.

Third, attitudes often need radical surgery. Willingness to change is critically important. Read books, attend seminars join fitness groups, and make friends with health-conscious people.

Finally, look for a weight control plan that is consistent with a life time of good health. This will include regular exercise, a low fat, high fibre diet and a physical, mental and psychological outlook that meets your needs in every area of life. Weight control should be only part of a full and fulfilling life— not its main preoccupation.

Questions:

1. On the basis of your reading of the passage complete the following as briefly as possible. Write your answers in the space provided.

(a) Obesity is harmful because ____________

(i) ____________

(ii) ____________

(b) Quick changes in diet patterns may reduce obesity but lead to ____________

____

(c) Shortening of lifespan by one year is caused due to

____

(d) One can fight obesity with the help of ____________

____

2. On the basis of your reading of the passage complete the following:

(a) Managing obesity is more than a dietary problem because

____

(b) Excess fat ____________

3. Answer in one sentence only:

(i) What is the most difficult thing for a person to do?

Ans. ____________

(ii) What do you mean by 'health conscious people'?

4. Select the words from the passage that are similar in meaning to the given words:

   (i) Ultimately ____________________

   (ii) Remove ____________________

   (iii) Basic ____________________

5. List 3 activities that one should plan out in order to have control on obesity.

   (i) ____________________

   (ii) ____________________

   (iii) ____________________

Passage 7

Our Son the Between-Ager

"Don't talk with your mouth full."

"I haven't got my mouth full."

"You are still talking with your mouth full. Stop it."

"I haven't got my mouth full." The boy said distinctly.

He opened his mouth wide so that I could observe the pink interior of the empty cavity.

"You had it full when I spoke to you." I said. He knows it. I look at the lanky kid sitting across the table from me, clicking his teeth with his fork and laughing at me secretly, and I know he has won again. True, I could use brute force and send him off to his room, but the use of violence would only prove that I'd lost.

Do you know what is happening? It's Young Bull trying to take over, and the Old Bull hanging on for dear life.

Take an example of my razor. Now, to me my razor is the symbol of my masculine maturity. It sets me apart from the rest of my family. So when the Young Bull wanted to use my razor, it cut me to the quick.

He does not need to shave. There is only the faintest shadow on his upper lip, but the way he waters it and croons to it you would think he was growing prize petunias. One day he darkened those sparse hair with his mother's eyebrow pencil and asked to use my razor. I gave him a reasoned answer; "Certainly not!" I suppose it was inevitable that the Young Bull should take this as an affront— and of course, he used the razor.

Questions:

1. Read the passage and answer the questions in one sentence only.

   (a) Who are the two people talking here in the passage?

   Ans. ____________________

   (b) What does the young boy insist to do?

   Ans. ____________________

2. Match the words from Column A with the meaning given in Column B.

Column A	*Column B*
(i) Masculine	(a) Inner most part
(ii) Violence	(b) Without disclosing it publicly
(iii) Secretly	(c) very less
(iv) Sparse	(d) related to males
(v) Interior	(e) anger intended to hurt physically.

Ans. (i) _____ (ii) _____ (iii) _____ (iv) _____ (v) _____

3. Substitute the word with similar meaning word chosen from the passage:

   Ans. (i) Clearly __________

   (ii) Sign __________

   (iii) Unavoidable __________

4. Complete the given sentence, using the information from the passge.

   (i) The razor is the symbol of __________ of head of the family.

   (ii) The boy does not need to shave, still he wants to do it in order to __________________________

5. The title of the passage our son - between ages suggests some characteristic traits of young boys. List 3 of them.

   Ans. 1. ________________

   2. ________________

   3. ________________

Passage 8

Only The Moon

When I was a child I thought
The new moon was a cradle
The full moon was granny's round face.

The new moon was a banana
The full moon was a big cake.

When I was a child
I never saw the moon
I only saw what I wanted to see.

And now I see the moon
It's the moon
Only the moon, and nothing but the moon.

Questions

1. Read the given poem and answer the questions below in one sentence only.

   (a) Why would a new moon appear like a cradle?

   Ans. ____

(b) Why did the poetess not see the moon when she was a child?

Ans. ____________________________

(c) Why does she see the moon as only the moon now?

Ans. ____________________________

2. As a child, the poetess saw so many things in the moon list them.

Ans. ____________________________

3. Write at least 3 words from the poem that are related to childhood.

Ans. (a) ____________________

(b) ____________________

(c) ____________________

4. The last 3 lines of the poem have repeated reference of the word 'moon'. What does it signify?

Ans. ____________________________

____

5. Give some other suitable title to the poem.

Ans. ____________________________

Passage 9

Ranthambhor— A Natural Wildlife Resort

Nature has been generous to Ranthambhor and the park is criss-crossed with streams and rivulets flowing through great rock formations and steep scarps. The interior of the park abounds in wide grasslands as well as thick forest cover, and a vast variety of animals can thus avail of the habitat that suits them best.

To protect the habitat and avoid conflict between man and beast, 12 villages have been shifted out of Ranthambhor. The villagers, though sad to leave their ancestral homes, were very well compensated and are better off today than they ever were. The authorities are to be complimented on the successful implementation of this crucial plan, for all over India, the growth of human population levels is exerting alarming pressure on wildlife areas. Cattle, essential to villagers, transmit diseases and compete with wild game for fodder. Wood, necessary for village fire, is lifted from jungles, thus causing severe denudation and disturbance to game. Today the shifted village sites are a vivid example of nature's regenerating powers where grasses and shrubs have overrun fields, and mosses and lichens have carpeted the stone walls of abandoned dwellings.

The Ranthambhor management plan has been to leave nature to tend its own wards. Most of the personnel perform 'watchdog functions to ensure that poaching, illegal grazing, wood cutting and other such human intrusions are prevented. Others traverse the forests on predetermined routes to report on game activity, road conditions, fire prevention and tracking.

These people are well versed in jungle lore and are familiar with the habits and behaviour of animals.

Questions :

1. Read the passage and complete the sentences given below on the basis of the information.

   (a) Nature has been generous to this place as ____________________

   (b) Many of the people keep a watchdog function in order to____________________

   (c) 12 villages have been shifted from Ranthambhor as to ____________________

2. Match words from Column A with the meanings given in Column B.

Column A	Column B
(i) Habitat	(a) Make use of
(ii) Transmit	(b) Natural home
(iii) Illegal	(c) To pass from one to another
(iv) Generous	(d) Not according to Law
(v) Avail	(e) Kind

Ans. (i)______ (ii)______ (iii)______ (iv)______ (v)______

3. Give one word substitution from the passage for the given phrases.

   (a) To praise somebody or something

   Ans. ______________

   (b) to grow/develop/produce again.

   Ans. ______________

   (c) One which is already decided.

   Ans. ______________

4. Read the passage and select words opposite in meaning to the words given below:

   (a) Exterior ______________

(b) Unfamiliar ________________

(c) Acquired ________________

5. Write two major steps that Ranthambhor management plans to take?

   (a) ____

   (b) ____

Passage 10

Basis of Breakfast

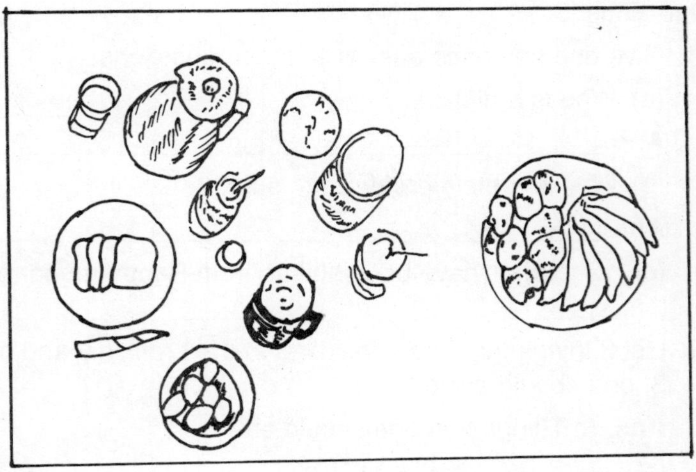

All in all, it appears that we'd be better off enjoying a good breakfast. What makes a good breakfast? Not just tea and toast. And certainly not 'puris' floating in oil. Or 'jalebis' swimming in syrup. What we need to start the day well, is a high protein, high-carbohydrate snack. Protein to stimulate mental alertness, carbohydrates (starches, not sugar) for physical energy. Sarala Mathew, Chief Dietician at Breach Candy Hospital, provides the general guidelines: "The first meal should be about a quarter or a third of your daily intake of calories, proteins and carbohydrates. For a normal person, some fat and sugar for taste is okay, but a high-fat, sugary meal would be the right breakfast for anyone." Oddly enough, low blood sugar is best replenished by protein, not sugar as it is commonly believed. Sugar gives you a quick boost but lets you down equally fast. Protein turns into blood sugar within the body at a steady rate and keeps you going over a longer time. Pick your protein from any of these all dals and their flours, whole grains of beans like chawli, moong, rajma, etc. (best if sprouted), fish, chicken, eggs, nuts (especially groundnuts) and of couse milk (skimmed) and its products like paneer (cottage cheese), curds and buttermilk. Grains of corn, jowar, wheat, etc. provide the right kind of carbohydrates so does the potato.

Questions.

1. Give one sentence answer to these questions:

   (a) Who is a dietician?

   Ans.____

   (b) Why is protein preferred to sugar?

   Ans.____

   (c) 12 villages have been shifted from Ranthambhor as to

   ____

2. List 3 things that one should eat in the breakfast and other 3, one should avoid.

   Ans. (i) Things that one should eat.

   (a) ____________________

   (b) ____________________

   (c) ____________________

   (ii) Things that one should avoid.

   (a) ____________________

   (b) ____________________

   (c) ____________________

3. Give 3 crucial tips for a healthy breakfast?

Ans. 1.________________________

2.________________________

3.________________________

4. Match the following items of Column A with functions of Column B.

Column A	*Column B*
(i) Protein	(a) Provide taste only
(ii) Carbohydrates	(b) Stimulate mental alertness
(iii) Fat & Sugar	(c) Gives physical energy

Ans. (i)______ (ii) ______ (iii) ______

5. Write two more words that sound similar to Dietician.

Ans. 1.________________________

2.________________________

Bibliography

Alavandar, R. 1992: "A Study of Selected Variables related to English reading competency of high school pupils". Ph.D. Thesis ; Annamalai University.

Alkin, C., 1984: Writing: Doing something constructive, *Young Children* 40, 3-7.

Allen , R.V. and Allen, C., 1966: "Language Experience in Reading" : *Teacher's Resource Book,* Chicago, Encyclopedia Brittanica Press.

Aranha, Mabel, 1988: "Reading Attitudes of Indian Students"; *Indian Educational Review,* Vol. 23 (4), 51-59.

Barr, R.C. 1974-75: "The Effect of Instruction on Pupils' Reading Strategies." *Reading Research Quarterly,* 10, 555-59.

Barrett, Thomas, C., (1972): "Taxonomy of Reading Comprehension In Reading". Lexington, Mass: Ginn-Axerson Education Company.

Bhatnagar, R.P. 1967: "A Study of Some of the Personality. Variables as Predictors of Academic Achievement". Ph.D. Education, Delhi University.

Bloomfield, Leonard 1942: *Linguistics and Reading.* London, George Allen and Unwin Ltd., Museum Street.

Bridges, L.H. 1941: "Speed Vs Comprehension in Elementary Reading" *Journal of Education Pyschology,* 32, 314-20.

Buch, M.B., 1974: "A Survey of Research in Education". Baroda, Society for Educational Research and Development.

Buch, M.B., 1979: "Second Survey of Research in Education". Baroda, Society for Educational Research and Development.

Calfee, R.C. 1977: "Assessment of Independent Reading Skills; Basic Research and Practical Applications." In A.S. Reber and D.L. Scarborough Eds., *Towards a Psychology of Reading,* Hillsdale, NJ: Erlbaum.

Calfee, R.C. and Priseilla, D. 1986: "Research on Teaching Reading", *Handbook of Research on Teaching,* III Ed., AERA Mac Millan Pub. Company, New York.

Carroll, J.B. 1964: *Language and Thought.* Englewood Cliffs, N.J. Prentice Hall.

————1976: "The Nature of the Reading Process." In H. Singer and R. Ruddell (Eds.); *Theoretical Models and Processes of Reading* (II Edn.) Newark, International Reading Association.

————1977: "Development Parameters of Reading Comprehension." In J.T Gutherie (Ed.); *Cognition, curriculum and comprehension,* NEWARK International Reading Association Pub.

Chall, J.S. 1967: *Learning to Read: The Great Debate.* New York, Mc Graw, Hill Publication.

Chaplin, F.S. 1928: "A Qualitative Score for Rating the Home and Social Environment of Middle Class Family in an Urban Community." *Journal of Educational Psychology,* Vol. 19, 99.

Chan, Jimmy (1980) : "Parenting Styles and Children's Reading Abilities: A Hongkong Study", *Journal of Reading,* May 1981, Vol. 24, No. 8. A Publication of International Reading Association.

Cutts, W.G. 1953: "Dealing with Reading Problems at the Pre-College Level". *Journal of Educational Administration and Supervision,* Vol. 10. 168-73.

Dave, P.N. and Venkatesh Murthy, C.G. (1988-1992): *Educational Research and Innovations. A Bibliography;* NCERT Publication.

Davis, F.B. 1968: "Research in Comprehension in Reading". *Reading Research Quarterly,* 3, 449-545.

Dechant, V. Emrald 1969-70: "Improving the Teaching of Reading." Ist & IInd Ed., Englewood Cliffs N.J. Prentice Hall, Inc.

Deshpande, V.S. 1973: "Teaching Reading to Beginners. A Methodological Study", Ph.D. Thesis, Poona University, Poona.

Elliot, J.A. and Hewison, Jenny 1991: "Comprehension and Interest in Home Reading." *British Journal of Educational Research,* June 1994, 64(2) The British Psychological Society Publication.

Engle, R.W., Carulld, J.J. and Collins, K.W. 1990: "Individual Differences in Working Memory for Comprehension and Following Directions." *Journal of Educational Research,* May-June 1991, 84(5).

Fries, C. Charles. 1963: *Linguistics and Reading.* New York: Holt, Reinehart and Winsten Inc.

Fry, Edward 1963: *Teaching Faster Reading.* London: Cambridge University Press.

Fotheringham, J.B. and Creal, Dorothy. 1971: "Family Socio-economic and Educational Emotional Characteristics as Predictors of School Achievement." *Journal of Educational Research,* July-August 1980, 73 (6).

Gage, N.L. (Ed.) 1963: "Handbook of Research on Teaching." Chicago, R. and McNally.

Gates, Arthur, I. 1947: *The Improvement of Reading. A Programme of Diagnostic and Remedial Methods.* U.S.A., The Macmillan Company.

——1949: "Character and Purposes of the Year Book: Reading in Elementary School", *Forty Eighth Year Book of the National Society for the Study of Education, Part II,* Nelson B. Henry, Ed. Chicago, The University of Chicago Press.

Garrett, H.E. 1958: *Statistics in Psychology and Education.* New York, Longmans Green and Co., Inc.

Gray, William, S. 1960: "The Teaching of Reading." Chester A. Harris, Ed. *Encyclopedia of Educational Research* (3rd Ed.) New York, Macmillan, 1114-35.

Gray, W.S. 1925: "Summary of Investigation Related to Reading." Chicago, Illinois, University of Chicago, 97-98.

Gray, William S. 1956: "How Well Do Adults Read? In Adult Reading." 55th Yearbook Part II, NSSE. University Chicago, 29-56.

Grover, Santosh 1991: "An Investigation into the Standards of Reading Ability in English in Govt. and Central Schools of Delhi." Ph.D. Thesis, Jamia Millia Islamia University, Delhi.

Guthrie, E.R. 1952: *The Psychology of Learning.* New York, Harper & Brothers.

Harri et. al. 1982: *Reading to Learn,* Methuen. London and New York.

Harris, Albert J. and Sipay, Edward R. 1971: "Effective Teaching of Reading." 5th Ed. (13), New York: Dand McKey Company.

Hashway, R.M., Duke, L.I. and Farmer, V.F. 1993: "The Reading Habits of Adult Learners—Reading Improvement." *Journal of Reading,* April 1994, Vol. 37, No. 7, A Publication of International Reading Association.

Hickman, C.W., Greenwood, G. and Miller, M.D. 1994: "High School Parent Involvement: Relationship with Achievement, Grade Level, SES and Gender", University of Florida, *Journal of Research and Development in Education*, Vol. 28, No. 3, Athens, Georgia.

Hollingsworth, P.M. 1993: "Effect of Fluency Training on Second Graders' Reading Comprehension", *Journal of Reading,* April 94, Vol. 37, No. 7, A Publication of International Reading Association.

Johnson, N.L. 1983: *How to Insure Your Child's Success in School. Fresnoca:* Milk Murach and Associates.

Kennedy, Alan 1952: "The Psychology of Reading." Methuen, London.

Lambert, W.W. and Lambert, W.E. 1964: "Social Psychology." 50, Englewood Cliffs, New Jersy; Prentice Hall Inc.

Lovinger, Jane 1940: "Intelligence as Related to Socio-Economic Factors." The 39th Year Book of NSSE Part I, School Publishing Co. Bloomington, Illionis, 159-210.

Melkin, Amelia and Merrit John 1974: *Reading Today and Tomorrow.* Open University Press, University of London, 48-102, 190-285, 293-370.

Mezynski, K. 1983: Issue concerning acquisition of knowledge; Effect of vocabulary training on reading comprehension. Review of Educational Research 58, 253, 279.

McCall, W. and Leath Crabbs 1961: *Standard Test Lessons in Reading.* New York: N.Y. Teachers College Press.

Mohan, Shashi 1991: "A Study on the Role of Aptitude, Attitude and Motivation in English Acquisition." University of Delhi. Ph.D. Thesis, CIE, Department of Education.

Munby, J. 1968: *Read and Think.* Cambridge: Cambridge University Press.

————1978: *Communicative Syllabus Design.* Cambridge: Cambridge University Press.

Muthayya, B.C. 1965: Some Correlates of Achievement Motive Among High and Low Achievement in Scholastic Field. *Journal of Psychological Rev.,* 9(16).

Neuman, Susan B. and Prowda Peter 1978-79: "Television Viewing and Reading Achievement." *Journal of Reading,* April, 1982, 25 (7)

Pal, Anusuya 1977: "Developing a Reading Oriented ELT Strategy— A Psychological Study", Ph.D. Thesis, Hyderabad: CIEEL.

Parikh, V.P. 1976: "An Inquiry into Factors Affecting Reading Speed and Comprehension." Ph.D. Thesis, Baroda: M.S.U.

Pearson, P.D. 1978: "Some Practical Applications of a Psycholinguistic Model about Reading." In S.J. Samuels (Ed.); *What Research Has to say About Reading Instruction?* Newark, Del. International Reading Association.

Philip, Rotham. 1954: "Socio-Economic Status and the Value of Junior High School Students." *The Journal of Educational Sociology,* Special Issue, New York University, Nov. 126.

Pineel, G.S. and Galloway, C.M. 1987: "Human Development, Language and Communication; *Then and Now. Theory into Practice* 26, 353-57

Rangaswamy, T. 1969: "Socio-Economic Status of Students in Some Long Established High Schools in Coimbatore and After Independence." *Journal of Educational Research and Extension,* July, p.14.

Raven, J.C. 1960: "Guide to the Standard Progressive Matrices Sets." A, B, C, D and E, H.K. Lewis and Co., London.

Reutzel, D.R. 1993: "Effect of Fluency Training on Second Graders' Reading Comprehension", *Journal of Reading,* April 94, Vol. 37. No. 7, A Publication of International Reading Association.

Richardson, 1977: "Reading Attainment and Family Size— An Analogy". *The British Journal of Educational Psychology,* 47(1) 75-77.

Robinson, Helen, M. 1946: *Why Pupils Fail in Reading?— A Study of Causes and Remedial Treatment,* University of Chicago, 256-57.

Rowe, Kenneth, J. 1991: "The Influence of Reading Activity at Home on Students' Attitudes Towards Reading— Classroom Attentiveness and Reading Achievement": *British Journal of Educational Psychology,* Vol. 61, 19-35.

Russell, David 1961: "Personal Values in Reading." *The Reading Teacher,* Vol. 15, (Dec. 1961), 172-78.

Russell, David, H. 1954: "The Dimensions of Children's Meaning Vocabulary in Grade Four Through Twelve." U. California Public Ed. II (Nos. 5), 315-415.

Russell, D.M. and Fea, H.R. 1963: "Research on Teaching Reading." In N.L. Gage Ed., *Handbook of Research on Teaching,* Chicago.

Sabharwal, Veena 1989: "A Study of Reading Skills of Precocious and Average Readers in First and Second Language Learning." A Ph.D Thesis, Deptt. of Education, Jaipur: University of Rajasthan.

Salinger, T.S. 1988: *Language Arts and Literacy for Young Children.* Columbus, OH: Meriee.

Sankarrappan, R. 1992: "A Study of Some Variables Related to the Achievement in English of IX Grade Pupils in Madurai District." M.Phil-Study Tamil Nadu: Annamalai University.

Schickedang J.A. 1986: *More than ABC's. The Early Stages of Reading and Writing.* Washington DC: National Association for the Education of Young Children.

Schofield, H.L. 1976: "Reading Attitude and Achievement—Teacher-Pupil Relationship." *Journal of Education Research,* Nov./Dec., 1980. 74(2).

Searls, D.T., Mead, N.A. and Ward, B. 1981: "The Relationship of Students' Reading Skills to T.V. Watching, Leisure Time Reading and Homework". *Journal on Reading,* Nov. 1985. 29 (2).

Shah, J.H. 1979: "A Comparative Study of Some Personal and Psychological Variables and Reading Comprehension." III Survey of Research in Education 1972-78. NCERT Publication.

Shastri, S.V. 1972: "The Teaching of English as a Second Language in Bombay with Special Reference to Structural Approach." Ph.D. Thesis, Bombay University.

Singh, B.N.K. 1965: "Some Non-Intellectual Correlates of Academic Achievements." Ph.D., Arts. Pat. Uni.

Singh, Bir 1981: "Some Experiences in Teaching Reading." *English Teaching Forum,* Vol. 19, Jan. 1981, 37.

Singh, Manju 1989: "A Study of Achievement in English in Relation to Intelligence, Interest, Socio-Economic Status and Facilities Available for Learning the Language of High School Stage." Ph.D. Education, U.P. University of Gorakhpur.

Srinivasan, R. 1969: "A Comparative Study of Language Abilities and Scholastic Achievement of Secondary School Children Belonging to Certain Social Class Categories." Ph.D. Education, Delhi University.

Smith, Donald, E.P. and Carrigan Patricia M. 1959: *The Nature of Reading Disability.* New York: Harcourt Brace Journorich, Inc.

Smith, Frank 1971: *Understanding Reading: A Linguistic Analysis of Reading and Learning to Read.* New York: Holt, Rinehart and Winston Inc. 1971, 12.

Smith, P. Henry and Dechant, V, Emrald (1961) : *Psychology in Teaching Reading.* Englewood Cliffs, New Jersey: Prentice Hall, Inc. 22, 198-201.

Spaai G.W.G., Reitsma P. and Ellermann, N.H. 1987: Effect of several feedback methods for correcting reading errors by computer assisted instruction. IPO Annual Progress Report, 22, 87-96.

Stauffer Russel, G. 1969: *Directive Reading Maturity as a Cognitive Process.* New York: Harper.

Stevens, K.C. 1980: "Can We Improve Reading by Teaching Background Information?" *Journal of Reading,* Jan. 1982. 25(4).

Thorndike, L. Edward 1971: "Reading as Reasoning: A Study of Mistakes in Paragraph Reading". *Journal of Education Psychology.* (June) Vol. 8, 323-32.

Thorndike, R.L. 1973-74: "Reading as Reasoning: *A Reading Research Quarterly.*" Vol. 9, 137-147.

Venon, M.D. 1977: *Backwardness in Reading.* England: Cambridge University Press.

Wagner, Lily 1980: "The Effects of TV on Reading." *Journal of Reading,* 24 (3).

Young, K. 1942: *Sociology.* American Book Co.

Zenker, E.R. and Frey, D.Z. 1981: "Relaxation Helps Less Capable Students." *Journal of Reading,* Jan. 1985. 28(4). A Publication of International Reading Association.

Ziller, Robert. C. 1964: "The Social Psychology of Reading." *The Reading Teacher;* Vol. 17 (May 1964), 587.

Index